THE SEA'S BITTER HARVEST

THE SEA'S BITTER HARVEST

THIRTEEN DEADLY DAYS
ON THE NORTH ATLANTIC

DOUGLAS A. CAMPBELL

CARROLL & GRAF PUBLISHERS
NEW YORK

THE SEA'S BITTER HARVEST
Thirteen Deadly Days on the North Atlantic

Carroll & Graf Publishers
An Imprint of Avalon Publishing Group Inc.
161 William Street, 16th Floor
New York, NY 10038

Copyright © 2002 by Douglas A. Campbell

First Carroll & Graf edition 2002

Library of Congress Cataloging-in-Publication Data is available.

ISBN: 0-7867-0970-7

Printed in the United States of America
Distributed by Publishers Group West

*For Monica Campbell, whose patience and encouragement nurtured this book,
and for Loring E. Hart, whose wisdom made it possible.*

TABLE OF CONTENTS

	PROLOGUE	1
ONE	*Happy, Harrowing New Year*	3
	The Crew of the *Adriatic*	5
	Fill-in	12
TWO	*A Promise of Prosperity*	16
THREE	*The Floating Factory*	28
FOUR	*Loyalty's Price*	38
FIVE	*Dredging for Dollars*	49
	Fill-in: The Clam Pump	50
	Fill-in: Regulating the Pirates	53
SIX	*The Touch and the Terror*	60
SEVEN	*Intoxicating Sea*	72
	The Crew of the *Beth Dee Bob*	72
	Fill-in: The Edge Men	79
EIGHT	*Your Money or Your Lifestyle*	83
NINE	*Making Your Trip, Heading for Trouble*	90
TEN	*Clam Boat Down*	99
ELEVEN	*A Fisherman's Mother Remembers*	103
	Fill-in: A Day on the *Debbie & Jeanette*	110
TWELVE	*Salvation in the Air*	113

THIRTEEN   *The* Beth Dee Bob *Sighs Its Last*   123

FOURTEEN   *Alone in the Blackened, Sloshing Sea*   134

Fill-in: A Matter of Minutes   139

FIFTEEN   *The Promise*   144

SIXTEEN   *Father and Son*   148

SEVENTEEN   *"There's No Future in This"*   154

EIGHTEEN   *A Winter Weather Window*   162

The Crew of the *Cape Fear*   164

NINETEEN   *Love and Death*   176

TWENTY   *The Many Ways to Sink a Boat*   183

Fill-in: Doomed by Design   190

TWENTY-ONE   *Death Roll*   199

TWENTY-TWO   *A Search and Some Answers*   211

TWENTY-THREE   *Securing the Future*   220

TWENTY-FOUR   *George's American Dream*   228

TWENTY-FIVE   *Tough Men, Treacherous Seas*   236

The Crew of the *Ellie B*   237

TWENTY-SIX   *Ready to Sail the* Adriatic   243

TWENTY-SEVEN   *Sleepwalking*   250

TWENTY-EIGHT   *Sorrowful Sea Dollars*   255

EPILOGUE   268

ACKNOWLEDGEMENTS   281

INDEX   283

Four boats down, ten lives lost in the course of thirteen days.

There's more than ends meeting ends riding on them waves.

Fortune seekers, bottom reapers, love slaves of the sea—

The widow maker, father taker, it can steal your breath away.

From "Four Boats Down"
Words and music by Michael Troy

THE SEA'S BITTER HARVEST

PROLOGUE

January 8, 1999

EVEN now, after one wave had flooded across the rear deck of the *Cape Fear* and refused to drain back to the sea, Captain Novack's stoicism comforted his crew. He could have been teetering on the edge of panic here in the storm-tossed black of night a dozen miles at sea, yet his practiced expression revealed nothing but calm. In fact, he was confused. He had never seen anything like this before. In six- to eight-foot seas, the stern of the big, black clam boat seemed to be sinking. Novack knew that could not happen, not to this, the queen of the clam boat fleet. He had been shown the proof.

Only a year before, the *Cape Fear* had survived much worse. Novack and his crew had been dredging for quahogs in the ocean south of Martha's Vineyard, Massachusetts, and had not yet taken their full load when the wind, blowing from the northeast, stiffened and became a gale, with gusts up to 70 miles per hour. The *Cape Fear* could work in a 15-foot, rolling ocean swell, but these were "wind waves" six to eight feet high, and work was no longer possible. The bow hammered into the steep walls of water, which stopped the boat dead, and so Novack told his crew to prepare for the trip home. He steered close to the Vineyard shore, where, sheltered by the land, the seas were more docile. But to make it back to New Bedford, the *Cape Fear* had to leave the protection of the island and steam northeast, directly into the onslaught of even more ferocious waves, before cutting between smaller islands and making the final seven- to eight-mile dash across Buzzards Bay.

Novack trained the boat's floodlights on the seas ahead, and he cut the throttle to zero when the biggest waves loomed. But he could not see beyond these foaming mounds to steer, so he kept his face close to the radar screen while steering his course.

Suddenly he found himself looking up at the biggest wave he had ever seen, a mound of green water that slammed over the wheelhouse, obliterating the outside world from view. The *Cape Fear* seemed to be lifted and moved to the left, as easily as a child moves a toy boat. Just as quickly, another mammoth wave pounded the boat and there was an awful crashing sound. Novack, now keeping his eyes on the radar alone, called to his crewmen to look to the rear. He suspected one of the boat's outriggers—long poles that extend from the side of the boat to give it stability—had been ripped away. But when they looked aft, the crewmen saw only that the entire rear of the *Cape Fear* was submerged. More than 80 feet of steel boat was underwater. The deck and the outriggers were nowhere to be seen.

And then, like a submarine surfacing in an emergency, the clam boat surged up through the water and over the next wave, escaping the sea with its outriggers intact and almost no damage.

Now, on this January night when the sea roiled but was not monstrous, Novack thought back to that experience and was certain the *Cape Fear* and its 230 tons of clams simply could not sink. But if he was not yet alarmed, he was puzzled and concerned. Why *was* the water, which only a moment before had flooded the deck, now advancing toward the wheelhouse, and what did it portend? In less than five minutes, he would learn the harsh answers from a lethal sea indifferent to the lives of the men who work its waters.

ONE

HAPPY, HARROWING NEW YEAR

SAILING through the cold, winter holiday darkness, a commercial clam boat—painted like Santa in crisp red and white—was three hours off the New Jersey coast with a full load when the clocks ticked past midnight and the celebrations began onshore for January 1, 1999. As it steamed ahead, the boat crossed a time line into what soon would become the deadliest year ever in the clamming industry. But on this night, none of the four bone-weary fishermen aboard the 84-foot *Beth Dee Bob* had any concerns. They were all headed for a fat payday after they reached the dock in Point Pleasant Beach. As was his habit, Ed McLaughlin, the captain, snoozed in his stateroom below the boat's wheelhouse. His first mate was on watch. An autopilot steered the boat. The mate had only to watch the radar screen to see that the path ahead was clear and to check two television monitors that showed what was happening below deck in the engine room at the rear of the vessel. The boat's high bow pushed through the modest seas, and white foam boiled along the hull's red paint, some of it splashing through the scuppers and washing across the deck, which rose only inches above the sea. At midship, in the hold under flat steel hatch covers, were 48 five-foot-tall steel cages, into each of which the crew had loaded 32 bushels, or 3,000 pounds, of quahogs, a black-shelled clam about the size of a hockey puck. Eleven cages were stacked on the deck near the stern. And eight cages were loaded and stacked on top of the others at the front of the hold, up near the wheelhouse, preventing the hatch covers from closing completely. This was the way the *Beth Dee Bob* always came into port, even though the naval architect who had surveyed the boat several years earlier had warned that it was unsafe to load this way.

In the 37 years leading up to this New Year's Eve, more than 100 commercial fishing vessels had sunk along the New Jersey coast. Among those were 19 commercial fishing boats that had sailed from Point Pleasant Beach, never to return to shore. Forty-five men on those boats were lost. But McLaughlin let personal history be his guide. There had never been a problem loading the *Beth Dee Bob* this way in the eight years he had been on the boat, four of them as skipper. He slept comfortably.

The *Beth Dee Bob* was not yet close enough to shore to see the lights that, observed from the water, decorate New Jersey's beachfronts like a glittering necklace from New York harbor south for 45 miles. But somewhere behind those lights, other members of the 48-boat clam fleet—a community of perhaps 200 regular participants—were engaged in their individual and innocent welcoming of the cruel year that would pluck ten men from their midst.

Consider the men of the *Adriatic*, an 86-foot clam boat that usually held a crew of four but was currently one man short. For two weeks, the boat had been tied to the dock in Point Pleasant Beach while major repairs were made to its machinery. These men would, before setting out to sea themselves, bear witness to events that would frighten even the bravest members of the clamming community.

The Crew of the *Adriatic*

George Whitely Evans, 51, had been the captain of the *Adriatic* since 1994. He was of average height and build, with dark, curly hair and blue eyes that crinkled at the edges when he smiled. Although some people thought he looked like movie star Tom Berenger, his voice was the first thing people noticed because it was quiet, with a refined Virginia lilt. His dress was reserved, his temper even. He might've been a banker or a concert violinist. Few would guess he worked on clam boats.

On December 31, 1998, Evans was in the Pilot House Restaurant in Brick, New Jersey, just inshore from Point Pleasant, as midnight approached. The place was nearly empty and the wait staff, by their restlessness, made it clear they wanted to close. Evans had come here with his New Year's Eve date, Joan Nowicky. She was luminescent in a black chenille sweater and black slacks. Her dark hair framed a face dominated by large, brown eyes. Evans was entranced, and it may have taken longer than necessary for him to notice they were the last customers in the place.

Evans had met Nowicky, 45, the night before in Moby Dick's Tavern. He had entered the raucous Point Pleasant bar in search of a place to spend New Year's Eve within walking distance of his garden apartment. As if guided celestially, he had found the empty bar stool beside Nowicky. Although he was known to his crew as a man who seldom spoke, Evans had found the words to begin a conversation. Despite the wailing of karaoke performers in the distant corner beyond the kidney-shaped bar, the hearty conversations of a capacity crowd and the undertone from seven wall-mounted televisions, he and Nowicky had talked. And talked. They had both been dating for many years, but the spontaneous reaction they experienced was extraordinary. At closing time, they carried their conversation into his Jeep Cherokee, and it was 3 A.M. when they parted, he with her phone number and a date for New Year's Eve.

Now they were on that date. She looked into the brilliant blue of his eyes and saw a gentleman. His smile was unforced and genuine. After the meal, she smoked. He did not. He paid the bill, and then, with his arm around her, walked her to the Cherokee and drove to her town house, not far away. The neighbors were outside, banging pots and pans together, and they wished the couple a happy new year. The brightest of fireworks were going on inside Evans and Nowicky. They sat on her couch and talked until 5 A.M. They hugged. They kissed. And then they planned to meet again the next day, Saturday. They could feel the future. It was glorious!

George Evans had reached a point in his life where his financial concerns had been eliminated. He had worked hard and invested wisely. And now, with a woman capable of appreciating him, it looked as though his life might come into complete balance.

Evans's two regular crewmen had found no such equilibrium in either their financial or their romantic lives. But then, Evans was more than 20 years older than either of them.

Frank Jannicelli was Evans's regular deckhand on the *Adriatic,* which normally sailed with a captain, a first mate, and two deckhands. The other hand had quit in the fall over a pay dispute, and since then Evans had hired a fill-in crew member for each trip until the boat docked for repairs in December. Jannicelli had been on the *Adriatic* for a little more than a year. It was his first job on a clam boat, and the work had changed him from a boy with baby-fat features to a 24-year-old man with a strong, chiseled jaw and a lean body. The work of deckhand on the *Adriatic* was pure and unending physical labor, and Jannicelli did not consider the job a career. Still, he had no other plans for his future. A high school nerd who had studied electrical engineering in college, Jannicelli had dropped out of the New Jersey Institute of Technology five years earlier to follow a young Point Pleasant woman home. Now he was spending New Year's Eve with that woman, Amy Cavanaugh, in the apartment they shared in Brick. Although Jannicelli longed for a relationship with Cavanaugh, this was not a date. She loved him like a brother. They shared debts. They owned a two-year-old, gray-and-white, in-your-face cat—Cinder—and an older gray cat—Patches. But there was no romance. Cavanaugh had a boyfriend. On this night, Jannicelli and Cavanaugh sat innocently in front of the television with a couple of bottles of champagne, waiting to see the madness as the ball dropped above the mayhem in Times Square while her boyfriend, Dominic Ascoli, worked the midnight shift in a gas station 15 minutes away.

But then the phone rang. It was Ascoli. He was alone in the kiosk-style office of the four-pump-and-a-car-wash gas station. He wanted company. So Frank and Amy grabbed their champagne, jumped into Jannicelli's aging Buick, and joined Dominic in his cramped quarters to welcome the new year.

The kiosk had a front room, about six feet by eight feet with windows on three sides. Racks of cigarette packs formed a curtain over one window; air fresheners were stacked on one counter, and the controls for the gas pumps sat on another. A wooden stool with a ripped red rag over its tattered foam seat shared the floor with a cane-backed chair. The other room had no windows but did have a toilet, a sink, and, on a counter, a cube-style refrigerator with a tiny microwave placed on its top. A typical night out for Jannicelli, who could make up to $900 a week on the *Adriatic*, was to accompany Cavanaugh on a visit with Dominic in this gas station. It was so tiny there that to pass someone, you had to turn sideways. A typical New Year's Eve for Jannicelli included a requirement to watch the Times Square ball drop. But there was no television in the kiosk, and so they went outside, opened the Buick's door, turned on the car radio, and listened to the countdown to midnight, hugging each other in celebration. They opened the champagne and drank until they got a buzz. Then they hung out until three in the morning, when the buzz had worn off enough for Cavanaugh and Jannicelli to drive back to their apartment. Earlier, Cavanaugh had put a tape in the VCR and set the machine to record the televised Times Square chaos. They watched the video in the company of Cinder and Patches. Jannicelli's New Year's Eve was complete, so he and Cavanaugh went to their separate beds.

MICHAEL SCOTT HAGER, the *Adriatic*'s first mate, had financial strains and romantic woes, just like Jannicelli. He was a tall, broad-shouldered, lanky man who, at 31, had already spent 13 years as a commercial fisherman. Hager loved what he did, even though it had led to his breakup six months earlier with the mother of his five-year-old son, Mikey. He would take almost any opportunity to work at sea. Indeed, he had been offered a chance to work this very New Year's Eve, sailing on the *Beth Dee Bob*. The economics of the trip made sense. While the *Adriatic*, on which he was second in command, was undergoing repairs, Hager earned only $350 a week doing maintenance on the boat and assisting with the repairs. But he would earn more than $500 on the *Beth Dee Bob* spending less than two days at sea. And Hager needed the money. The *Adriatic* had been in port since mid-December, and Hager's expenses—rent on his two-bedroom ranch house in Brick, support for Mikey's mother, Susan Cornell, and all the rest—had continued. So when Capt. Ed McLaughlin had asked Hager to fill in for three trips in December and January, he had jumped at the offer. He made the first trip, cut short by foul weather, just after Christmas. The *Beth Dee Bob* had caught 28 cages, less than half its normal load, and McLaughlin headed for port to avoid the windstorm and rough seas that he knew were coming. Crewmen and captains alike are paid a share of the catch, so the trip was a financial dis-appointment for Hager. But Hager, the son of a clammer, had

experienced the effect of short trips all his life. A clam boat captain will go to sea if the winds are predicted to be less than 25
knots, but rougher seas make the work impossible, so Hager
knew McLaughlin's decision was the prudent one.

The next opportunity for a trip came on December 29, but
when Hager got the call, he decided to stay home. There were
two important things in his life: clamming and Mikey. And on
this occasion, he decided to stay with his son.

There was an added incentive. Susan Cornell, 28, had told
Hager she would spend the evening with him and their son.
There was one thing Hager wanted most of all: a home and
family to return to when his trip at sea ended. He and Cornell
had shared their lives for several years before the breakup. Now
there was a chance for at least the illusion of Hager's dream—
an evening at home with woman and child.

But the dream evaporated shortly before the new year
arrived. Hager fell asleep with Mikey in his living room in front
of the television, and Cornell walked out of the pale blue
ranchhouse with the cream-colored trim and spent the last
couple of hours of 1998 talking with the fellow next door.
Perhaps, Hager thought later, he should have gone with the
Beth Dee Bob.

THE CHOICE TO work on a clam boat is a decision to engage in
the most deadly occupation in the nation. Commercial fishing
took 380 lives between 1992 and 1996, a rate of one of every
714 fishermen, 28 times as dangerous as the average for all
industries. Fishermen were washed overboard, taken down
with their boats, drowned, frozen to death, or assaulted by their
machinery.

Through good fortune, the East Coast clam industry had, by
1998, experienced a run of six consecutive years without a fatali-
ty. The last two boats to be lost, taking eight men with them, went
down in 1992. But in that year, the industry was just beginning to

operate under new regulations designed to make the work safer. At one time, the federal system that limited the number of clams harvested had encouraged clammers to head to sea when the weather was bad. Allowed by law to work only on a specific day of the week, the clammers went out on that day regardless of the weather conditions. The new federal rules instituted in 1990 gave the clammers complete latitude in choosing when to work and when to stay in port. The quantity of clams they could catch was still restricted by a rule requiring them to attach a numbered tag to each cage of clams they landed. But they could gather those clams at any time. And for six years, no clammer had been killed at sea.

Little else had changed, however. The boats were still floating factories made of steel or wood. They gathered quahogs or, closer to shore, surf clams, shellfish that were used by processing plants to make chowders and clam strips. These were not the dainty cherrystone clams served in restaurants as appetizers. They were larger animals whose meat was in constant demand by canning plants up and down the coast. Summer or winter, there was always a need to catch clams.

To "catch" a clam is something of a misnomer. Clams can maneuver along the ocean floor, but not at great speed. Unlike a scallop, which can squirt this way and that, a clam buries itself in the mud or sand of the ocean floor to await the arrival of food at its open shell. A clam boat gathers its catch by lowering a steel cage, called a dredge, in 50 to more than 200 feet of water and dragging the dredge through the sand or mud. The dredge is lowered on a heavy steel cable. When the dredge hits the ocean floor, the cable goes slack as a fixed length of polypropylene rope thick as a big man's wrist and made fast to the stern of the boat takes over the towing. The rope, which unlike a steel cable can stretch, protects the boat from sudden impact should the dredge snag on the ocean floor. When the clam boat captain thinks his dredge may be full, he begins collecting the steel cable on a powerful winch, raising the dredge from the sea and dumping the clams on the boat.

Dredges can get tangled in wrecks or communications cables or other obstacles on the sea floor. They can get tossed from the boat's deck by violent waves, yanking the vessel precariously. Machinery can break. Engines can malfunction. Fires can erupt. But in most cases, these are not the problems that will sink a clam boat.

Rodney Bart, a friend of Ed McLaughlin's who captained the quahog dredger *Victoria Elizabeth* in January 1999, explained that the greatest danger faced by a clam boat is the water on which it floats. "Someone asks you to carry a two-hundred-and-fifty-pound man across the parking lot on your back, you can do that," said Bart. "That's a clam boat with a full load of clams. If they ask you to carry a second two-hundred-and-fifty-pound man on top of the first, you can't do it. That's a clam boat with a full load, taking on water."

In Bart's example, the extra water is the problem. But first there is the full load. On a boat that carries 70 full clam cages, each weighing 3,500 pounds—about 500 for the cage and 3,000 for the clams—the boat's total load weighs a quarter of a million pounds. Each extra cage adds nearly two tons to the load. For safety's sake, fewer clams on board would be better.

But both the captain and the crew are paid according to how many clams they bring ashore. More clams, more dollars. Consequently, there is greater incentive to overload or, when the weather would suggest otherwise, to continue to harvest clams.

Clam fishing is not a free-for-all, however. Only boats with federal or state fisheries permits may harvest clams. In federal waters more than three miles offshore, where most of the surf clams and all of the quahogs are taken, the entire fleet is limited by government rules in the number of bushels that may be taken in any year. Each licensed boat owner is allocated a portion of the total annual catch based on his catch prior to 1990, when the new regulations went into effect. The more successful the owner was prior to 1990—the more risks they, their captains, and their crew members took and survived, or the more laws they broke—the higher their allotment is. These quotas can be sold, but the total allotment of clams the fleet may harvest remains unchanged in any given year.

The result is that a boat's captain and crew know on January 1 precisely how much they can earn by the end of the year if they bring back all of their allotment. And they can go to sea whenever they want. Only the weather—and the boat owners and the clam processing plants—influence a clam boat captain's decisions. Processing plants have production schedules and need clams on a regular basis, regardless of weather. And owners, who are paying the huge fuel and repair bills that keep their boats at sea, have an incentive to make each trip count. The more clams that reach the dock, the more profit is made.

These were the factors that governed the lives of captains Evans and McLaughlin and crewmen Hager and Jannicelli as the year 1999 began. These and one other: opportunity. Evans, McLaughlin, and Jannicelli, although they each had a year of college, were not so much different from Hager, who dropped out of school at age 16 and went to work on the docks until he reached 18, when he could go commercial fishing. Each of these men had found a way to make more money at sea than they could onshore. A clam boat captain can do as well as a high school superintendent, and an uneducated deckhand can earn as much as a teacher with a masters degree. In weighing the inherent dangers of their trade against the income, these men felt they had but one choice—to reap the sea's harvest.

So they would head out again in 1999. Before the year was 18 days old, it would become the deadliest in the clam fleet's history as the ocean exacted its bitter price. In sickening succession, four boats would be lost in the Atlantic. Six men would survive. But ten men would lose their wager with the sea and their lives.

FILL-IN

A FILL-IN ON a clam boat is a person who is not part of the regular crew but who, for one trip or from time to time, does the work of an absent member. This could be a fill-in deckhand or a fill-in captain. Michael Hager had been invited by Ed McLaughlin to be a fill-in because the *Beth Dee Bob* was short one crewman after Christmas, and on New Year's Eve he was to have been the fill-in first mate, but chose to stay onshore. The *Adriatic* would be calling on a fill-in once repairs were finished.

Allow me as you read this story to serve as a fill-in, a voice that comes when it is needed. This is a tale at times of riveting terror and at others of human strength and frailty. Yet for a complete understanding of the world in which these daring men work, one needs help at times with arcane information about the clamming industry—its regulation, for example—or some technical aspect that is relevant but that may not be easily understood. I would also like to use these sections to fill you in on why this reporter came to think this story should be told in a book.

I had arrived at work at the Cherry Hill, New Jersey, office of the *Philadelphia Inquirer* at nine o'clock on Monday, January 11, and was talking with my immediate editor, Porus Cooper, when his phone rang. He listened for a moment and then handed me the receiver.

"You know about the clam boat that sank?" asked Robert J. Rosenthal, the *Inquirer*'s top editor. I did not, having been out of town for four days. Rosenthal gave me a general outline of what was known. Then he said he wanted the complete story behind the headlines. "I don't care if it takes a week or a year," he said.

Rosenthal knew that I wanted to work on the longer, more complicated stories that take time to develop. And the *Inquirer* had a history of going after those pieces. I took him at his word, got in my car, and drove to Point Pleasant Beach, a town about 60 miles to the east.

More than 25 years earlier, I had taken a trip on a clam boat sailing out of Wildwood, New Jersey. My faded recollection was of a middle-of-the-night departure, a ride that slammed from one big wave to the next, and of my surprise that the 15-year-old son of the captain would make $300 on this one-day trip while I, as a newspaper reporter with about five years' experience, would earn $165 in the entire week.

These were insufficient facts to support any pretense that I understood the clamming industry, and so I took my time getting to know the men and women in Point Pleasant Beach for the *Inquirer* piece. I went from boat to boat, interviewing captains and crewmen and asking, in the end, if they would take me on their next trip so that I could write authentically about their world. None extended an invitation, although most talked openly about their lives and those of the men who by that time were missing at sea.

Within a week of my arrival at the Point Pleasant clam dock, three more boats had been lost. My face had become sufficiently familiar in the small clamming community that I was phoned at home by the clam dock office manager when each of the last two boats sank. Within days, I attended a memorial service for one man and the funeral of another, whom I had just met. The warmth with which I was received on these occasions and the eagerness among many of the survivors and relatives that the story of those lost be told fully and accurately was a strong motivation to get inside this dangerous industry.

It took a year to finish reporting and writing the story for the *Inquirer,* which published it as an eight-part serial on the anniversary of the events. Before the final segment was printed, I realized that there was much more to tell. The serial drew only crude sketches of the ten men who had died and of their six companions who had survived. And it was the human story that I most wanted to tell.

One reason for the scanty portraits was the lack of access I had had to some of the individuals' personal histories. Among the survivors, there were those who remained silent in the face of lawsuits that had already been filed. Among the lost, there were those with few relatives or friends, phantoms apparently, who drifted from boat to boat. And there were men whose families simply wished to be left alone.

But there were as many families and as many survivors who would talk. I had pieced together enough of a picture to write a newspaper story. Now I went back, looking for the rest of the details. As this book goes to print, the story remains incomplete for many of the same reasons. After repeated offers to listen to their recollections of the lives of their men, some families chose, understandably, to remain silent. Yet others among the families and the surviving fishermen have become my friends. Three years after the last boat sank, this is my effort to do justice to all of those brave men.

TWO

A PROMISE OF
PROSPERITY

MICHAEL Hager was born to the sea. His father, Richard, had been a fisherman before him. For 25 years, until his heart quit working right and he became tethered to an oxygen tank, Dick Hager came home from work reeking with the vapors of fish and rotting rubber boots. While some of his siblings may have gagged, Mike, the youngest of Dick's six children, loved every part of his father's life. He knew what he wanted to be when he grew up.

It was the inglorious part of that work to which Hager, a tall, slender, broad-shouldered man with sandy, hacked-off hair and a broad mustache, returned on Saturday, January 2, 1999. The *Adriatic* was still tied to the dock, an invalid in need of nursing, and there was foul work to be done in her belly. Already, Hager and deckhand Frank Jannicelli had cut away steel walls and removed the old clam pump from the engine room, a cold steel cavern under the deck. But the welders had not yet wrestled the big new pump into place. It would be a while before Hager's boss, George Evans, was ready to head back to sea. So Evans was using this time to keep other parts of his 20-year-old boat in good repair. In the salty ocean air, every nick in a boat's paint bleeds rust, and paint buckets and brushes are as much a part of the fisherman's life as dredges and nets.

Each morning, Hager was first to arrive at the *Adriatic,* whose dock lines were knotted around pilings in front of Laurelton Welding, a waterfront business that specialized in working on Point Pleasant's commercial fishing fleet. The welding shop was on the bank of Wills Hole Thoroughfare, a swirly gray-green tidal creek that curved south and then washed west just inside Manasquan Inlet, Point Pleasant's opening to the sea. It was also next door to the clam dock operated by Point Pleasant Packing Inc. Working clam boats tied up at this dock or to the west, at a bulkhead along the thoroughfare. Cranes at those locations loaded empty cages onto the boats before they sailed and removed the cages loaded with clams when they returned. Tractor-trailers backed up to the dock and the bulkhead to be loaded with the cages full of surf clams and ocean quahogs, which were trucked to canneries from New England to Delaware.

When Hager reached the clam dock parking lot in the long shadows of that clear, cold morning, he could see that the *Beth Dee Bob* was back from its New Year's Eve trip. He did not yet know if his welcome was worn out with Captain McLaughlin. By Tuesday, Hager had his answer. On that day he arrived at the dock as usual, and before he had unlocked the padlock on the *Adriatic's* wheelhouse door, he saw the *Beth Dee Bob* was making another trip but he had not been invited to go on it.

UNLIKE MICHAEL HAGER, Edward McLaughlin had no seaman father to guide him. That was inconsequential. He had taken his first fishing job as a 19-year-old college dropout. By the time he was 32, he was the captain of the million-dollar *Beth Dee Bob*, entrusted by its owner, PMD Enterprises of Cape May, New Jersey, with all aspects of the boat's operation. In the last year, he had earned $82,531 from PMD, more money than he could make at any other job, and the way his life was headed, that was an important consideration. With a wife and a two-year-old son, McLaughlin had acquired a focus that he lacked in his younger days. When the owners said, "Go," McLaughlin went. Now, five days into the new year, he was headed out past the coast guard station and through the stone jetties of Manasquan Inlet. He had his regular first mate aboard—Jay Bjornestad, 38—and his regular deckhand —Roman Tkaczyk, 48. He had also signed on a new deckhand, Grady Gene Coltrain, 39. Coltrain filled the bunk Hager would have slept in had he not stood McLaughlin up in December.

The routine on the *Beth Dee Bob* saw McLaughlin at the helm for the eight- to ten-hour trip 70 to 90 miles from port to the clam beds, while the rest of the crew slept in their bunks below the wheelhouse. Once the boat reached the fishing grounds off the coast of Long Island, New York, Bjornestad would relieve McLaughlin, and the two deckhands would prepare the boat for dredging. Then, each time the dredge was filled and hauled out of the water, they would handle the chores involved in moving the quahogs—pronounced "ko-hogs"—from a hopper where the dredge had dumped them and loading them into the cages. The work would typically proceed for up to 18 hours, with the mate and the deckhands trading off breaks for sleep, and McLaughlin taking a turn at the helm. They each would grab a meal in the galley when they could. When the boat was fully loaded, Bjornestad would steam back to the dock while McLaughlin once more sought the comfort of his bunk.

So it was on Tuesday morning, January 5, 1999, that McLaughlin was alone in the pilothouse, overseeing the progress of the *Beth Dee Bob*, while the crew had the chance to snooze. Soon after he left the jetties of Manasquan Inlet, he had lowered the outriggers, booms 30 or more feet long that were hinged near the deck behind the wheelhouse and, when deployed, stretched out at right angles from the side of the boat, nearly level with the sea. From the tips of the outriggers, McLaughlin would lower heavy steel "divers" or "birds"—objects shaped like yard-long space shuttles and suspended by cables. Dragging through the water 20 feet below the surface, the wings of the birds would cause them to dive, pulling down on the cables and keeping the *Beth Dee Bob* from rolling violently in heavy seas. For now, the birds still dangled from the outriggers as McLaughlin sat facing forward in the black, swivel-mounted vinyl captain's chair at the center of the wheelhouse, his elbows propped on the folding armrests and a newspaper—the *Atlantic City Press*—unfolded on his lap. As the autopilot steered the course to a corner of the ocean where McLaughlin had found quahogs before, the captain scanned the real estate advertisements, his interest focused on finding a new home. On this beautiful day, he had no reason to be concerned about the ocean. That was a luxury in the winter on the Atlantic. The treachery of this sea was notorious, particularly in shallow coastal waters where a sudden windstorm that weather forecasters could not anticipate might pile wave on top of steep wave. McLaughlin and all the other East Coast fishermen had been given a reminder of this potential fury when, only eight days earlier and about 300 miles to the south, a small commercial fishing boat—the *Predator*—had sunk off the Virginia coast. The 33-foot *Predator* was overloaded with 113 pots used to trap conch, a large, spiral-shelled mollusk. Each pot weighed 40 pounds. The *Predator* was returning to port at 11:30 on the morning of December 28 when the captain noticed water on the deck. He slowed the boat to find the source of the water, and the sea washed up over the stern, sinking it and leaving only the bow above water, pointing toward the sky. The captain had only enough time to holler one Mayday into his radio before he and his one crewman were forced into the cold water in their work clothes. The life raft deployed automatically some time later and the two climbed in. But the captain, soaked and cold, died of exposure before help arrived.

The *Predator* was one of a dozen commercial fishing boats nationwide to have sunk since the beginning of December. A total of nine fishermen had lost their lives in six of those cases. And less than an hour before McLaughlin had steered away from the Point Pleasant clam dock, another boat—a 49-foot shrimp boat—sank off of Savannah, Georgia. Most of these cases were unknown to McLaughlin and his friends in the clamming fleet. But it was all prelude to the tragedies lying in wait off the eastern shores.

AN HOUR AND a half after the *Beth Dee Bob* left the Manasquan Inlet jetties and steered northeast, McLaughlin passed over a notorious section of the sea referred to by local watermen as the Mud Hole. At times when the waves are rising, their size can be doubled at the Mud Hole. An ocean floor ravine lies hidden here beneath the waves in about 100 feet of water. The headwall of the ravine is near the entrance to New York Harbor, and the sidewalls extend southeast about 14 miles offshore. Rising waves pushed at right angles to this ravine—for example, during a blow from the southwest or northeast—slam into currents climbing the walls, and the combination creates steep, troubled seas.

McLaughlin had seen the Mud Hole angry. Now he saw it docile. The sun shone down on the sea from his right, pouring through the Plexiglas windows that encircled the wheelhouse. From his seat, McLaughlin could see the green circular screen of the radar scanning the water 12 miles ahead of and behind the boat. He could see the two television monitors that relayed constant images from the engine room at the rear of the boat. Directly in front of him was the stainless-steel wheel with which the boat could be manually steered. Behind the captain's seat was a console with the levers, knobs, and dials for the dredging machinery, as well as a duplicate set of controls for running the boat. There were radios with microphones both on the dashboard to McLaughlin's right and overhead, above the console. Without moving from his seat, the captain could run the boat either facing forward or turned around. Facing the rear, he could watch the entire dredging operation. This room atop the boat was functionally neat, its lower walls trimmed with blond paneling, its floor clear of clutter. One of the few personal touches in the wheelhouse was a photograph taped to the wall above the helm—a child riding a hobbyhorse while a woman looked on.

The child's name was Liam. The woman was Lisa McLaughlin, Ed's wife.

At about 9 A.M., as he crossed the Mud Hole, McLaughlin picked up his cell phone and dialed his condo in Absecon, New Jersey. Lisa, who often talked with her husband two or three times a day when he was at sea, answered. They discussed their plans to buy a town house, and Ed gave Lisa a few phone numbers he had found in the paper. They decided that they would spend time house hunting on the weekend. Then Lisa handed the phone to Liam, who had celebrated his second birthday on December 12. When Ed was home, he and Liam were inseparable. Ed, who carried 250 pounds on a five-foot-eleven-inch frame, would get down on the floor with his tiny son to play cars, or he would sit at the computer with Liam in his lap, playing video games. Now, when he heard his son's voice on the phone, McLaughlin asked him about the sharks on a CD-ROM they had used Monday night, before Ed had given Liam his bedtime bath.

The phone call lasted ten minutes before the captain had to return to work. Lisa had learned to live with the demands of clamming. There had been times when her husband was gone for weeks on end, and other times when he had to leave with little warning. One such trip had begun on December 29, when McLaughlin got a call from PMD. The company had some federal tags left for 1998 and they wanted him to make one last trip. He had just finished a trip that began the day after Christmas, the one for which he had hired Michael Hager as a fill-in. It had lasted until December 28, and then McLaughlin had made it as far as Lisa's parents' house in Pennsylvania before he got the next call from PMD.

Ed and Lisa had planned to go out New Year's Eve. They had arranged to hire a baby-sitter for Liam. Lisa was out shopping on the twenty-ninth when Ed got the call. When she returned, Ed and Liam were sitting at the computer and she could see the grim set to her husband's face.

"I have to go to work," he said. The implication was clear. New Year's Eve was off. "I'll make it up to you," he said.

The *Beth Dee Bob* made that year-end trip, and on Saturday, January 2, McLaughlin got home in time to take Lisa out at seven o'clock for her consolation dinner. They ate at the candlelight-and-linen Ebbitt Room in Cape May. She had steak. He had fish, the house special. Then, arm-in-arm, they strolled the cold, deserted streets of the Victorian resort town at the southern tip of New Jersey. They looked at displays in the windows of several real estate offices. They entered the Ugly Mug and had hot chocolate. They talked of their plans to move and of a February vacation in Florida. It was less a celebration of the new year than a date between friends who had first met in Cape May.

MCLAUGHLIN WAS FIVE years into his fishing career and was living in Cape May in the fall of 1987. A friend, a fellow named Bob, visited McLaughlin's apartment and, in the course of conversation, told him that he had been at a bar and had seen a woman named Mimi and "that girl from the Harbor House Deli, the one with the nice ass and the great legs." Lisa was substitute teaching during the school year in Stone Harbor and nearby Avalon, both upscale resort communities with multimillion-dollar summer homes along the oceanfront dunes, and she was working part-time in the delicatessen.

Inspired, McLaughlin drove to the deli, where he ordered a ham-and-Swiss sandwich on rye with mustard, to go. He was wearing shorts and a T-shirt and a ski coat with ski-lift tickets dangling from the zipper. He flirted with Lisa. She thought he looked athletic. She threw his change at him, embarrassed by his staring. The next time McLaughlin entered the deli, he sat down for lunch and then asked his waitress if he could make dinner for her.

"The only thing I eat is lobster," Lisa shot back. She got it.

Their first big date was the Clammers' Cotillion, a Christmas extravaganza. They dated for seven years, and were engaged in 1994 and married on September 29, 1995. By that time, McLaughlin was steaming the *Beth Dee Bob* out of Shinnecock, Long Island, and came home only once every three to four weeks. It was in May 1997, when Liam was five months old, that the *Beth Dee Bob* finally returned to New Jersey. Sometimes McLaughlin would sail from Point Pleasant Beach, an hour's drive to the north of the condo in Absecon. Other times he would unload—or "pack out" as the industry terms it—in Atlantic City. That put him only ten miles from the apartment, so he could go home for lunch. Occasionally Lisa and Liam would pack a picnic lunch and meet Ed at the dock.

Since his return to New Jersey ports, Ed had been making up for lost time. Lisa could not count the number of weddings she had attended alone in those earlier days. It was a sacrifice she made because she understood Ed's job and accepted its demands. The couple made a point of eliminating the inessentials when they had time together. She saw Ed take off his captain's face when he got home. They did not talk about the boat, only about themselves.

ON MONDAY NIGHT, January 4, when he left their condo, McLaughlin had shared a group hug with his son and wife in the doorway, and then he rode to Point Pleasant in the blue pickup driven by Bjornestad, who lived in the same town. Now it was the next morning and Ed was at sea and on the phone with Lisa. He knew they would talk later in the trip, and he ended the phone call with "I love you." Lisa did the same, and the phone call was over. There had been no discussion—nor was there ever—of the danger of McLaughlin's trade. If he was concerned about the safety of his occupation—if, for example, he was troubled by the loss of the *Predator*—he did not share that with Lisa. The only hint he ever gave Lisa concerning the dangers of clam-ming—one that she let pass unexplored—was that he had for-bidden her to read Sebastian Junger's best-selling book about the sea and commercial fishing, *The Perfect Storm.*

Worry would have served little purpose for either husband or wife. McLaughlin, like many, if not most, fishermen, simply *had* to go to sea. It was a matter of economics. At 36 years of age, he had no other skills that would earn him the same income, and his formal education had stopped after a year in community college.

That is not to say that McLaughlin was without talents or intelligence. His best friend since high school, Fred Smith, went on to graduate from college and found no one who was any smarter. McLaughlin was an Irish Catholic Democrat, and he would debate politicial issues with Smith, a Republican. In the end, Smith would find himself agreeing with McLaughlin, who he thought would find his true calling as a politician.

McLaughlin had already proved himself in the clamming industry. His management of his crew was sufficiently shrewd to place his reputation among those of the top skippers in the 48-boat clamming fleet. He had the skill to diagnose and repair mechanical problems aboard the *Beth Dee Bob.* He handled the boat's payroll and its expenses well. In short, he was a success-ful small businessperson, although not the owner of the small business. He accomplished through the force of his personali-ty what others might need a college degree to achieve. His was the personality of a natural leader.

McLaughlin's family had moved to New Jersey when he was

seven and his father had retired from the air force. He became the captain of the high school football team, playing tackle on both offense and defense. In his senior year, he and Smith were voted co–class clowns. He seemed to have friends everywhere, and his leadership among them was not just a given but a source of comfort to them. If a fight was going to happen—and somehow when McLaughlin was present it often did—Ed was the guy you wanted beside you. He was able on the one hand to bring people together. But if a friend got in a fight, McLaughlin finished it.

Kevin McLaughlin, Ed's older brother, saw in his sibling a man without a mean bone in his body, and Kevin felt he could judge these things. He was a municipal police detective and encountered the worst of humanity in action. But Kevin would be the first to admit that Ed did not argue long with someone trying to get the better of him. He would say, "Okay, no problem." And then his fist would settle the issue. Quickly.

When McLaughlin was an adult, the frequency with which his toughness was tested may have been connected to the places he ventured. Waterfront bars are more physically threatening places than quiche parlors. If you let someone show you disrespect, the lapse may cause you problems later. Better to deal with the man up front.

Having been raised in a large family with little extra money, McLaughlin gave less importance to wealth than he did to having friends. He was offered a football scholarship to the University of Delaware but turned it down because none of his pals was going there. Instead he enrolled in Gloucester County College, a two-year school in southern New Jersey where Smith also enrolled. At the end of the first year, McLaughlin went to the docks in Cape May and found a fishing job. With the certainty of a man who knows himself well and who has found his calling, he stayed on the boat in September. His formal education was finished.

At first he was a deckhand on scallop boats, vessels that are at sea for two weeks at a time. Then he tried long-lining for swordfish, a segment of commercial fishing where the trips are a month or longer. Finally he settled on clamming, happy to return to shore every other day, for at shore, the true Ed McLaughlin could let loose.

Wherever McLaughlin was on land, there too was a party. He would round up his buddies when they were home from college and he would finance their weekend flings. Even as an adult, when he reached shore he wanted a good time. He would visit his married friends and, because he treated their wives with affection equal to that which he showed their husbands, they let their men go with him. Neither wives nor husbands seemed to be able to say no to Ed McLaughlin's call to party.

And always, he was free with his money. There was plenty of it, too. On at least one occasion, he bought a car from a friend just to get home from a party. Each of his sisters and his brother had inherited cars from him at one time or another, a gift when he decided he wanted new wheels. As a young fisherman, he would bring a duffel bag of dirty clothes home from his boat, trash them, and buy a new wardrobe. He bought rounds for his friends, paid for fishing trips for his relatives, and when it was time for a McLaughlin family picnic, no one needed to bring burgers because Ed would show up with filet mignon and lobsters for everyone.

Charging at everything, ready to consume it, McLaughlin believed he could do anything, and people responded to him. A crowd would be waiting for him when he arrived at a party. When he was on the *Beth Dee Bob*, the captain's character was unchanged. He thought his vessel was the best boat in the clam fleet and that it would take care of him. As a result, he wanted to take care of it. There were men whom he would not hire to work on the *Beth Dee Bob*, he told his brother, because they did not care as much as he did. Since he became captain in 1994, he had gone through 47 deckhands. There was money to be made, and McLaughlin wanted men willing to work for it.

Buried in the money, however, was a hook. As Smith would later observe, "You start making money at twenty-one or twenty-two that most guys out of college don't make until they're thirty-five; you get trapped into staying. It's a risk-reward relationship."

The risk didn't bother McLaughlin until he married Lisa in 1995. By then he was 32 years old. Friends he had made at the docks saw the man turn from a fellow always ready for a good time ashore to one who would rather head home to be with his wife and son, born in 1996. When he ran into clam boat captain Rodney Bart around Christmas, they had a few drinks and talked about all the great times they had shared. But it was clear to Bart where McLaughlin's interest now lay. What he really wanted to talk about was his son. Liam was the moon and stars, and all else faded into black night.

THREE

THE FLOATING FACTORY

THE perfumed mingling of brine and raw seafood is not the dominant fragrance aboard a clam boat. Whether at the dock or at sea, a clammer's nose is stung by cigarette smoke, diesel fumes, or both. Onshore, Ed McLaughlin would bum cigarettes from the clam dock manager, Bill Becica. But no clam boat captain would put to sea without loading lots of grub and smoking supplies. Cartons of cigarettes were as certain to be aboard the *Beth Dee Bob* as the 12,300 gallons of fuel pumped into the boat's tanks, and, as on every other clam boat, they were as vital to keeping the crew happy as fuel was to a functioning engine. For a captain, there are many long hours with little to occupy his idle hands except a cigarette. Steaming to the clam beds on the morning of January 5, 1999, was one of those times for McLaughlin. While the crew slept, there was scant activity in the wheelhouse. The big engine hummed in its room below the deck, about 50 feet to the rear. Trapped at his post, McLaughlin was limited to the option of reading or smoking. Sometimes when he was truly bored, he challenged himself by trying to tie a drinking straw into knots with one hand. But he always had a book he was reading. At the helm, he could read while alternating glances between the book, the navigational equipment and the television monitors.

The *Beth Dee Bob* made a steady ten knots, or about 11 miles an hour, through the water, a normal speed for a clam boat. It presented a silhouette typical of the more modern style dredger. The wheelhouse was at the front, just behind the bow, a configuration called a western rig. Occupying the middle of the boat was the clam well or hold, essentially a large steel box welded below the deck. The hold was just large enough to place 48 clam cages, each three feet by four feet by five feet high, side by side and end to end, with no room to spare. Large flat steel lids called hatch covers rode above the hold on steel tracks in a telescoping fashion. When hauled by cables, they could be drawn up like bedclothes to cover the yawning hold or pulled one way or the other to expose the cages for loading.

Just forward of the *Beth Dee Bob*'s stern, a tubular steel A-frame rose perhaps 30 feet above the deck, and a ramp consisting of two heavy steel rails slanted up from the stern and forward, to the top of the A-frame. As the boat headed toward the fishing grounds, the dredge, a large steel box made of welded rods and weighing several tons, rode on the ramp, held in place by a steel pin and raised and lowered by a thick steel cable that could be gathered up by or dispensed from the drum of a large winch positioned several feet above the deck between the ramp rails.

When the dredge was hauled, the clams fell from a trapdoor at its rear into a hopper under the A-frame. The clams then were funneled onto a shaker, a grooved and tilted table that shook out the ocean-floor debris and left only clams and large objects. Next, the clams and large objects were dumped onto a conveyor system that ran up the center of the deck, over the hold. Moveable chutes attached to the conveyor shot the clams down into the cages, filling first one cage and then, when moved by the crew, filling another.

This configuration classified the *Beth Dee Bob* as a stern-ramp dredger. When it was first built in 1990, it was designed as a side dredger, from whose deck two dredges were lowered over the sides by booms.

Another feature that marked the *Beth Dee Bob* as a clam boat was that it rode low in the water. While steel bulwarks—walls about two feet high—were built from front to rear at the edge of the deck, the 26-foot-wide deck itself was only 18 inches above the water. Scuppers—holes built into the bulwarks— allowed the sea to slosh in and flood the deck when the boat rolled to the side. If a clammer went on the deck while the boat was moving, he either wore rubber boots or had wet feet.

In the winter, wet decks become icy if the air gets cold enough to freeze salt water. And since winter is prime clam chowder season, to be a clammer means to accept snow and ice as part of your life.

Louis Lagace, who owned the clam boat *Ellie B*, had a unique way of describing the clamming environment. Lagace, 47, had the flat vowels and droll wit of his native Fall River, Massachusetts. His answering machine there casually informed callers that "I am currently on a three-state killing spree," and invited them to leave a message.

Turning to the subject of work aboard a clam boat, Lagace dropped the humor.

"Take a factory, remove the roof, remove the walls, maybe dim the light. Get a hose and hose down the floor, and then maybe rig up these huge hydraulic pistons to make it move, and that's your fishing boat: a factory that is wet, open to the elements, and is moving back and forth."

Like a factory, a clam boat has big machinery moving quickly most of the time. There is the constant movement of the convey- or belt. Crewmen stand on small platforms welded along the conveyor's sides and reach over the moving belt to remove from the clams the dogfish, horseshoe crabs, scallops, starfish, bolts, nuts, and other seabed items that the undiscriminating dredge scoops from the sand and mud. There is the dredge itself, and the big winch that hauls it, each capable of catching and crushing a man's arm or leg if he gets too close. There are booms and cables that can swing unexpectedly. And there are the cages, which weigh 500 pounds empty and are at times stored on the deck, where they can topple on top of a man.

Under coast guard regulations, only the more severe injuries aboard the *Beth Dee Bob* were required to be recorded. These included the time a Polish fisherman, Bronislav Orkapski, was hit by the conveyor and knocked overboard. Luckily, he was saved. On another occasion, crewman John Senger fell into the cold November sea. He had been fixing the hydraulic lines on the rigging and slipped. Luck was with him because another crew member saw him go and someone put the boat in neutral. He had no life jacket on. Fishermen never wear them. He was hauled aboard without injury but he was drenched right down to his thermal underwear. "I've seen people fall in and not try [to save themselves]," Senger recalled later. "The cold water takes over. [You] hit that water and it paralyzes you."

Fingers were among the body parts most frequently assaulted by the *Beth Dee Bob*. First mate Jay Bjornestad had lost part of a finger in 1996. Deckhand Roman Tkaczyk suffered a severe cut to a finger in 1998 when, while he was working on another boat, a clam cage pinned the finger against a belt.

The most severe injury recorded on the *Beth Dee Bob* occurred on June 21, 1994, a few months after PMD Enterprises bought the boat. A solenoid—a switch that is part of the controls for raising and lowering the dredge—had failed and the dredge was sitting on the ocean floor. The boat was dead in the water and could not be moved unless the dredge was either raised or cut free. No clam boat captain with the option of saving his dredge, a custom-built item that costs thousands of dollars and that would take perhaps weeks to replace, would choose to lose it. One option was to tie a buoy to the end of the rope used to tow the dredge, set the rope free, and mark the location so that when repairs were made ashore, the dredge could be retrieved.

McLaughlin chose to fix the problem at sea. He went to the engine room with Senger, his deckhand, and started the work of replacing the solenoid. This involved removing hydraulic hoses. One of the hoses was filled with highly flammable hydraulic fluid under pressure. Somehow the hose became detached and sprayed fluid onto the hot diesel engine, creating a ball of fire that flashed through the tight compartment below the deck. Senger was in front of McLaughlin, heading for the ladder that climbed to the deck. McLaughlin could not move out of the fire's way fast enough and received second- and third-degree burns on his chest and arms. Senger was burned on his hand.

The coast guard was called, and McLaughlin and Senger were taken from the *Beth Dee Bob* by a helicopter. McLaughlin's burns healed only after a long convalescence, and frequent phone calls from lawyers promising him great riches if he would sue PMD. He chose not to, in part because the company supported him through his recovery and in part because he had plans for the future. A month later, the nervous sea captain, his face growing red as he sat on a park bench, would propose marriage to Lisa. To provide for a wife, he needed his job, and, he told a friend, he didn't want to get blackballed in the industry.

DURING MCLAUGHLIN'S RECOVERY from his burns, the *Beth Dee Bob* was hauled out of the water to make repairs where the fire had been. PMD's boat manager, Ernest Riccio, used that time to persuade Peter LaMonica, a co-owner of the company, to convert the boat to a more efficient stern-ramp design. Some people felt the boat would be unsafe with a stern ramp, but Riccio was adamant and LaMonica finally agreed. Tests were performed on December 21, 1994, precisely six months after the fire, to determine with what loads and in what sea conditions the *Beth Dee Bob* with its new ramp would be stable. By this time McLaughlin was back on the boat with his crew, and a naval architect performed the test, which involved moving weights about on the deck to determine the vessel's center of gravity. When the test was completed, the naval architect made some mathematical calculations and presented PMD and McLaughlin with his conclusions, a thick report bound like a book explaining the safe loading conditions of the *Beth Dee Bob*.

A so-called stability letter does not guarantee that a boat is always safe. There are many ways that a normally stable boat can sink, and if that happens, the crew's safety would depend on the survival equipment it carried.

The most fundamental pieces of equipment—the first line of defense against a disaster—were the boat's systems that detected problems. The television cameras in the engine room and their monitors in the wheelhouse were there to alert the crew to flooding. There also were bilge alarms, which sounded in the wheelhouse and throughout the boat if more than a foot of water was sloshing around in the depths of the hull. There were low pressure and overheating alarms to warn of problems in the main engine or the hydraulic and pump engines.

Once a catastrophic problem was discovered—a fire that could not be extinguished or flooding that could not be halted—McLaughlin and his crew had numerous items at their disposal both to save themselves and to alert others to their problems.

First, the boat carried two types of radios—a VHF unit that could take an incoming call from as far away as 25 miles, and a single sideband radio, which could send a signal around the curve of the earth, reaching land-based receivers no matter how far away.

Flares and smoke canisters were stored under the control panel in the wheelhouse, also of use in signaling for help. And a life ring was hung from the wall outside the door to the wheelhouse, where it could easily be grabbed and thrown to a man who had fallen overboard.

Once the decision was made to abandon the *Beth Dee Bob*, the crew's best option for survival would be to use the life raft. It was inside a case that was mounted on the wheelhouse roof. A device called a hydrostatic release kept the lid of the case shut. The lid could be opened manually or, if the boat sank, the hydrostatic release would open once it hit water and the raft would automatically inflate and float to the surface, tethered to the boat by a long plastic rope. Since the *Beth Dee Bob* traveled only in water no more than 400 feet deep, a rope longer than 400 feet would assure that the raft remained on the surface if the boat sank.

The other option—one that would always be employed in a winter catastrophe—would be for each crew member to get into an individual immersion—or survival—suit. These suits—some red and some orange—are made of neoprene and cover the entire body from head to boots, and once zipped shut, they keep water out and body heat in while allowing the person to float effortlessly.

On the *Beth Dee Bob*, the immersion suits were stored in a rack above the galley table, and there were enough for all the crewmen. Each suit was packed in an orange or dark green vinyl bag that was closed at one end with snaps and had a strap at the other end. The quick way to get into the suit was to hold the strap so that the bag was hanging toward the floor, then jerk upward on the strap. The motion would pop the snaps and the suit would fall out on the floor.

Also nicknamed a Gumby suit, perhaps because of its similarity to the costume worn by comic Eddie Murphy on *Saturday Night Live*, an immersion suit would be almost worthless as working gear. The gloves are thick, making the use of fingers and thumbs all but impossible. Suits are made large, so that a big man with his boots on can get into them. The result is that the suit folds uncomfortably at the chest when a person bends. And once the zipper up the front is closed and the hood is properly pulled over the head, only the eyes and a little skin around them are exposed, making conversation difficult. Getting into an immersion suit takes practice and a relatively flat and uncluttered piece of floor. With the suit unfolded on the floor and face-up, a sailor sits down and pushes his feet—boots and all—into the legs, then stands to pull the suit up to his waist. The motion is roughly the equivalent of a child getting into a snowsuit. Experienced fishermen keep plastic shopping bags in the legs of their suits and pull the bags over their boots to help them slip into the neoprene, the way people often get into rubber over-shoes. With arms shoved into the sleeves, the sailor's greatest difficulty in donning an immersion suit follows. With the hood pulled over the head and ears, and fingers encased in the suit's thick gloves, the wearer must now grab the toggle at the end of the zipper and yank it to chin level. Finally, a flap is pulled across the face and attached by a hook-and-loop fastener, sealing the mouth and nose behind protective neoprene. The fisherman must be able to complete this whole process on a rocking, sinking boat in about one minute. Then he steps into the water and, if it is night, turns on the plastic strobe light attached to the suit's chest and waits.

The shipwrecked clam boat crew has one more lifeline. On the *Beth Dee Bob*, it was in a small box mounted on the wheelhouse roof with a hydrostatic release mechanism to open the box if the boat sank.

The device is called an electronic position indicating radio beacon, or EPIRB. If the box containing the EPIRB opens, an electronic gadget floats free, rising to bob on the ocean waves and transmit a signal that has been registered by the boat owner with the National Oceanographic and Atmospheric Administration (NOAA). All commercial vessels are required to have an EPIRB. Within minutes of the EPIRB's being activated, the coast guard knows what vessel is in trouble and approximately where it is. Satellites in space triangulate the EPIRB's signal, giving rescuers a target in the vast ocean.

In April 1998, a marine surveyor inspecting the *Beth Dee Bob* found that the hydrostatic release on its EPIRB was out-of-date and that the periodic inspection of the life raft was overdue. The surveyor, Stephen Sperlak, revisited the boat in August and found that McLaughlin had changed the EPIRB release and that the life raft had been inspected. While the captain was lax on the timely maintenance of the EPIRB and life raft, he, like many other clam boat captains, showed even less interest in a federal law that required him to assure that his crew was trained once a month in ten separate safety procedures, from fire fighting to putting on their immersion suits. Jimmie Brown, a former mate on the *Beth Dee Bob*, recalled a time when the boat was about to get a courtesy inspection by the coast guard.

"We had a list of things that had to be done and checked over on the boat before we got our initial inspection, and one thing on the list, it said, 'Log records of drills performed on the boat.' Now I said to Ed, I said, "What do you want to do about this? We've never performed no drills.' He said, 'Just fill in a couple of pages in the book in different months, just write down that we did the drill,' [but] we never did perform the drill."

Unlike some clam boat captains, McLaughlin had no trouble putting his hands on the stability letter for the *Beth Dee Bob*, which summarized all of the conclusions made by Lynn T. White, the naval architect who had determined that, under specific circumstances, the boat was safe to operate. When in April 1998, Sperlak had asked to see the book, McLaughlin pulled open a drawer on the starboard side of the wheelhouse, right near the door, and took it out.

The time bomb aboard the *Beth Dee Bob* as it headed to sea on January 5, 1999, however, was the fact that while McLaughlin knew where the book was and knew what was in it, he routinely ignored White's instructions.

When he tested the *Beth Dee Bob* after its conversion to a stern ramp, White concluded that by stacking some clam cages on the deck, the boat could safely carry 70 cages. That number was significant because each tractor-trailer hauling clams to a cannery can hold 14 cages. Five full trucks would be 70 cages, and that would be the most economical load.

But White was aware that in years past, the *Beth Dee Bob* had often sailed with cages double-stacked in the hold. That meant that the hatch covers could not be completely closed. With the hatch opened, seawater could flood the hold, making the boat unstable. In his stability analysis given to PMD, White typed in capital letters: "NO CAGES SHOULD BE DOUBLE-STACKED IN THE CLAM WELLS." He did not put the same blunt warning in the stability letter that would be taken aboard the boat, but in that document he directed that the hatch covers be completely closed and weathertight for the letter to be valid. That meant no double-stacking of cages.

McLaughlin felt otherwise. He began almost every trip since he had received White's instructions—including this trip—planning to steam home with 48 full cages in the hold, another 8 stacked on top of the cages in the front of the hold, and 11 cages riding on the deck for a total of 67 cages, three under the absolute limit. This January 5 trip would be routine. At the end would be another hefty payday.

FOUR

LOYALTY'S PRICE

TWO types of clams are dredged off the Atlantic Coast—qua-hogs and surf clams. The meat of both types is processed into clam strips, chowders, and other canned goods. Neither the product from the quahog nor the surf clam is typically served in restaurants, where a sweeter, smaller cherrystone clam is favored.

The quahogs that Edward McLaughlin set out to hunt on the morning of January 5 may have been among the oldest living beings on Earth. Quahogs can live to be 225 years old, according to some scientists. Such an ancient animal, had the *Beth Dee Bob* dredged it, could have been alive since Ludwig van Beethoven was in his teens. Even scientists who give more modest estimates believe that quahogs may live to more than 100 years old.

There is, of course, little exertion in the life of a clam. Pumping water between its shells, it buries itself in the ocean floor and awaits food. Even sex is effortless. The male sends its sperm into the passing water and the female does the same with its eggs. On their own, the sperm and eggs float freely, unite, then form larvae that grow and finally drop to the ocean floor, where they mature into adult clams. Quahogs become sexually mature in five or six years. They grow rapidly for about 20 years and reach a length of about five inches. Quahogs, formally known as *Arctica islandica,* are found in coastal waters of the Atlantic, north of Cape Hatteras, North Carolina, all the way to Canada. They live only in water that stays at 60 degrees Fahrenheit or colder, which means that the farther south they are found, the farther offshore they must go to find deeper, colder water. Before the early 1990s, most quahogs were harvested off the New Jersey, Maryland, and Virginia coasts in about 200 feet of water. But in the last decade commercial harvesting had moved north and captains like Ed McLaughlin routinely set their autopilots for spots off the Long Island coast. The clams they caught averaged about 50 years of age, according to scientists, whose estimates are based on growth rings similar to those found in trees.

Clam boats that go after surf clams have less distance to travel from Point Pleasant than those seeking quahogs, because the greatest concentrations of these larger mollusks are in 150 feet of water or less. Surf clams live at most to their mid-30s. They reproduce the same way as quahogs but much more quickly, reaching sexual maturity in their second year. Surf clams, called *Spisula solidissima,* are found predominantly off the coast from New Jersey to Virginia, although there are concentrations off of New England, as well. They grow rapidly until they are seven years old, reaching about nine inches long.

Surf clams are often smaller when they are sold, but a biological peculiarity of the surf clam limits its attractiveness as a substitute for dainty cherrystone clams, according to Rutgers University biologist Kathryn Ashton-Alcox. "Since it is such a fast-growing clam, its metabolism is all ramped up when it is small, and therefore it has a short shelf life. Its enzymes, et cetera, are very active. You can shuck a small *Spisula* and watch it crawl right off its shell, which would probably throw a lot of raw-bar customers for a loop and make them reconsider that last cocktail they drank."

One reason surf clams are found closer to shore, Ashton-Alcox theorizes, is because they are stronger burrowers. This means that when storms toss the shallow coastal waters and stir the mud and sand at the bottom, the surf clams can stay in their foxholes longer than quahogs can.

Because both the quahog and the surf clam were traditionally found off the shores of New Jersey, Maryland, and Virginia, the ports of these states became the natural homes for the clamming fleet. As more clams were found in northern waters, the ports in Maryland and Virginia became less significant, and clam boats began working out of Long Island and New England ports. But New Jersey has remained the heart of the clamming fleet. Its coastline, which provides several ports within close range of many of the clam beds, is one reason.

The sandy New Jersey coast is, from Point Pleasant Beach south, a series of barrier islands separated from the mainland by a string of shallow bays. Between any two islands are inlets through which the sea floods and drains the bays. The Intracoastal Waterway begins at Manasquan Inlet, which separates Point Pleasant Beach from the town of Manasquan to the north. The ICW then snakes through the bays—Barnegat, Little Egg Harbor, Great Egg Harbor, and a dozen others—until it reaches Cape May, about 95 miles south of Point Pleasant Beach. (The ICW continues for 1,200 miles to Florida.) To the north of Manasquan Inlet, there are no barrier islands. The beach is the beginning of the New Jersey mainland all the way to Sandy Hook, a narrow cape that curves north and west into Lower New York Bay.

To the south of Manasquan Inlet, several inlets lead to docks where clam boats can unload. Occasionally clam boats will dock inside Barnegat Inlet. More often, they enter Absecon

Inlet for the docks of Atlantic City, or Cape May Inlet for docks in Wildwood and Cape May.

Manasquan Inlet is about 25 miles south of Sandy Hook, a spit of land at the southern edge of New York Harbor, with a view of Manhattan. The banks and jetties of Manasquan Inlet are built of huge boulders trucked and barged there when Manhattan's bedrock was excavated to build its subway system. A fishing boat or a pleasure boat captain entering the inlet from the sea is faced with an immediate decision just inside the inlet. There, the water divides around a sandbar, some of it flowing northwest in what is called the Manasquan River and some of it bending sharply to the south, the beginning of Wills Hole Thoroughfare. Straight ahead is Gull Island, an uninhabited mound of sand overgrown with reeds. Long-distance mariners seeking the protection of the ICW stay right, keeping Gull Island to their left, or port side. Local traffic, including the port's substantial commercial fishing fleet, bears left. The docks begin immediately, with net boats and long-liners and scallop and head boats, or party boats, tied to piers or pulled into slips. A few clam boats dock in this first section, before the gray-green water of the thoroughfare turns abruptly to the west. But when returning from the sea with a load of surf clams or quahogs, all clam boats (and some other fishing boats) make that turn around a red buoy and travel a quarter mile until, on the port side, the clam dock is reached. This is a hub of the East Coast clamming industry.

Day and night, seagulls perch and screech on the ridge of a white-and-aqua-colored shed that extends the length of the clam dock. The shed's waterfront wall rises from the edge of the dock, about four feet above the average tide. Boats parallel park beside the dock, which can accommodate about three vessels, each near one of the three large doors in the shed's waterfront wall. Inside those doors is a dock-long passageway, paved in concrete, over which forklift trucks whine. Inshore from the passageway and still under the roof are two structures. To the east is a large ice room from which a bucket loader scoops ice for the holds of those boats that need it. While this is the clam dock, other types of fishing vessels unload here as well, and they use ice to keep their catch fresh for several days at sea. To the west of the ice room and still under the shed roof, another concrete-block structure is divided into three spaces—a lounge where workers or crewmen gather to get out of winter winds or summer heat, a rest room, and, no larger than the rest room, the clam dock office.

In January 1999, Kathy Becica, 50, was the office manager at the clam dock and her husband, William, 52, was the dock manager. On most days Kathy could be found in a haze of cigarette smoke at her desk, which was wedged into a corner of the small office. Behind her seat, a wall chart under a sheet of clear plastic listed the clam boats that used Point Pleasant as their home port. In grease pencil on the plastic was noted the status—in port or at sea—of each boat, along with other pertinent information. At the side of Kathy's desk was one chair where Bill could be found when he was not outside tending to boats. A computer was on top of the desk. A television sat atop a file cabinet behind Bill's chair, and daytime shows—*The Montel Williams Show*, *The People's Court*, and various soap operas—created a diversion for those times when there was no one with whom Kathy could be talking.

But there was almost always someone either in her office or in the lounge area, a no-frills workplace space where men with fish-smeared clothes could rest comfortably in chairs or on a couch. Kathy Becica talked by radio or on the phone with most of the clam boat captains or mates several times a day when they were at sea, keeping track of when they would arrive at port and how many trailers she needed to order to haul away their catch. And like brothers or sons, they and their deckhands found her office a pleasant place to linger when they were ashore. She knew their language. Her husband, Bill, had been a fisherman and clam boat captain for 27 years before he had docked for good in 1993.

Bill, a man of average height and ample belly, full gray jawline beard, tattooed arms, and a rolling walk, had last skippered the *John N,* one of the largest clam boats in the fleet. He had sailed out of Point Pleasant and all of the other New Jersey clam ports as well as Ocean City, Maryland, and Chincoteague, Virginia.

While clams are stationary, clammers are an itinerant group, following the flow of dollars. A crewman will hop from boat to boat, seeking the best income. And a clam boat captain can dredge wherever he wants, wherever he can find clams. He can land his catch in any of the major ports where he can find a buyer. But in most cases, it would be the boat owner's decision where the clams are landed, for the owner holds the contracts with the shucking houses and determines which ports mean the most income. As a result, a clam boat captain frequently works the clam beds closest to the port chosen by the owner.

For example, Ed McLaughlin had spent three years sailing from Long Island, including the first two years of his marriage to Lisa. He went where the work was. Only when Liam was born did the *Beth Dee Bob* return to New Jersey ports, including Point Pleasant, and that decision was made by the boat's owner, PMD.

REGARDLESS OF WHAT port they called home, the clammers were treated like family in Point Pleasant, and the Becicas, whose home was a one-story house on the far side of the clam dock parking lot, were the warmhearted uncle and aunt. Their son, William J. Jr., worked at the dock, and another son, Sean, had been first mate on a number of boats, including the *Adriatic.* The Becicas knew most of the other men at least by their first names. They knew wives and girlfriends and had seen photos of the clammers' children if they hadn't met the kids themselves.

One of the men the Becicas knew was Mike Hager, who had worked with Sean Becica on the *Adriatic.* Mike was a typical example of the footloose fisherman.

Hager had quit Point Pleasant Borough High School at 16. His father's rule was, "School or work, take your choice." He worked with his father, first mate on the clam boat *Marie Kim*, for a bit. But as a minor he could not be a full-time fisherman. So he got a job at the fish co-op at the bend in Channel Drive, not far from the clam dock, and worked there until 1985, when he was 18 and old enough to sign on as a fishing boat deckhand. His first job was on a 68-foot net boat, *Tuisu*, owned by a man known as the Chinaman, who taught Hager the trade.

Fishermen are loyal to their income only. A boat that is capable of catching more fish or dredging more clams provides bigger shares for the crew back at the dock. Hager moved on from the *Tuisu* to richer boats, then returned to the vessel when a new owner gave him a shot at being captain. But the owner refused to let Hager select his own crew—normally the captain's prerogative—and Hager stayed with the *Tuisu* only a few months. By the early 1990s, Hager and his brother Timothy were working on one of the premier scallop boats, the *Christian Alexa*, a vessel known as a gentleman's boat. The owners, the Ochse brothers, screened potential employees to avoid hiring heroin addicts and other riffraff, and they offered their crew generous shares. There were ten crewmen on the *Christian Alexa*, and when the boat returned to port, the first thing the crew did onshore was to head for the Broadway Bar & Grille, a popular waterfront restaurant. It was their time to wind down from ten or eleven intense days of scalloping. Even for the family men among the crew, the Broadway was the first stop ashore. But the fishing life—including its ritual visits to the Broadway—was wearing thin for Timothy Hager's wife, and she would demand within a year that he quit commercial fishing despite the irreplaceable sea wages.

Mike Hager, on the other hand, was single, and there was no incentive for this 25-year-old to quit. Still, there was an aching in his soul. He told Tim, "I want what you have." He had dated several women and had given himself unequivocally to a couple, only to be left brokenhearted. This was often the fate of fishermen. Away for long periods, they frequently came home to a woman who had found companionship elsewhere. Hager nevertheless clung to a vision of a little home with a wife and baby and a nicely painted fence around his yard. It was a dream based on his childhood.

Dick and Judy Hager, who in the early 1960s had migrated to the seashore from a paper mill town in western New Jersey, bought a house in Point Pleasant Borough the year before their last child, Michael, was born. The area was still rural. The neighbors were the Shaugnessys, who had four children, and the Connorses, who had five. There were always enough players for a coed game of baseball or football. They had backyard tree houses. The Point Pleasant Canal, part of the ICW, was a few hundred feet from the front door. Although Dick Hager was at sea most of the time, Michael's oldest sister, Terri, taught him how to fish and catch crabs in the canal. The Hager house was filled with little peanut-butter-and-jelly-smeared faces, both Hagers and neighborhood children. And although there was a weary father who collapsed in his recliner between clamming trips, there was a strong sense of family.

Michael was a towhead with a pageboy haircut, a child who thought for himself. At age eight, he took his dog for a walk one day without telling anyone and returned with a ribbon, the top prize in a municipal dog show. When he was fourteen, he ran off to Florida with his best friend, Sean Domingo, and Sean's girlfriend. The girlfriend was old enough to drive, and the trio reached Florida but then split up. Michael spent a night under a bridge with homeless people and another night in a shelter before he was shipped home to his angry yet relieved parents.

Most of the time he was growing up, Michael had several of his three brothers and two sisters at home. The oldest, Richard Jr., was 18 when Michael was six. As the family baby, Michael was the object of unceasing affection. And from this nurturing, he grew into the most affectionate of the brood, a man who always had hugs and kisses for his parents and siblings.

Hager carried his affection and his dreams of domesticity with him like a piece of luggage. He arrived by bus in New Bedford, Massachusetts, in September 1992, looking for a boat that offered better shares. New Bedford, once a whaling capital and later a mill town during the Industrial Revolution, is on one side of a harbor that empties into Buzzards Bay. The bus terminal was in the downtown area, a hillside rising from the waterfront. In the terminal, Hager saw a pretty young woman with dark hair and dark eyes. They exchanged glances, and then she came toward him. He looked like a rock star, with his shoulder-length sandy hair and lean body. They talked until her bus arrived. She gave him her phone number, and he said he would call.

Susan Cornell was 20, worked in a factory hand-folding curtains, and was going through a divorce. She guessed she would never hear from Hager. But he called from New Jersey, and then he flew back for a weekend. A few weeks and several visits later, Hager took a job on a New Bedford scallop boat, and he and Cornell took an apartment together. He told her he was making enough as a commercial fisherman that she did not need to work, and she quit the curtain factory. Their son, Mikey, was born the next June, and it was not long before Hager, pressured by Cornell to spend more time at home, took a land job as maintenance manager for a clam processing plant.

The young couple had some obstacles to overcome. One was Hager's passion for the life of a fisherman, which he was reluctant to give up but which demanded long hours and offered little shore time. There were also the strong attachments each of them had to their hometowns. After two years in New Bedford, Hager persuaded Cornell to move to Point Pleasant. They rented a condominium, and he once again looked for work on a boat.

For a while, Hager worked on the scallop boat *Discovery*. Then he was invited to join the *Adriatic* as a deckhand. Cornell saw less of him and complained about it regularly. She had no driver's license and felt imprisoned when Hager was away. She said that all he wanted to do was work.

On the *Discovery*, which made long scalloping trips, Hager had been dissatisfied because he had so little time to be with Mikey, now two years old and walking. But when in 1996 he took to clamming, accepting George Evans's offer to work on the *Adriatic*, he was home every other day, had enough money, and had time to be with his son. The couple moved from their condo into a neat, two-bedroom home in Brick, the town just south of Point Pleasant Borough. Helen Sacchi, who had lived for 30 years in the house across the street, would see the fisherman come home from work and, in minutes, step outside to play ball or ride a bicycle with his son, who was obviously glad to see him.

For Hager, the world was as it should be, but Cornell was miserable. Moreover, she was unsettled by the nature of Hager's work. She thought clam boats were dangerous, and worried about her life if something happened to Hager. When he took her aboard the *Adriatic* to show her his bunk and the galley, she felt claustrophobic in its confines. Back in New Bedford, she had asked him what would happen if his boat sank.

"To be honest with you, Sue, I'm gone," he replied. "The water's too cold."

Mortality was not the big issue that tore at the bonds between the couple, however. Their breakup was fueled by Cornell's feelings of isolation. Six months of counseling did not improve the relationship, and by the fall of 1998, they separated. Each had sought restraining orders against the other as they struggled over custody of Mikey. Cornell wanted to return with her son to Massachusetts. Hager wanted to have him whenever he was in port. By January 5, 1999, there was a court decree giving Hager custody of Mikey on weekends, and visitation on those afternoons when he was ashore. He had had Mikey on Christmas. He and his friend Sean Domingo took their children on a spur-of-the-moment trip to Pennsylvania's Pocono Mountains, where they went snow tubing. And every weekend, Hager and Mikey had played sleep-over hosts to the Domingos and their two children.

The separation had actually improved relations between Hager and Cornell. No longer in close contact and at each other's throats, they managed pleasant conversation when Hager arrived at her apartment to pick up or drop off his son.

Yet it was at this time that Hager sought the skills of a tattoo artist and gave him instructions for the image of blood drops spattering across his back—for the women who had stabbed him.

FIVE

DREDGING FOR DOLLARS

IN the belly of the *Adriatic,* Hager and his companions had
found trouble. They had come into Point Pleasant Beach on
December 15 with a plan to replace the boat's clam pump, a
large, critical piece of machinery mounted below the deck at
midship, in the engine room. They backed the *Adriatic*'s rust-
streaked stern between two columns of weathered pilings in
front of Laurelton Welding's shed and tied off their dock lines.
Then, with Evans in charge, Hager and Jannicelli began the
work of removing the old pump. It was heavy, dirty labor. And
as with an old house, in which fixing a door often leads to
replacing the wall in which it hangs, so with the *Adriatic.* Below
deck, the sea was exacting a price in serious rust that would
have to be dealt with before the new pump could be installed.

On the morning of January 5, the *Adriatic*'s crew members were three weeks into their stay in port and still had nearly two weeks of work in front of them. The steel bed on which the pump sat had rusted away from the dripping of salt water. Also, some of the frames of the boat—the steel ribs that give shape and support to the steel plates that make up its hull—were terminally rusted. All of that corruption had to be replaced by professional welders before the new clam pump could be installed. No clams could be caught without it.

Clamming may offer an independent lifestyle, but what shapes the industry are economic considerations. While there is big money to be made, there are also big expenses to pay. The operation of any boat is a constant battle with the corrosive effects of seawater. Keeping a boat safe and efficient requires unceasing maintenance. Replacing the clam pump was but one example of the economic factors with which a boat operator like George Evans had to contend. With a functioning pump, he could make money. Replacement of a broken pump was unavoidable. It was essential to the dredging operation.

FILL-IN: THE CLAM PUMP

A CLAM DREDGE is built with a horizontal "knife" blade across the bottom of the dredge mouth. The blade cuts into the sand or mud on the ocean floor where the clams live. But the knife is not strong enough to cut through raw mud or sand, and even with a huge diesel engine, the clam boat lacks the strength to drag the dredge through the bottom. The answer is the clam pump.

Mounted near the *Adriatic*'s engine but driven by its own, smaller engine, the pump sucked seawater through an opening in the bottom of the boat. A huge valve with a wheel on top was opened to let the water in. On the other side of the pump was a pipe, attached by bolts to a flange on the pump. This pipe crossed the bottom of the boat and then turned up toward the deck. After passing through the deck, the pipe ran to the rear of the boat along the port bulwark. At the stern, the pipe had a valve and a coupling.

When the valves in this line were opened and the clam pump was turned on, an enormous amount of seawater was driven through the piping and then into a ten-inch black rubber hose that was attached to the coupling at the end of the pipe. The other end of this hose—which was about 300 feet long—was attached to a pipe welded across the front of the dredge, above its blade. This pipe had a dozen or more nozzles spaced along its entire length. When the dredge was dropped, the hose went with it to the ocean floor.

The clam pump sucked up and delivered several thousand gallons a minute of seawater to the nozzles, which then shot high-pressure jets toward the ocean floor, churning the seabed in front of the dredge blade, eroding the mud or sand. The dredge was then able to scoop up the boiling soup of mud, sand, and clams without strain.

FOR SOME TIME, George Evans had been unhappy with the way his clam pump was functioning. Catching a load of clams was taking more time than it should, which meant fewer trips or fewer cages in the same amount of time. And that meant less income for everyone on board. On a good trip, Jannicelli, the lowest-paid member of the crew, could bring home $350. On a bad trip, one when the boat returned with some empty cages, his share might be only $180.

So Evans had bought a pump and, to the surprise of some, was actually going to install it. He had for some time talked about modernizing the deck machinery on the *Adriatic*, and he had purchased a conveyor system. But the deck machinery remained uninstalled, and all of the work aboard the *Adriatic* was still done by hand. Evans was earning money with the *Adriatic*, but he was investing it in Virginia real estate before improving his boat. Another example of his financial priorities was the fact that Evans would not pay Laurelton Welding to prepare the *Adriatic* for the new pump. Instead, the captain hired his crew at $350 a week to cut away steel bulkheads and to haul out the big, old pump.

If he pinched pennies on the *Adriatic*, Evans's decisions were driven in part by the economic reality of operating this particular vessel. Each clam boat has a unique set of finances, shaped by the number and type of clams it catches and the number and amount of its expenses. The *Adriatic* sought only surf clams, which brought about $11 a bushel at the dock, because its allotment for clams, based on the boat's catch before 1990, was for surf clams, not quahogs. Ocean quahogs earned about $4 a bushel, clearly a less lucrative product for a boat owner. At one time prior to 1990, quahogs were abundant, while surf clams were scarce, and some boat owners had fished for quahogs to stay in business. Those boats now had allotments for quahogs, or some combination of surf clams and quahogs.

Using the allotments available to the *Adriatic*, Evans could expect to land between 60,000 and 70,000 bushels a year, for a gross revenue of as much as $770,000.

The cost of operating the *Adriatic* began with Evans's lease payment—$3,569.26 a month. Then there were the crew members' shares. That amounted to more than $1 per bushel, and in 1998 had totaled more than $70,000. While a job on some boats could make a deckhand more than comfortable, the *Adriatic* jobs paid less. Hager, the first mate, made $48,000 in 1998. The deckhands got far less. The *Adriatic* carried 12,000 gallons of fuel in two tanks and used up to 1,000 gallons on each trip. Evans paid an annual insurance premium of $23,100. And he paid to lease many of the permits that allowed him to harvest surf clams.

So when it came to maintenance, every penny saved aboard the *Adriatic* counted. And the *Adriatic*, built in 1977 by Master Marine Inc. in Bayou La Barte, Alabama, was old enough to need regular repairs. It had been two years since the boat had been hauled from the water and its bottom cleaned and painted. But from time to time, winches had to be rebuilt, seals replaced, bearings and shafts packed. The bills chewed into Evans's share from the *Adriatic*'s catch.

Still, there was enough going into the captain's pocket that he could foresee the day he would own the boat. His dream was of retirement, when he would turn the *Adriatic* over to another captain—perhaps Michael Hager—and live in one of the homes he had purchased on the mouth of the Chesapeake Bay in Virginia Beach. He had signed a lease-purchase agreement in December 1994, with Bernard Rubin, a Salisbury, Maryland, man who owned a series of fishing boats. Evans had worked for Rubin aboard the *Miss Toby* until Rubin bought the *Adriatic* in 1992. The lease-purchase agreement gave Evans the right to buy the *Adriatic* by August 1, 2001, for $10,750.

Rubin had last seen his boat in 1996, and he played no role in deciding how the boat would be used by Evans. He had observed the skipper for several years and believed he was cautious and careful. When asked about Evans, Rubin would reply that he "trusted in his ability, his judgment when we went into the contract, and that's how we left it." In return for the lease-purchase contract, Evans became not only the owner-operator but a traveler through a regulatory labyrinth. Clams may not simply be caught and sold. A boat used to dredge clams must gain a state or federal permit allowing it to gather clams. States have authority up to three miles from shore, and the federal government controls clamming farther out to sea. Assuming a clam boat captain wants to sell the clams he harvests, however, he has to possess a quota.

FILL-IN: REGULATING THE PIRATES

THE INDIVIDUAL TRANSFERABLE Quota system was instituted in October 1990 by the Mid-Atlantic Fishery Management Council, a quasi-governmental body charged with managing the East Coast fisheries, including clamming. The ITQ system was created as a means of controlling the quantity of clams harvested each year. It was by no means the first attempt to limit the catch, however. The first efforts at conserving fish populations on the open ocean were made in the 1970s, when all of the clams and other immobile aquatic life off the New Jersey coast died. At the time, it was assumed that ocean dumping of sewage was responsible. Since then, Rutgers University researchers have theorized that a natural phenomenon—a coastal upwelling—was responsible. An extended period of southwest winds had driven the warm surface water away from shore. Cold water from the deeper offshore sea replaced the warm, bringing with it microscopic plants that are the base of the food chain. Exposed to the sunlight, these plants grew rapidly and, completing their short lifespan, died and fell to the ocean floor. There they rotted, consuming all of the oxygen in the water. As a result, the clams and other animals that could not escape—including predators—suffocated. For more than a year, the clamming industry was dead in the water.

In the wake of that disaster, the federal Fisheries Conservation and Management Act was passed, creating a system of regional fishery management councils composed of biologists, conservationists, and fishing industry representatives. The job of the councils was to devise plans for preventing the extinction of various species of fish and shellfish. Because surf clams were among the species killed by the disaster, they and their cousins the quahogs were among the first species to fall within the sights of the Mid-Atlantic Fishery Management Council.

Biologists have three ways to protect the populations of the sea: close off certain areas from fishing, prohibit fishing during breeding seasons, and restrict the mesh size of nets used in the industry.

The first restrictions put on clam boats involved the number of days and the hours of the day they could work. By the late 1980s, each clam boat was allowed to go to sea only 24 days a year. On each of those days, the boats were allowed to dredge for only six hours. Enforcement officials from the National Marine Fisheries Service and the coast guard were responsible for catching violators. The clam boats would schedule their trips with the shucking houses, and the regulators would use those schedules to oversee the harvest. If the weather was bad one day, boats were allowed to go out the next day. But the regulators would not be more flexible. A boat that tried to work on its allotted day was charged with using that day, regardless of whether the conditions forced it to turn back with less than a full hold. And if the captain chose to stay in to avoid bad weather, his only option was to fish on the next assigned day, regardless of the condition of the sea.

"Well, unfortunately, if the sea gets really kicked up from one day to the next, it's likely to be rough the next day," observed Clay Heaton, an official with the Mid-Atlantic Fishery Management Council. "They would have the freedom to stay in port, but that's money you're giving up and you'd rather not do that. They were faced with the dilemma of giving up the money or braving the weather."

If the system encouraged decisions to sail that ignored dangerous weather, it also encouraged outlaws.

"We lived like pirates," recalled Timothy Hager. "A lot of clams were stolen. Back then, everybody did it. Catch at night the day before you were assigned for catching. If a [regulator's] plane came nearby, douse the lights, haul the rig, and steam to sea."

The purpose of the restrictions was to preserve the stock of clams in the ocean. But the government was saving the clams while risking the fishermen's lives and encouraging them to harvest illegally. A new system was needed, but for that to happen, someone had to give up something. No clammer wanted to be that someone.

Finding a balance that would please all the clammers was the first hurdle regulators had in reaching their true objective: creating a system that would leave enough clams in the water so that reproduction occurs and new clams hatch to replace the ones that are harvested. In 1998, for example, scientists decided that 4 million bushels of ocean quahogs could be harvested without damaging the stock, and 2.656 million bushels of surf clams could be taken. For 1999, the scientists upped the quota to 4.5 million bushels of quahogs but kept the surf clam quota unchanged.

The new management scheme of individual transferable quotas began in 1990 and dropped the government restrictions on when a clam boat could work. Instead, the fishery council decided simply to limit how many clams could be taken each year. The tricky part was deciding who got to harvest the clams. That was where the debates started in the 1980s. One group of clammers argued that since they had been in business a long time, they should get a bigger slice of the limited supply. Another group—those newer to the industry—countered that their investments in new boats and equipment should be taken into account.

Clammers had been submitting logbooks of their catches since 1979. The logs recorded the number of bushels harvested and the location from which they were taken. The government used these logs to divide the annual catch for the next year, taking into consideration a clammer's entire history but giving greater weight to his catch in recent years. The formula dropped each clammer's worst annual harvest from the calculation while adding a factor for their investment and another for the size of their vessel.

"Some thought fishing rights should be put up for auction, like oil rights," said the council's Heaton. But federal law prohibited auctions, he said. "Another problem we had to deal with was that a major portion of the formula is based on catch history. Some may have cheated on the regulations, fishing in closed areas or fishing longer than allowed. We tried to respond to that, too." Regulators pored over the records of fishing infractions recorded by the coast guard and the National Marine Fisheries Service, looking for ways to penalize the outlaws. But lawyers told the council that fishermen who broke the law had already been penalized by fines and seizure of their catch.

When the council finally instituted the ITQ system, it divided the overall annual quota among those who were in the industry at that time. Each clammer got a piece of the action, allowing him to take a specific number of bushels in the coming year. He could catch the clams himself, he could lease his quota or part of it to another clammer for the year, or he could sell the quota outright.

"We wanted to create a system in which fishermen see this fishery as the family farm, and they have a reason to protect it," said Heaton. "When an individual fisherman has harvest rights that don't expire, you have an incentive to want that fishery to be healthy. They also have something of value that would be at risk of forfeiture if they violate the regulations. Ultimately, after being fined, if this individual is a flagrant violator of harvest rules, he stands to have his allocation revoked. We have found that the fishery is much more self-regulating. When someone cheats with this type of system, each one of the industry participants is really invested in it." In other words, someone will rat.

The new system was much less costly to enforce than the previous one, which required a small armada and air force to check on clam boats at sea. Each time a crane lifts a cage from a clam boat's hold or deck, a numbered plastic tag is attached to the cage. Every cage arriving at a processing plant has to have a tag on it. There are only a handful of processing plants, so inspectors can focus their efforts at these locations, making surprise inspections.

"One of the impetuses behind changing over to the ITQ system was vessel safety," Heaton said. "Now the government is not concerned with what day you're on the water." And there is no official pressure to go out on a dangerous sea.

But even with the government pressure removed, Heaton said some boats still sail in bad weather, and at times stay at sea as conditions deteriorate, in order to get a full load.

"There is still a motive for the fisherman to go out," he said.

"The processor has a processing plant and wants to have stable, continuous operations of that plant. They want to be able to fill those orders and plan to . . . deliver when buyers want it. They in turn pass those needs along to the vessels. They say, 'We want deliveries on this day, this day, this day, and this day.' They make schedules for the boats. Those needs are regardless of the weather."

George Evans was required by his contract with Rubin to deliver his surf clams to one processor, Sea Watch International Limited. The company removed the meat from the clams (a process called shucking) at its plant in Milford, Delaware, and sold the meat to canneries. Evans had three sources of federal tags to attach to his clam cages. He had an agreement under which Sea Watch would sell him federal surf clam tags. As part of the lease for the *Adriatic*, Rubin supplied tags for several thousand bushels of surf clams. But under his agreement with Rubin, Evans first had to purchase tags from another firm with which Rubin had a long-standing business arrangement. If Evans needed more tags to keep clamming once these three sources were exhausted, he could buy tags on the open market from other owners, who sat at home and earned clamming wages without taking the risks at sea.

Unlike Evans, Ed McLaughlin had no snarl of contracts to follow, no collection of tags to sort through. He was a hired driver, employed by PMD to take its boat to sea and bring it back with clams. PMD alone had to worry about the source of quotas for the *Beth Dee Bob*. Formed in 1994 by fishing industry entrepreneurs Peter LaMonica and Daniel LaVecchia, the company purchased the ship the same year. LaMonica had never been involved in the harvesting of clams, but his family had been in the seafood business for 60 years and in the processing business—shucking, freezing, and canning—for 50 years. LaMonica's interests became vertically integrated with

PMD's purchase of its first clam boat. He owned 40 percent of Dockside Packing, a company that trucked clams from the dock to the processing plant. He also owned half of Surfside Products, a plant that shucked quahogs, and half of Cape May Foods, which shucked surf clams that it sold in three forms: fresh, canned, or frozen.

By January 1999, PMD owned three clam boats—including the *Danielle Maria* and the *Judy Marie*—and a related company, Ocean Quahog Corp., chartered three other boats—the *Christopher Snow*, the *Cora Jean Snow*, and the *Lisa Kim*. LaMonica still knew little about clam boats, however. He made no attempt to provide his boats with standard operating procedures or safety guidelines. He told a coast guard investigator that he thought his company had a policy on fire and abandon-ship drills, but he didn't know what it was, assuming his captains would take care of it. PMD had a zero-tolerance policy on drugs and alcohol, he claimed, testing its employees for such substances. But he did not know, when asked, whether any employees had ever been fired under the policy, and he did not know if the company had an outside contract to perform drug testing.

PMD had no policy whatsoever concerning clamming in heavy weather. "We really aren't boatmen," LaMonica explained. Better to leave those decisions to the captain. If the weather was "fit," they would go out.

SIX

THE TOUCH
AND THE TERROR

THE captain of a clam boat has three major enemies at sea: storms, mechanical failure, and his own hunger for success. Maintenance can eliminate some of the threat from mechanical failure, so a good and financially able captain sees to these chores regularly. And most captains stay in port when severe weather is forecast. But the best clam boat captains push the limits in both areas because they are judged not by their prudence as seamen but by the regularity with which they return to the dock with a full load—or, in the terms of the industry, make their trip. Ed McLaughlin was known as one of the very best.

One element in the drive that sent McLaughlin to sea on January 5 was the needs of the industry. Clams are caught alive and must be delivered to the shucking house alive. Since most clam boats have no refrigeration system, the summer heat can be lethal to the product, and trips are cut short to keep the clams alive. The result is that more clams are caught in the winter, the very time when the sea is most deadly.

But another factor that urges captains on is competitiveness. A captain who is willing to push his boat and crew hard is rewarded by the industry with bigger boats that earn more money. He also gets bragging rights in the dockside bars, where he can crow, for example, that he made his trip in only 20 hours.

"It's a very competitive profession," said Capt. Tom Dameron, skipper of the *Christi Caroline*, one of the largest clam boats, at 133 feet and with a load of 112 cages. "For a younger captain, it's scary because he's got to try to keep up with the guy who's got the touch." Some captains, Dameron said, are able to feel through their boats what is happening on the ocean floor as their dredge moves along the bottom. By the motion of the boat, they can sense when they are catching clams. They can get into a groove during which each time the dredge rises, it is overflowing with clams. They can tell by the angle of the cables suspended from the outriggers that tow the stabilizers through the sea whether they are making adequate headway, even before their sophisticated electronic devices in the wheelhouse give a hint. And the captains play the weather reports like a horse bettor studying a handicapping sheet, looking for ways to squeeze in trips when others might not.

"They used to call me Hurricane," said Dameron, who was the same age as McLaughlin. "I was actually supposed to be fired at one time. I had a hot little spot off Atlantic City. The rest of the fleet was heading in. All these guys called the dock and said they were headed in." But Dameron was looking at a different weather forecast than his colleagues, and he believed he could fit in a trip before the next front came through, so he headed to sea. He was working for PMD at the time, and the owner, Peter LaMonica, anxious that Dameron was going against the common wisdom, asked the coast guard to check on him. Dameron caught his load in 20 hours and got back to the dock before the storm hit. Later, Dameron said, PMD's boat manager told him he had orders to fire Dameron when he returned to the dock. But the boat manager argued with LaMonica that Dameron was only doing what he was paid to do—to make his trip—and his job was spared.

Ed McLaughlin was among that elite group of captains with "the touch." Another was Steven Novack, captain of the *Cape Fear*, which normally worked out of New Bedford, Massachusetts. Both were 36 years old. Both captained profitable boats. And if they pushed the limits, they always knew, at least theoretically, the perils of their trade. If a captain like McLaughlin did not talk about the dangers at home, he was nonetheless deeply fascinated by the terror the sea could wreak. There was one book among the many McLaughlin had read that held him tighter than rivets—*The Perfect Storm.*

He was sailing out of Shinnecock, Long Island, in 1997 when the book was published. Often away from home for weeks at a time, he was sometimes happy to spend some nights in local bars but kept other free time for reading. When he finished Sebastian Junger's book, about the violent October 1991 storm that took the Gloucester, Massachusetts, fishing boat *Andrea Gail* and its crew, McLaughlin was obsessed with the story. Junger had detailed how the storm and its huge waves, reaching 100 feet high, were generated by the collision of three weather systems. He described the environment in which oceangoing fishing boats work along the East Coast, and he re-created, to an extent that amazed McLaughlin, the lives of the people aboard both the *Andrea Gail* and other vessels caught in the same storm.

When McLaughlin had a day off, he drove to Gloucester and visited the various locations mentioned in the book. A gregarious fellow who made friends easily, he talked to the people he met in Gloucester, hoping to fill in more details of not only the storm and the people from the *Andrea Gail* but also about Junger. McLaughlin thought he would someday like to write his own book about the fishing life. He had 17 years of experience from which to draw. Like anyone who frequents the fishing docks, he had also heard many stories of others who had been on boats that were lost while they survived. And he knew the tales of the vessels whose crews never came home. More than 100 boats that sailed from New Jersey's ports had been lost in the last four decades, according to one tally.

The *Beth Dee Bob* was considered a state-of-the-art vessel. With McLaughlin's respected experience at the helm, there were few concerns about the ship's safety. Perhaps this absence of undue concern is why the captain could immerse himself in a story of tragedy at sea. The stories of men who had survived clam boat wrecks were chillingly instructive if not directly applicable to McLaughlin in his position aboard a clam boat that others in the fleet called top-of-the-line.

McLaughlin was thirteen years old in 1975 and so probably had not heard the tale told by John Goulart, who survived a clam boat sinking that year off of Rhode Island. Goulart was a 22-year-old deckhand on the boat *Pvt. Frank T. Kessler*, a green-and-black dragger/clammer working out of Point Judith, Rhode Island. The 65–foot-long boat had been dredging clams offshore from Point Judith one day in May. The *Kessler* had no deck machinery, so the work was all done by hand. Nor did the *Kessler* have a hold, so the 32-bushel cages were simply set against each other on the deck, where their weight alone kept them in place.

Goulart's job was to shovel the quahogs into bushel baskets and then lift the baskets and empty them into the cages. This wasn't the worst work a clammer could encounter. On some boats, the clams were handpicked and placed in burlap bags, which were then stacked on the deck.

When the *Kessler's* cages were filled on that day and the boat was steaming back to Point Judith with the dredge stored on the starboard rail, Goulart went into the galley for something to eat, and the captain, Roger Brayton, and another crewman, Ted Morse, were in the wheelhouse, above the galley. It was about 5 P.M., daylight savings time, and the boat was only 20 minutes from the dock.

"In that time of year, you get these southwest winds coming in," Goulart recalled. "It must have been blowing about twenty-five knots on the way home. The term we used back then was a queer sea." Today it would be called a rogue wave. The wave slammed the boat on the starboard stern quarter, and the boat rolled sharply. When the wave passed, it left a hole in the ocean, and the *Kessler* tipped back to starboard. At this point the entire load shifted to the starboard side, which already bore the weight of the dredge.

"I didn't realize what was happening. It was like slow motion. It went over that way and I kind of waited for it to come back. Everything just kept going. The captain yelled down that she was going to go," Goulart said. "I made my way up the companionway and I remember looking over at the glass in the wheelhouse and thinking, *I have to look away because the glass is going to break.*" Just then, the rolling boat hit sideways on the water. In the same instant Goulart grabbed the door handle and turned away. The glass in the wheelhouse windows shattered, the door slammed open into the boat, and the sea rushed in.

The ocean water off Rhode Island is cold in May, reaching little more than 50 degrees. And Goulart was not the sort of person to jump right in, even if he was swimming. But his adrenaline was pumping and he didn't feel the water, only found himself submerged in a boat gone dark. He pulled himself out through the upside-down door, searching for the surface.

The captain and the other deckhand had managed to get out of the boat before Goulart reached the wheelhouse, and the captain saw his vessel go belly-up, its propeller still turning. But underneath that hull, Goulart was feeling his way below the boat. One of his boots ripped from his foot when it caught on the companionway steps. He gave it no thought as he groped for a recognizable shape. He felt a familiar object, a pipe that ran along the deck and carried the steering cables aft from the wheelhouse. But as he tried to work his way along the pipe, he banged his head on the steel deck. There was darkness and there were bubbles, and Goulart kept going but again banged his head. More than a minute had passed, and when he hit his head a third time he thought he might not make it. But just then he cleared the edge of the boat and bobbed to the surface. With the other crewman, he climbed up on the upturned bottom of the boat. The captain had already found a floating object to grab onto. Goulart was worried that if the boat sank, it might suck him down with it, so he told his companion to jump and they went back in the water, where they grabbed the clam hose, floating nearby. As they struggled to stay afloat, big, cold waves periodically dunked the two fishermen. Fortunately, they were not alone. The captain's brother had been clamming on another boat, the *Carol & Peg*, and within twenty minutes he reached the *Kessler*. One by one, the men were hauled aboard. Goulart, suffering from hypothermia, was unable to stand when the crew of the *Carol & Peg*, attempting to hoist the last drenched sailor out of the water, told him to make room.

In the next week, some fishermen raised the *Kessler* from where it sank in 40 feet of water. Goulart went to the shipyard where it was taken to look for his belongings. But he did not return to the ocean for another year. "You don't think about [sinking] until it happens," he said. "Sometimes on those rides home, if the water was rough, you would think about it. But after a while, you don't."

When finally he returned to the ocean, however, Goulart thought about the dangers enough that he decided the open sea was not for him. In January 1999 he was 45 years old, and although he was still making his living on the water, he stayed within the saltwater bays near Point Judith, where he worked from his own 22-foot boat.

Roger Brayton, the *Kessler*'s owner and captain, did not quit the quahog business. Instead, two years later he had built a new boat, the *Ellie B*, a 65-foot wooden clam boat, a vessel with a star-crossed future.

ONE CLAMMER SELDOM seems to learn from another's mishaps, or if he does, he nevertheless may still be doomed to repeat history. An example was Goulart's friend, Andrew B. Rencurrel, of Warren, Rhode Island. He was 34 years old on September 24, 1995, when he steamed toward port in New Bedford with a load of quahogs he had dredged off of Shinnecock, Long Island. The 75-foot steel, stern-ramp clam boat he had captained for the past three months was called the *Troydon*. The *Troydon* had had a chronic problem with its system for pumping water out of the holds. The discharge pipe met the hull under the waterline, and due to a defective valve in the system, the boat would siphon seawater back into the holds after they had been drained. Rencurrel stopped late in the afternoon to the south of Block Island, Rhode Island, and pumped the holds dry once again. A tug with a barge in tow that had been following the *Troydon* passed the clam boat during the twenty minutes it was stalled. When Rencurrel finished pumping, he left one of his two deckhands on watch and went to his bunk to sleep.

About 90 minutes had passed and it was dusk when the hand woke Rencurrel and told him the boat had taken on a severe list. Climbing to the wheelhouse, Rencurrel looked out to see the starboard stern quarter dipping underwater. He told the hand, William Lanseardia, to wake the other crewman, Michael Staab, who served as the boat's engineer, and for the two of them to start the boat's pumps. Lanseardia had barely left the wheelhouse when Rencurrel suddenly realized the *Troydon* was about to capsize. He grabbed the microphone and yelled "Mayday" twice. The boat was on its way over, and he dropped the microphone without giving his location, jumped down the three steps to the galley, grabbed three survival suits, and threw them out the door. But he had no time to follow as the boat spun swiftly over. The sea smashed most of the glass out of a small galley window, and Rencurrel saw green water coming in as if he were standing by a waterfall. Instinctively, he threw his arms up to protect his head, and just as quickly the flooding water swept him off his feet. The boat continued to roll, and the fluorescent cabin lights glowed for a bit as the torrent washed him into the head, which was now upside down, and into the shower stall. With his arms still stretched above his head, he sensed through his hands that they were in an air pocket, so he floated up to take a breath and then sank back into the water.

The captain was scared. All he could think was that he would never see his wife and children again. But, keeping his head, he knew the force of the water entering the boat would prevent his escape until the boat was filled, and so he waited as the lights were finally extinguished. Then his upstretched hands felt the air pocket above him growing smaller. Air was escaping through the shower drain. He surfaced to take another breath of air, and then he began his swim, trying to find the door. Instead, Rencurrel found the shattered window and, swimming through it, was slashed on his legs and back by the remaining glass shards. Bleeding, he swam in the 70-degree water for the surface, where he found Staab and Lanseardia. Staab, who had been on deck with Lanseardia, had been caught between the boat's conveyor system and a sliding cage that broke from its chains during the capsize. His pelvis had been crushed, but he was able to float.

In the drawing darkness, the three men clung to one life ring. The *Troydon* still floated upside down nearby, and the men found the life raft as well. It was still inside its canister, tied into its cradle, which had ripped from the wheelhouse roof during the roll. They pulled a cord to open the case and inflate the raft, but all they heard was a hiss. The crewmen looked at Rencurrel as if he should have an answer.

Finally the men pried the canister open and dragged out the uninflated raft, inside of which there should have been a hand pump. As the useless raft floated on the surface, they rummaged through it but were able to find only a survival pack, from which they took a couple of flares. They lit the flares and waited in the growing darkness.

Meanwhile, the tugboat captain had heard Rencurrel's Mayday and had dropped his barge. Although Rencurrel had given no location, the tug captain had been tracking the *Troydon* on his radar and knew the general direction he should head. Two hours after the *Troydon* rolled, the tug spotted the flares and picked up Rencurrel and his crew. Rencurrel received thirty stitches to close his slash wounds and took two months off before returning to the sea.

On January 6, 1999, he was the skipper of the clam boat *Beth & Lisa*, another New Bedford clam boat, still fishing the same waters where the *Beth Dee Bob* worked.

IF ED MCLAUGHLIN ever decided to get serious about writing a book, he needed to go no farther than the office of the Point Pleasant clam dock to get an up-close story about a clamming tragedy. Kathy Becica, the office manager, remembered as if it were yesterday the last trip she made with her husband, Bill. It was, in fact, in 1971. The Becicas, both on their second marriages, had met earlier in the year, when Bill's mother introduced him to Kathy. Bill, who was 24, had a son and a daughter, and Kathy, 22, had a son. Kathy had an arrangement with the wife of another clammer to care for each other's children so that each wife could make clamming trips with her spouse. It was summer, and Kathy had already made several trips out of Oyster, Virginia, serving as cook on the *Eleanor Marcher*. The men were dredging on this warm day and Kathy spent some time sunbathing on the boat's bow. "I remember the only thing I saw out there was a cardboard box and a Styrofoam cup. You couldn't see land. Some sort of little bird landed on the boat." At some point, with the boat more than 50 miles at sea, she decided to take a nap in the wheelhouse, which was at the rear end of the boat. As she came out of her slumber, Kathy looked out the wheelhouse windows. It was dark, and wherever she looked, she saw water. A storm had come across the ocean, with winds of 50 to 60 knots scooping the sea into towering waves on which the boat now rolled and thrashed. Bill was out on the deck, chaining down the clam cages. There was no hold, and he feared that the load might shift, the cages tearing out the wood at the rail where the deck met the hull. When Bill returned to the wheelhouse, Kathy was shaking. "Are you cold?" Bill asked. "No, I'm scared shitless," she replied. Then she pointed to an aluminum johnboat, the *Marcher*'s only lifeboat, which was strapped against the outside of the wheelhouse wall.

"I said, 'If anything happens to this boat, my ass has that lifeboat,'" Kathy recalled. A huge gust of wind ripped the boat from its straps at that moment. "I was pointing at it as it left. I didn't get my mouth shut."

There were no survival suits on the *Marcher*. There may have been life jackets. It had taken seven or eight hours to reach the clamming beds, but now the boat was taking twice as long to return to port. At one point the boat made seven miles in two hours. Bill told Kathy to go to bed. "I told him if I was going to die, I wasn't going to be asleep."

In the midst of this storm, as the *Marcher* bent and creaked, its hull conforming to the shape of the waves, voices could be heard on the boat's radio, clammers talking back and forth. One of them was the captain of the *Salty Sea*, another old, wooden boat more than 100 feet long. The boat was also in trouble, struggling toward shore some distance in front of the Becicas. In the darkness, the captain radioed a Mayday call, and boats that were near him converged on his location. The *Salty Sea*'s crew of three had all been sleeping in bunks under the deck near the front of the boat. The ferocious waves had taken a toll on the boat's planks; the bow opened and the boat sank almost immediately. The captain was found hanging on to the companionway steps. All three crewmen, however, were taken to the ocean floor by the *Salty Sea*.

The *Marcher* made it to the clam dock in Oyster, Virginia, and Kathy Becica got off. In the 28 years since, she had never again taken a ride on a clam boat. "That was the end of my sea-faring days," she said in an interview.

However, up and down the Atlantic coast, scores of men continued to return to the sea every year. Many would never make it home. A record of boats lost at sea existed in a desk drawer not far from the Point Pleasant clam dock, in the office of Laurelton Welding. Thomas A. Gallagher, owner of the welding and marine repair shop where the *Adriatic* was getting a new clam pump, had developed a fascination with lost boats, and over the years he had logged the passing of each one. Some of the events were recorded on yellow-lined paper. Others were written in ballpoint pen or in pencil on the cardboard backs of writing tablets. Some of the boats were draggers, some were long-liners, some were scallop boats, and many were clam boats. There were 130 boats on Gallagher's list, only a handful of them vessels that were not involved in commercial fishing. Some exploded, some burned at the dock., and some were involved in collisions. The majority sank at sea sometime between 1960 and 1999. In that period, there were 77 commercial fishermen lost in the Atlantic, 43 of them on clam boats, according to Gallagher. The worst years to be on a clam boat had been 1975, when four men were lost on one boat; 1981, when four men were lost on two boats; 1983, when seven men were lost on two boats; and 1992, when eight men were lost on two boats.

The last fatal clam boat sinking had been in 1993, when the *Gulf Air*, a 95-foot steel, stern-ramp boat from Cape May, sank in Buzzards Bay, four miles off New Bedford, Massachusetts. Two crewmen were saved but one was lost.

And the very last clam boat to have been lost was the *Troydon*, the boat on which Andrew Rencurrel had nearly lost his life. The vessel was owned by Warren Alexander, a major figure in the clamming industry.

Among the boats on Gallagher's list were 22 for which he had scant information and no dates for their sinkings. But where he could, he included little scraps of information. For example, when the dragger *Bettie T* went down, it took the lives of "one man and [a] dog."

Then there was the *Wally Fox*, a 95-foot steel clam boat owned by Robert Kelleher, that sailed out of Atlantic City. On Sunday, November 5, 1989, the boat was 40 miles offshore when the captain turned the boat around and it rolled over. John Senger was 21 at the time and was working on the *Wally Fox*. "The boat rolled over like a log," he recalled. He crawled up on the boat's bottom, the only part exposed, and then jumped into a life raft. "There was a boat right next to us fishing and [they] saw it happen and picked us up." The next year, when the *Beth Dee Bob* was launched, Senger joined the crew, with Ed McLaughlin as the first mate.

But before that, there was another clam boat sinking of note. On December 12, 1989, a 75-foot stern ramp clam boat was working four miles off of Wildwood, New Jersey, with three men aboard. The boat had recently been sold, and the new owner named it the *Tammy D II*.

The Kelleher family had bought the same boat, used, in 1983 after tragedy had struck them. Beth Kelleher, her son, Bobby, and her sister-in-law, Melissa—who was called Dee—were killed in an automobile accident, and the family named their new vessel for the three. Sometime later, the family sold the boat and had the new *Beth Dee Bob*—the one now run by McLaughlin—built. The former *Beth Dee Bob*, now the *Tammy D II*, was sailing under its new ownership on December 12, 1989 when it capsized. No one ever knew why it sank. The three men on board were lost at sea.

SEVEN

INTOXICATING SEA

ON its way to the clam beds on January 5, 1999, the *Beth Dee Bob* carried empty cages but a valuable cargo: the fathers of two girls and four boys. McLaughlin's two-year-old son, Liam, smiled at him from the snapshot above the helm, while three more fathers slept below the wheelhouse. Each of these men had stepped aboard the clam boat with his own seabag and his own history, filled with hopes and habits, skills and second thoughts.

THE CREW OF THE *BETH DEE BOB*

ROMAN TKACZYK, 48, was the oldest man on the boat and the most mysterious, if only because he spoke English poorly. A native of Gdansk, Poland, he had worked both ashore and on boats earning wages that he sent home to support his wife and a fourteen-year-old son. He had helped PMD's boat manager to rig the company's boats, and when he joined the *Beth Dee Bob*, he was its welder.

Tkaczyk had a reputation as a good worker, a fact that kept him employed in an industry where sober, reliable workers are not always available. He also had a record of quitting boats with no explanation and little warning, a quality that in most other industries would have made him unemployable. On one trip, he had refused to work any more at midtrip. He explained to PMD's boat manager on these occasions, "I just decided I didn't want to work on this boat anymore." Before McLaughlin hired him as a deckhand on the *Beth Dee Bob*, Tkaczyk had worked in 1997 on the *Lisa Kim*, a clam boat operated by PMD's sister company, Ocean Quahog. He left the boat on September 12, 1998. Between then and the end of 1998, he earned $15,818 on the *Beth Dee Bob*, for an annual pay rate of about $60,000.

Tkaczyk's movement from boat to boat was not unusual in the industry. Nor was it unusual for the *Beth Dee Bob* to have relatively new crew members. McLaughlin had had a particularly tough time during his nearly five years as captain keeping a crew together. While some change of crew was expected, the fact that he had been through 47 deckhands in that period was extraordinary. The other captains of boats owned by PMD and Ocean Quahog had little turnover among their crew. The disparity between McLaughlin and his peers did not concern the boat's owner, however. The only number that counted was bushels of quahogs landed. And the high turnover among the crew never seemed to keep the *Beth Dee Bob* from sailing. Many was the time McLaughlin told PMD's boat manager, "I'm looking for a warm body to go." And then he went.

Jay Bjornestad was an exception to the longevity rule aboard the *Beth Dee Bob*. Tall and scrawny, the first mate had been aboard the clam boat since 1995. Bjornestad, 38, was born in Dallas,

Texas, and had been fishing since he was about 20. He had fished on longline boats out of Florida and had captained a few fishing boats before he moved to New York and got a job on a dragger, the *Megan and Betsy*, out of Shinnecock, Long Island. It was in Shinnecock, at Captain Norm's Bar, a place where clammers congregate, that Bjornestad, another warm body with some experience, met McLaughlin, who hired him as a deckhand.

When McLaughlin brought the *Beth Dee Bob* back to New Jersey, Bjornestad came with the boat from Shinnecock, moving his wife, Charlene, and his daughter, Theresa, to Absecon, within a half mile of McLaughlin's condominium. He worked his way up to first mate, and in 1998 he earned $62,216 from the *Beth Dee Bob*'s harvests.

Not all of Bjornestad's time in New Jersey was spent on clam boats. Some was spent in a program designed to deter first-time offenders from a life of crime. His offense occurred on the night of September 16, 1997. It was the first year Bjornestad worked out of New Jersey, and on this particular night he was in Cape May and had been drinking when he wandered into a home on Lafayette Street. The police arrived and charged Bjornestad with criminal trespass and criminal mischief. PMD posted his $10,000 bail, and, after a year, his record was expunged when he completed the first-time offenders' program.

His record with PMD and McLaughlin was golden because, when he was needed, Bjornestad was there. Such had been the case on the New Year's Eve trip. Arrangements had been made to replace him as first mate, and Bjornestad planned to take the trip off. It was Theresa's birthday, and he wanted be at home to celebrate with his daughter. The *Beth Dee Bob* was important to him. He had a scrapbook filled with pictures of the boat, and he had made a home video of work on the boat and of the scene at the Point Pleasant docks. He had a right to have a day off, however, and McLaughlin agreed that Mike Hager could fill in.

Then Hager decided to stay home with *his* child on New Year's Eve. So McLaughlin called Bjornestad back. Theresa's birthday came and went with her father on the Atlantic.

Grady Gene Coltrain, the final member of the *Beth Dee Bob*'s crew as it steamed east on January 5, was making his first trip with McLaughlin. Coltrain had been fishing for most of his 39 years, but he had been clamming for only the last two months, when the captain of his scallop boat took a job running the 84-foot steel clam boat *Victoria Elizabeth*. Coltrain came aboard the black-and-white *Victoria Elizabeth* as first mate. But he and the captain had had a falling-out in December. He stayed home in suburban Cherry Hill, New Jersey, with his girlfriend and their two children for two weeks, celebrating Christmas and New Year's. Then he returned to a motel across Channel Drive from the Point Pleasant clam dock and waited for a new job on the sea. At 2:30 A.M. on Tuesday, January 5, he called his girlfriend, Anna Puglisi, at work. She was a hospital nurse working a 12-hour graveyard shift. Now Coltrain told Anna he had signed on with McLaughlin and was waiting to ship out. They said their I-love-yous and she said, "Have a safe trip." Later, when the *Beth Dee Bob* had cleared the jetties off Manasquan Inlet, but before it had lost sight of shore, Coltrain called Anna at home. She had fallen asleep as soon as she returned from work, so he got no answer and left her a message.

It had not always been the case that Puglisi could rely on hearing from Coltrain. Their life together over the last 13 years had had its rough patches. But his fortieth birthday loomed in February, and he seemed intent on capturing part of life that had eluded him. He had recently proposed marriage. Puglisi had on other occasions dismissed the idea. "Why jinx a good thing with a piece of paper?" she would say, although she had reason to decline based on Coltrain's proven unreliability. This time, however, it was New Year's Eve, a time for new beginnings, and she accepted. It would be her first marriage and Coltrain's second.

Coltrain brought more baggage than a prior marriage into his relationship with Anna Puglisi. He had a lifetime of troubles that shaped the man he became. He was the oldest of six children.

His mother and father separated when he was young, and he left school in the eighth grade. He had grown into a big man—six feet, four inches and 240 muscular pounds. As a fisherman, working on net boats and scallop boats out of the ports near his home in Hampton, Virginia, he made good money and, in his younger days, was the life of any party.

One night in 1982, the 23-year-old fisherman blew into the Zodiac, an after-hours bar in Hampton. The pockets of his leather outfit were stuffed with cash earned on the sea. In his eyes was a look of authority. He cast those eyes on an 18-year-old barmaid named Jenni and she felt anointed. Coltrain had a way with women that hooked them and, even years after he had moved on, left them dreamy-eyed at the memory. To Jenni, Coltrain was "just the coolest guy!" He took her out the next three nights, and on his arm, she felt like *somebody!* He seemed to know everybody, and all whom he met seemed to admire him.

The whirlwind ended when Coltrain returned to his scallop boat for a 30-day trip. But it resumed at the end of the month when, upon reaching shore, Coltrain brought a ring with a tiny diamond in it, and he asked Jenni to marry him. Intoxicated by the big, bold man's charm, she did not hesitate. The couple visited a lawyer who was authorized to conduct marriages and, with Coltrain's brother and sister-in-law as witnesses, they were wed.

Coltrain continued to work on boats for a while after the wedding, but then he got a construction job and, within six months, he and Jenni moved to nearby North Carolina. It was a sojourn, not a career move. By their second anniversary, the Coltrains had returned to Hampton, where he worked on boats part of the year and in construction the rest. He was a good husband and clearly had a good heart, for he was able to overcome his darker impulses purely through willpower. He told Jenni he had seen his mother hit by the men she dated, and he felt he might have the same tendency. So when an argument would erupt between Jenni and him, Coltrain would walk away without responding.

He unfortunately found other ways, as well, to retreat from discord or uncertainty, finding sanctuary in alcohol and drugs. Jenni would see him using drugs in their apartment. Without any attempt at subterfuge, he would use cocaine when she was present. Later she would hear that he was involved with heroin.

But Coltrain took pride in the fact that when he was on a boat, he was clean. He took pride as well in his ability to work hard. At times it seemed to Jenni that he liked the sea because it kept him away from the self-destructive things he did on land.

In early 1984, Coltrain and Jenni decided it was time they had a child. He told her, "I want to have a son and be a father to him like my father wasn't to me." Grady Gene Coltrain Jr. was born on November 29, 1984. But life as a father was not what Coltrain expected. He wanted to choose partying over parenting. And his self-esteem seemed to be threatened when Jenni told him she wanted to go to college. He had street smarts, but he realized he lacked the knowledge an education gives, and that made him feel inferior to those who had stayed in school. Even before Jenni had a chance to enroll, the marriage began to disintegrate. By the time his son was six months old, Coltrain had left Jenni in search of that which would fix the gnawing emptiness he so often felt.

Soon he was no longer even in Virginia, having migrated with the fishing boats north, to Cape May, New Jersey.

Anna Puglisi was visiting friends in Cape May when she was introduced to Coltrain. His charm worked again, and she found herself thinking like a schoolgirl. He was such a guy! There he stood in his black leather jeans, tall and rugged, and, as always, everyone seemed to be his friend. She was swept away, and in less than a year, in 1986, she bore their first child, Sarah. They rented an apartment together in Cape May. But when Coltrain was off on a three-week scallop boat trip, Puglisi would return to her parents' home in Cherry Hill, New Jersey, about 80 miles to the northwest. And after their son, Justin, was born in 1990, she moved the family to Cherry Hill for good.

By that time, Coltrain had spent some long months away from home. On March 7, 1988, Coltrain had been arrested with another man in Middle Township, New Jersey. A month later he was indicted on charges of manufacturing, distributing, and dispensing cocaine, and illegal possession of a semi-automatic handgun. He pleaded guilty and on May 30, 1989, was sentenced to six years in the New Jersey State Prison. He got lucky. He was given credit for 30 days already served, and in December 1989 he was released and placed in an intensive-supervision program that allowed him to live in Cherry Hill. But in June 1991, while he was still enrolled in the program, Coltrain disappeared.

Nearly two years later, in March 1993, Coltrain was arrested in New Bedford, Massachusetts, as a fugitive and was returned to jail in New Jersey. He was released on parole in January 1994 and returned to the life of a fisherman and, in the winters, of a construction worker. He returned, as well, to Anna.

Puglisi did not like Coltrain's work on the ocean. "You have hands of gold," she would argue. "You can build anything. Why put your life at risk?"

Construction had its risks, however. During the winter of 1997–1998, while he was on a construction job, Coltrain fell a great distance to the ground. He was taken unconscious to the hospital where Puglisi happened to be on duty. When he was revived, she saw a big smile on his face. "I'm fine. Really," he told her, and then, minutes later, he climbed down from the hospital bed and walked out of the hospital.

If he was a rugged outlaw, Coltrain was also a romantic, a man compelled to express his inner torment, his passion, and his version of love. At sea, he spent some of his free time composing verse, all of it rhyming love poetry. He had written to his wife, Jenni, many years ago. Now he wrote to Anna. In one recent effort, he had pleaded obliquely for another chance. "Long ago you gave your love to me. Like a fool I could not see . . . how much that meant until all that love I spent . . . wasted it like a fool with his gold . . . Now I'm left lonely and cold. . . ."

This verse was one piece of the evidence available to Anna when she agreed to be wedded to the man she called her soulmate.

It was in the summer of 1998 that Coltrain met Rodney Bart, the captain of a Cape May scallop boat. Bart was in the process of refitting the boat for fishing, and he hired Coltrain to help him finish rigging the boat and then signed him on as first mate. They became fast friends and Bart introduced Coltrain to the leisurely sport of bass fishing. Coltrain was an enthusiastic student, and when he got home to Anna and the kids, he wanted to teach them to fish. He took them to a small pond in the suburbs, where Anna caught a fish on her first cast.

Their son, eight-year-old Justin, had for some time had his love of soccer to share with Coltrain. Now Sarah, who was 12, had fishing to enjoy with her dad, and she seemed to excel at the sport. Coltrain did most of his fishing with Bart, however. He would spend all night on a pond, fishing for bass with his new friend. Then in November they left the fishing boat together and signed on as captain and mate of the *Victoria Elizabeth*. That arrangement lasted about a month before they encountered differences that drove them apart professionally. Bart stayed on the boat. Coltrain left and took the next two weeks off to spend time with his family. He and Anna did Christmas shopping together. They went to a professional indoor soccer game. Their New Year's celebration included his marriage proposal and her acceptance. And then Coltrain returned to the dock. Anna visited him at his motel on the Sunday before he signed on with McLaughlin. The weather was too rough for the boats to leave Manasquan Inlet. Then she got Coltrain's message early on January 5. He would be gone for a couple of days. He would not be working in construction this winter.

FILL-IN: THE EDGE MEN

I WAS STANDING in the wheelhouse of a clam boat docked in New Bedford, Massachusetts, when I first learned of the role played by drugs in the commercial fishing industry. The boat's owner, Charles Brayton, told me he was quitting the business and selling his boat in part because it was too difficult to get good crew members. Drugs, he said, were the problem. He pointed up the Acushnet River toward one clam boat and then another and said, "That's a drug boat. And so is that one." He said that when those boats arrived at the dock, a Volvo was waiting in the parking lot and the crew members headed directly for it to exchange their pay for their painkillers.

Later the same day, a man who had been a clam boat captain told me he had quit the industry for good because of the difficulty he had finding clean deckhands. I decided to ask around and was astonished at what I heard.

"Some of these guys earn eighty, a hundred thousand dollars a year and they're broke all the time," said one crusty old hand who has spent sixty years on the New Bedford waterfront. "There's a lot of wasted talent that is dead."

The biggest killers on the New Bedford wharves are drugs and AIDS, contracted through intravenous drug use, a local journalist discovered in 1996. After studying thousands of death certificates, Ric Oliveira, a reporter then for the *New Bedford Standard-Times*, found that nearly 30 percent of the drug-related deaths in New Bedford and four surrounding communities in the early 1990s were of fishermen. Fishermen accounted for 30 to 40 percent of the 1,000 heroin users arrested in New Bedford, narcotics detectives told Oliveira.

Fishermen represented 12.3 percent of the AIDS deaths, the highest proportion for any occupation, Oliveira reported. Carpenters and construction workers accounted for 5.8 and 5 percent of the AIDS deaths, respectively.

One of the sources Oliveira met at the time was a laundry owner, Millie Barlow, whose establishment near the waterfront depended on the business of fishermen. She had hundreds of pictures of fishermen tacked to the two walls in the entrance to the laundry. The photos of the living were on one wall, the dead on the other. She told Oliveira that most of the dead were lost to AIDS or drug overdoses, while a few were victims of alcoholism.

"I call them all of God's children," Barlow told Oliveira, "and I call this corner [an area bounded by three bars] the devil's triangle" because fishermen gathered there in a climate that encouraged drug abuse. Barlow noted that not all of the fishermen were drug abusers or addicts. Many were hardworking men who never touched drugs. But others—whom she still considered wonderful people—could not escape from the lure of drugs in the open drug market that was the waterfront.

Barlow, who had closed her laundry and moved from town by the year 2001, told Oliveira that a dozen or more fishermen had died owing her money, some as much as $1,000. "Many of them can blow their whole trip's paycheck in a couple of days. Then they come to me and they have no clean clothes." So she would launder their dirty garments and send them back to sea. "When you get down to it, they are just super human beings, but it's the drugs. The drugs are killing them," she told Oliveira.

Barlow knew about drugs and fishing from personal experience. Her son had fished, and he had become an addict.

"I remember him hanging out here [at the laundry]. He stole everything from me," she told Oliveira. "I worked till sweat was pouring down my legs and he would come here and rob me blind." Her son did not recover until she banned him from her life and he fell to the gutter.

The attitude among the fishermen who used drugs was best expressed by one who told Oliveira, "You work hard and you play hard." That fisherman had lost his family and his reputation as a vessel captain because of his drug addiction. His wife became a prostitute when, at his side, she developed a drug habit. Eventually she got clean, divorced the fisherman, and left town. The fisherman clung to his addiction. "It's too hard to be here [on the waterfront] and stay clean," he told the journalist.

An anthropologist who studied the New Bedford fishermen and their drug and alcohol habits—Dr. Stephen L. Cabral—

went to sea with scallopers to understand their lives. He found that some used drugs as a medication at sea against the ever-present danger of death and for recreation on land. Heroin was often the drug of choice because it provided escape from fear on the ocean, while cocaine tended to generate paranoia and did nothing to relieve the fear. Drugs were also a means of escape from family stress. Fishermen are often ridiculed within their homes for being away at sea for long periods, Cabral found.

Cabral and two colleagues at the University of Rhode Island—Richard B. Pollnac and John J. Poggie—tried to find out what scares fishermen. For a report published in 1998, they interviewed New Bedford scallopers and broke them into three ethnic groups. Among Norwegians, Portuguese, and American fishermen, they found that the American-born scallopers were those who were the most fearless. They asked scallopers from the three ethnic groups if their findings sounded correct.

"One Portuguese draggerman said, 'These figures don't surprise me. Most of the American-born scallopers don't worry about risks because they're too stoned to care. They're not [concerned about] the welfare of the boat, the crew, or their families.'" The anthropologists asked an American-born scalloper about the conclusions he and his colleagues had drawn. The man replied, "There's no doubt that we're the most reckless and crazed motherfuckers on the waterfront. It's not that we don't get scared out there. It's just that most of us don't give a shit! That's why we get high. . . ."

Cabral, in another report, wrote that he had known working fishermen who had a heroin addiction for 20 years and continued to function.

"Oh, yeah, they're good workers," said the crusty old hand on the waterfront. "It's a fuckin' shame. The more money they have in their pocket, the faster they dip toward the edge."

EIGHT

YOUR MONEY OR YOUR LIFESTYLE

THE sun, in its low winter arc, was falling to the west when the *Beth Dee Bob,* steaming east, reached its destination 70 miles out in the Atlantic Ocean. It was closer to Long Island than to its home port in New Jersey, and Ed McLaughlin's long ride in the captain's seat was nearly at its end. It was McLaughlin's custom at this point to turn the helm over to Bjornestad, who began the work they had come to accomplish. The captain and his mate had a chance now to discuss the best place to dredge, based on past experience. Then the captain climbed down the stairs, passing through the galley, where he could grab a snack, before settling into his stateroom for a long nap. The rest of the crew had chores at the rear of the boat. Tkaczyk, being more familiar than the new man, Coltrain, with the *Beth Dee Bob*'s layout, was the likely candidate to open the watertight door in the port-side doghouse, a boxlike structure at the rear under the dredge ramp, and climb down into the engine room to check on the main engine, the pump engine, and the winch engine. Coltrain had been on a stern-ramp clam dredger for a month before joining the *Beth Dee Bob*, and knew to climb onto the ramp, where the long, flaccid loops of black clam hose were tied. Tkacyzk and Coltrain's job was to release the hose and let it float behind the boat. On this day, the sea was fairly tame, the roll from side to side not a concern even for the hand climbing the ramp.

A clam boat is a combination of high-tech gadgets and brutish machinery. Even on a state-of-the-art vessel such as the *Beth Dee Bob*, the working end of the boat depended on sturdy steel equipment meant for heavy lifting. The dredge, weighing several tons, was built specifically for the boat, without the benefit of a naval architect's drawings. Men experienced in clamming and handy with welding tools could fabricate a working dredge with nothing more complicated than a flat dock on which to arrange the steel bars and rods and a surveyor's transit, used to make certain the work was level and square. The dredge ramp was also unique to the boat, made of pipe and angle iron welded together and fastened to the steel deck.

The wheelhouse was a different matter. In it was a collection of instruments worthy of an electronics shop. Key among these devices—and sharing space with the television monitors, the global positioning system, the fish-finding depth gauge, and the radar screen—was the plotter. On the screen of this device, color-coded lines traced various routes the *Beth Dee Bob* had taken in the past, information stored in the plotter's memory bank. With a remote control, Bjornestad or McLaughlin could key in the precise location on the ocean floor where they had dragged their dredge on a prior trip, and then they could steer to that location.

The man at the helm—right now probably Bjornestad— steered until a small, white blip on the plotter reached the scrawled colored line that represented the desired path. Then a button was pushed and the autopilot began steering the boat along that course. At this point the helmsman, facing the rear of the boat, flipped a lever on the console at the rear of the wheelhouse. Looking through the broad windows before him, he could see the dredge slide down its ramp and disappear into the water. He could see the cable paying out from the drum, and then he could see it go slack as the weight of the dredge was taken up by the fixed length of thick polypropylene towrope tied to a post on the boat's stern. The towrope—more elastic than the steel cable and able to absorb the shock should the dredge become snagged on the ocean floor—now began to drag the dredge in about 200 feet of water.

Bjornestad spent most of the rest of his shift—up to ten hours—in the wheelhouse, facing the rear, watching the dredge and the two deckhands. Through the feel of the boat or the amount of time he had been towing, the first mate could judge when the dredge should be full. Then he flipped the lever, a diesel engine strained, and the winch hauled back the cable. Disengaging the autopilot, Bjornestad spun the helm and turned the boat around until it was pointed in the opposite direction, with the white blip on the plotter retracing the same path it had just followed, but in the opposite direction. He now dragged the dredge through the same mud or sand that he had crossed with the first tow. As long as the dredge splashed up with a load at the end of the tow, there was no reason to leave.

Quahogs and surf clams are not randomly scattered. According to seasoned clammers, they are what are known as "edge and hole" animals. They seek out depressions in the ocean floor where they can hide from seabed currents. Charts show some of these spots, like the top edge of an ocean-floor ravine. The boat's fish finder—a sonar device with a screen in the wheelhouse—traces the contour of the ocean bottom and can show even smaller depressions. A clam boat captain looks for these locations and, if they prove fruitful, records them in his digital library.

Down on the deck, where the only digital equipment was the fingers at the end of the crew's hands, Tkaczyk and Coltrain wore thick rubber gloves, shin-high rubber boots, and rubberized overalls. They might have worn a sweatshirt or a flannel shirt covered by a rubberized jacket, but even in the winter they did not need a heavy coat. Their labor kept them sweating.

Before the dredge came up the first time, the deckhands needed to have everything in place. The forward hatch cover was slid back, exposing the nine clam cages in each of the two forward wells. These cages would be filled first, and the conveyor system had to be set to deliver the clams forward.

When it was time to haul the dredge, Bjornestad started the winch, using controls on the console, and he watched the angle of the cable. As the dredge neared the surface, he used another control to cause a Y-shaped frame to pivot out from the transom toward the cable. As a pool shooter's leading hand guides the cue stick precisely to the cue ball, the job of the Y was to align the cable with the ramp so that when the dredge surfaced, it camp up right onto its tracks.

The dredge engine raced and whined, and black smoke puffed from the vertical exhaust pipe beside the ramp. The process was automated. Tkaczyk and Coltrain had no more to do at this moment than did a flock of seagulls that had gathered in the air over the *Beth Dee Bob*'s wake. The birds hovered in anticipation of the sea life that would be dragged up from the bottom with the dredge. Under the gulls' gaze, the dredge surfaced and, like an elevator arriving in an open shaft, climbed the stern ramp. Water cascaded from the dredge, flooding the machinery and deck below it. Just before the dredge reached the top of the ramp, a latch near its lower end was automatically flipped, a grated steel door opened, and a load of quahogs fell, as loud as gravel falling from a dump truck, into the hopper—a funnel below the ramp. One of the crewmen flipped a switch on the edge of the hopper, and the shaker began vibrating and the conveyor belts started moving. A short conveyor belt took the quahogs from the bottom of the hopper up to the top of the shaker. Small seabed debris began falling into a chute below the shaker. The debris was washed overboard, and the gulls dived like darts into the boiling wake beak-first. On board, the sorted quahogs slid down the shaker until they fell onto the end of the long conveyor belt.

Welded under the sides of the conveyor belt were steel rods bent into stirrups on which Tkaczyk and Coltrain stood. With their boots in these stirrups and their thighs leaning against the side of the conveyor, they culled the unwanted sea life from the quahogs. Dogfish and skates—members of the shark and ray families respectively—were grabbed by the tails and flung overboard. Starfish sailed Frisbee-style over the side as well. Scallops were tossed into a waiting basket for shucking when there were no more quahogs to cull.

The forward clam wells had been partially flooded to keep the quahog shells from breaking as they dropped to the bottom of the cages, about eight feet below the conveyor. Only the wells that were being loaded were flooded, a practice that kept the boat safe from swamping. The seawater in the well also muffled the sound of falling quahogs. But the constant clattering of the shells on the shaker and down the stainless-steel chutes from the conveyor was a din that, when combined with the diesel engine roar, made speech on deck impossible. There was a loudspeaker through which the captain or mate could speak to the crew. But Tkaczyk and Coltrain could respond only with hand signals.

When one cage was filled—a fact accompanied by a further increase in noise as the quahogs fell from the conveyor onto a mound of their brethren that had risen above the water—one of the deckhands moved the chute to the next cage. When all the cages in the first hold were filled, the hands moved the hatch covers to expose more cages. The work was constant. If they were not moving deck gear or culling quahogs, Tkaczyk and his new partner, Coltrain, might be shucking scallops in three simple movements: insert the knife blade between the shell halves and twist; sweep the guts and both shell halves into a basket; pop the pale beige meat into a pot hooked onto the side of the conveyor. On some boats, slack time would be used to cut the livers from monkfish. The livers would bring a good price for export to Japan.

There were housekeeping chores to be done, as well. The deckhands could wash the decks or, standing like aerialists atop the edges of empty cages, shovel the excess quahogs from the tops of the filled cages into the empties.

The *Beth Dee Bob,* which could cruise at a speed of ten knots, slowed below three knots while the dredge dragged along the bottom. Each drag might last ten or twelve minutes. The sea sloshed in through the scuppers and then drained from the deck, and to the west, the descending sun cast a white-gold band of glare across the surface of the ocean. The big halogen lamps, mounted on the superstructure that rose behind the wheelhouse and on the A-frame supporting the dredge ramp, would replace the sun when it was gone. But there was nothing to replace the labor of Tkaczyk and Coltrain.

McLaughlin slept in his stateroom below the waterline to the lullaby of the diesel engines, some 50 feet distant under the aft deck. As the dredge was towed, the sound was similar to an idling bus, and as it was raised, there was the groan of a straining bulldozer. The captain had lived with these sounds for 17 years, and to him they were the sounds of money. They were also the sounds of a chosen lifestyle.

One of McLaughlin's fellow captains, Edward N. Platter, 42, actually put the money he made—$1,500 or more a week—second among the reasons he sailed the *Debbie & Jeanette* out of Manasquan Inlet every good day.

"The money? No, it's the lifestyle. The money's always second to it," Platter said, sitting in the wheelhouse of his converted shrimp boat as he dredged for quahogs off Long Island. "It's not like being closed up in a factory, somebody yelling behind your back. The ocean is a beautiful lifestyle. It's just one you can never take for granted. If you figure hours, I'm making fourteen dollars an hour. The lure is money and freedom, not risk. I've never been that romantic. After twenty-seven years on the ocean, I'll never boast that I can beat the sea."

Platter had had his share of scares. One came on a day when the weather forecast called for a small front moving onto the Atlantic, with a southeast wind of 20 to 25 knots. Platter settled for half a load and headed for Manasquan Inlet, convinced he was taking the safe course. But in the four hours it took him to get there, the seas had built so high that waves were smothering the ends of the jetties, normally five to ten feet above the sea.

"I got three hundred yards off, with the sea coming up behind me. There was no way [to continue], with seas ten feet and winds thirty-five knots."

The captain turned sharply to starboard and headed north along the coast, toward Sandy Hook, 25 miles away.

"Within ten minutes, the sea went to fifteen feet. It came into a gale at seventy miles per hour. It took us two and a half hours to [get to] Sandy Hook," behind which the *Debbie & Jeanette* hid until the blow was over. "That was one of the days they didn't call for anything rough. We knew to come in. We quit early." Two other boats followed Platter to the refuge behind Sandy Hook. On the way, the boats wallowed in the troughs of the big sea, and anything loose was being thrown from one side of the wheelhouse to the other. It was night. The rain was blowing horizontally. Seas were coming over the wheelhouse. The only way to navigate was by radar.

"If you ever get relaxed in your job, something like that will wake you back up," Platter said. "Sailors and weather people can't predict how fast the weather can come up. Every once in a while, somebody's going to get caught."

NINE

MAKING YOUR TRIP, HEADING FOR TROUBLE

ED McLaughlin was a couple of hours into his shift at the helm at 3 A.M. Wednesday, January 6, 1999. Looking out the rear wheelhouse windows, he could see the crew working, their shadows as short under the powerful lamps mounted on the rigging as if it were noon. The sea was relatively calm and the big, red boat rocked gently one way and then the other, and the dredge came up and then slipped back into the water in its own rhythm. McLaughlin reached for the microphone of his VHF radio, depressed the button and called his sister ship, the *Danielle Maria*, another clam boat owned by PMD. Joel Stevenson, the captain, answered.

"Joel, where you headed? Where you at?" McLaughlin asked.

"I'm heading up to my spot up there off Long Island to go clamming," Stevenson replied.

Stevenson had steamed out of Absecon Inlet, under the glow of Atlantic City's bright casino lights, at about eight o'clock the night before, prepared for a 15-hour trip to his favorite clam beds off Long Island. Atlantic City is about 55 miles south of Point Pleasant, and Stevenson's clamming grounds were another 90 miles to the north.

"Man, did you hear that weather?" McLaughlin asked. "They upped that weather now."

"No, don't tell me they got weather. I'm looking for a nice day today." Stevenson's boat was owned by PMD, and he delivered his clams to Surfside Packing, another company owned by Peter LaMonica and Daniel LaVecchia. The plant manager at Surfside checked in with Stevenson several times a day, giving him weather updates from the Internet. Before he went to the dock, Stevenson always checked the Weather Channel, and on the boat he, like McLaughlin, relied on forecasts transmitted over VHF radio by the NOAA. Yet he was unprepared for McLaughlin's news.

"No, they got bad weather up tonight," McLaughlin said. "If you've got a spot to work inside, work inside. Listen to that weather. You'll see what I'm talking about."

Stevenson listened to the forecast, which predicted southwest winds arriving Wednesday evening. He would not have time to fill the 65 cages in the *Danielle Maria* if he continued to Long Island. He radioed back to McLaughlin.

"I got a spot right here in front of me. I guess I'll stop and work there," Stevenson said. "How are you doing where you're at?"

"I'm catching steady. I'm doing good," McLaughlin said.

For a moment Stevenson pondered joining McLaughlin, who was closer to Point Pleasant than his spot, known as Joel's Hole.

"Don't even think about coming off here," McLaughlin warned. "I'm seventy miles off. That's still a pretty good steam. By the time you get your trip, it's a pretty good steam [back]. It's going to be pretty nasty for you. You're better off finding some spot inside, close."

Stevenson was 38 miles southeast of Point Pleasant, and he decided that was good enough. He thanked McLaughlin for the advice.

By now it was four o'clock, and the *Danielle Maria's* dredge slid down its ramp to begin its work. McLaughlin told Stevenson that he had 19 cages yet to catch to make his trip complete.

An hour later and 30 miles farther east than the *Danielle Maria,* the crew of the *Beth Dee Bob* saw the blackness of night yield to the first touch of gray. A hint of the horizon appeared, and the rippled ocean surface was etched in black and gray crescents. In another hour, the gray sky blushed faintly pink. The fair-weather morning light show was about to begin, one of the benefits of McLaughlin's job.

On a morning like this, the distant clouds would begin as gray smudges, like puffs of smoke just above the junction of sky and water. The sky would turn a lighter gray, and the bellies of the smudged clouds would, in an instant, glow pink as they embraced the nearing sun. At about this point, seabirds would again follow the *Beth Dee Bob,* hovering behind the ramp, like shoppers on sale day eager for the store doors to open.

At about seven o'clock, an intense pink would light the eastern horizon, like the warning glow of headlights coming up over a hill. Suddenly it would be high beams, the blinding sun popping up into view from below the curve of the Earth. The sun might stay or go, but the gulls would remain until the sky again turned black.

At about eight o'clock, Coltrain took a break from his deck work. Dialing his cell phone, he called Anna Puglisi. She would be home from the hospital now. But when the phone rang, she did not answer. She was asleep already, dead to the world. So Coltrain left a lighthearted message and hung up.

By eleven o'clock—about 20 hours after the *Beth Dee Bob's* dredge first fell to the ocean floor—the last of the cages had been swung into place atop the filled cages in the front of the forward hold. Once these final cages were filled, Tkaczyk and

Coltrain began the work of securing for the long trip home. Bjornestad had taken over the helm, and McLaughlin was prepared to wind down from his ten hours at the controls. The boat headed west, into a breeze that had begun to blow from the southwest.

One of the deckhands now placed the locking pin in the dredge to keep it from falling off the ramp. One began washing down the deck with a high-pressure hose. Caked shell fragments and the same fine, gray clam grit that formed a crust on the crew's foul-weather gear coated the deck. If there were clams still in the hopper, they now had to be run through the conveyor system to fill the final cages.

The big black clam hose and the polypropylene towline now floated in the boat's long wake. One of the deckhands flipped a lever to shoot compressed air through the hose, blowing out the water so that it would float high. And one began the job of hauling in the towrope and stowing it under the ramp.

The next step was to haul in the hose. To do this, a strong rope was looped around the hose where it left the deck. The rope was tied to itself with a slipknot so that, like a noose, it could be pulled tight around the hose. Then the crewman eased the rope out and the loop slid down the hose until it reached the streaming water. The force of the water pulled the loop back along the hose, and when the loop reached the appropriate distance from the boat, the crewman pulled the loop tight and put the near end of the rope around a winch. With the winch engaged, the rope pulled a section of the hose up to the top of the ramp, where a crewman tied it. Then the process was repeated until all the hose was secured.

At the same time, it was the job of a deckhand—probably Tkaczyk, who was more familiar with the boat—to pump out the clam holds. On the starboard side, behind the holds, was a pipe with a collection of valves, one valve for each hold and one for the engine room. With the clam pump running, Tkaczyk opened each valve in turn to empty each hold. While the clam pump could be operated from the console in the wheelhouse, the valves had to be turned by someone standing on deck. There was no way to conduct this pumping solely from the wheelhouse. Nor could all the valves be left open to continuously pump the holds dry. If water were to get into a hold—a dangerous condition because it could make the *Beth Dee Bob* unstable—someone would have to go to the deck to turn a valve.

Once all the deck chores were done, Tkaczyk and Coltrain were free to go to their bunks. By this time, the *Beth Dee Bob* was heading west for Point Pleasant, its sharp, high bow cutting into mounting waves being blown from the southwest. Once again, the autopilot was doing the work as the mate sat in the swivel captain's chair. He reached for the VHF microphone and called the *Danielle Maria* on channel 66. When Stevenson answered, Bjornestad told him he was heading for the clam dock and was taking spray over the bow.

"Yeah, this wind came on quick," Stevenson replied.

An hour later, at noon, Bjornestad called again. "Man, I'm taking a lot of water over the bow. Joel, you're not still working, are you?"

In fact, the *Danielle Maria* was working. Stevenson had a rule: he would work until the boat rocked so furiously that he had trouble getting the dredge to stay on the ramp when he hauled it. Bjornestad was amazed, and Stevenson admitted, "Yeah, it's not nice but I can still work it. I'm trying to even my trucks up." The *Danielle Maria* already had enough cages loaded to fill one tractor-trailer—13 or 14 cages, depending on the trailer. Stevenson was now trying to get enough quahogs to fill the second truck.

Bjornestad checked in with Stevenson every hour, and each time he remarked on the roughness of the sea. Each time he questioned Stevenson's ability to dredge effectively.

At two o'clock, Stevenson's mate, Larry Kirk, got up and prepared to take over the helm. The wind was blowing 25 to 30 knots and the seas were building quickly. Kirk and Stevenson decided that the conditions were unsafe for dredging. They believed the *Danielle Maria* could handle any seas, but the dredge refused to stay on the ramp when it was hauled. They had only 23 cages filled by three o'clock, but they decided that would have to do. It was between three o'clock and 3:30 when the *Danielle Maria* raised its dredge for the last time. Jay Bjornestad came on the radio again, telling Stevenson and Kirk that he had lost a knot of headway because of the steep waves. He went on to say he was going to be in trouble with his wife, Charlene, because he had brought a microwave oven onto the boat from home. The company was going to have to replace it or risk losing a first mate, he joked.

At about 3:45, the *Beth Dee Bob* passed within a mile of the party boat *Jamaica II*, which was anchored about 20 miles east of Manasquan Inlet with 19 customers who were bottom-fishing for ling and had paid for 12 hours at sea. The captain of the boat was in the process of hauling his anchors because the trip was nearly over. He tried to take a video of the *Beth Dee Bob*, but with one hand on the helm and the seas tossing him, he had trouble focusing. Once his anchors were up, the captain turned for shore. He was ahead of the *Beth Dee Bob* and, with his superior speed—the *Jamaica II* could make 13 knots—he quickly pulled away from the clam boat.

By four o'clock, Ed McLaughlin was in the wheelhouse and on the radio. After five hours of trying to sleep, he was now reading a book and, he told Stevenson, looking forward to being at home with his wife, Lisa, and his son, Liam.

Stevenson had now been at the helm for 20 hours. He was thoroughly exhausted and had to get some sleep, so he left Kirk in charge and went to his stateroom. Kirk took over the helm, and when the deckhands had the clam hose hauled in, he began steaming toward Point Pleasant, to the northwest. Because the seas were coming from the southwest, the *Danielle Maria* was running parallel to the waves, in a trough now, and, in the next moment, on the crest of a wave. The *Beth Dee Bob*'s course was nearly head-on into the same waves, and the seas were increasing by the minute. The *Beth Dee Bob* pounded incessantly against the waves. The ride on the *Danielle Maria* was smoother but not entirely calm. Within a couple of minutes of falling asleep, Stevenson was awakened when a rogue wave smacked the side of the boat. Again he slipped into sleep, and then another rogue wave jarred the *Danielle Maria*. Stevenson persisted in his effort to sleep, and every couple of minutes another rogue wave would taunt him, a reminder of why he earned the big money.

THE MONEY ED McLaughlin made on the *Beth Dee Bob* afforded Lisa and him the luxury that she could stay at home to raise Liam. He wanted this. She would half joke with him about returning to work, but she accepted her role as mother. Ed was concerned that she not be trapped in their condominium, however, and he frequently asked his older sister, Patti Birchall, who lived about 30 miles to the south, to check in on Lisa. On this particular afternoon, he knew that his wife and his sister planned to go to a movie together, leaving their kids at Patti's house with her husband. He dialed his cell phone and reached Tom Birchall. The women had already left for the movies at four o'clock. McLaughlin was pleased and returned to reading his book. Bjornestad was still at the helm. The autopilot steered, but the mate controlled the throttle, and when the boat hit a big wave, he would ease off momentarily before resuming a normal speed.

Half an hour later, at 4:30, Bjornestad radioed the clam dock, where Bill Becica, the dock manager, answered. Bjornestad told Becica that the tides were running against him. He had just checked his Loran, an electronic device for determining the boat's location, and determined he was running a half hour late. He wanted to let Becica know, because the dock had to arrange for the timely arrival of trucks, and because the man who operated the crane that removed the cages from the boat would have to be summoned.

The radios in the *Beth Dee Bob* and the *Danielle Maria* now remained silent until 5:30, when Kirk decided to find out how conditions were closer to shore.

"Ed, is it any better in there?" Kirk asked.

McLaughlin, who was still in the wheelhouse, responded on channel 66. He was approaching the Mud Hole, that notoriously troubled stretch of water. The last tinges of daylight were on the western horizon. The New Jersey coast was not yet in view.

On this day, however, the Mud Hole was not an issue. "Yeah, once you get inside eighteen miles, it's good," McLaughlin replied. "I think because the sun's going down. Sometimes the weather changes at that time. Sometimes the sea will drop down."

"Oh, great, 'cause I'm getting my ass kicked out here," Kirk replied. Kirk had been on the water for 23 years and this was one of the nastiest seas he had experienced. He figured the waves were 10 to 12 feet high, and the wind was blowing at 40 knots. The *Danielle Maria* was now taking the waves hard on its port bow, which was about 15 feet high.

Ten minutes after the last call, McLaughlin's voice came over the radio in the *Danielle Maria*'s wheelhouse.

"*Danielle Maria*, are you there?"

"Yes, Ed, I'm here," Kirk replied. "What's going on?"

McLaughlin's voice was tense. "I'm taking on water, big-time."

Kirk heard the distress in McLaughlin's voice. "Where are you at?" he asked.

McLaughlin read off the coordinates of his location, and the radio went silent for five minutes as Kirk entered those numbers into his own Loran, which, connected to the autopilot, could steer the *Danielle Maria* for the *Beth Dee Bob*'s location, about 15 miles—or an hour and a half—to the northwest.

Now Kirk took his microphone and called the *Beth Dee Bob* on channel 66. There was no answer, so he tried channel 70, another frequency that the clam boats sometimes used for their casual conversations. Again there was no reply. Kirk switched to channel 16, a frequency reserved for emergencies and for hailing other vessels. He tried several times and could not raise McLaughlin. It was then, about ten minutes after he had last heard from McLaughlin, that Kirk radioed the coast guard station at Manasquan Inlet, letting them know the fishing vessel *Beth Dee Bob* was taking on water about 14 miles from the inlet. Kirk heard the coast guard issue an alert to other vessels in the area. Now a flotilla of boats at sea were converging on the Mud Hole, and others were casting off their lines to leave the clam dock. Help was on the way.

TEN

CLAM BOAT DOWN

THE coast guard station in Point Pleasant Beach bears itself amidst the bustle of seashore commerce—the restaurants and taverns, the bait shops and party-boat docks—with the stateliness of a dowager at a flea market. The two-and-a-half story center hall colonial stands within 200 feet of the vessel traffic through Manasquan Inlet. Its sides are clad in cedar shakes, painted white. Its shutters are green. Small arborvitae flank its small front porch, and a watchtower is perched on the center of its pitched red roof. Visitors enter through the front door under the porch roof and find themselves in a short hallway that ends at a visitor's window, looking into the communications room.

Keevan Walker, a coast guard fireman, was behind that window on Wednesday night, January 6, 1999. He was supposed to be aboard the station's 41-foot patrol boat on a training run.

But since he was already qualified as a crewman and his shipmate was not, Walker volunteered to take the other fellow's assignment as a watchstander in the communications room. The other fellow got aboard the patrol boat tied to a floating dock on Wills Hole Thoroughfare, across the street from the station. Walker took his seat at the sea-blue radio console in the communications room.

The radio console was the size and roughly the shape of an old desk. Its face slanted back on the right, and on its left was a cubbyhole. There were four radios—each serving a different purpose—mounted in the console. At the top of the slanting surface was a VHF radio that was always tuned to channel 16, the frequency on which vessels transmit Mayday and other distress calls.

Below the VHF radio was a larger receiver with a half dozen buttons for as many VHF channels. This receiver scanned those channels. If it received a call, lights came on that indicated the strength of the signal, allowing the watchstander to estimate the distance to the vessel that was calling. There was also a circular dial with a pointer—a radio direction finder that indicated the compass bearing of the calling vessel.

To the left of this receiver was a second VHF radio. The watchstander used this radio to communicate with coast guard vessels and helicopters.

Set back in the cubbyhole on the left was the fourth radio, dubbed a "high site," that allowed direct communication with Coast Guard Group Atlantic City, which was in charge of Coast Guard Station Manasquan Inlet.

To Walker's left as he sat at the console was one of three windows in the communications room that had views of the inlet to the northeast. The duty officer, Petty Officer Colin Reedy, was somewhere else in the stationhouse, and Walker was about halfway into his four-hour shift at five minutes before six— about an hour after sunset—when a voice came over the VHF radio at the top of the console, the one tuned to channel 16. Larry Kirk, the first mate of the *Danielle Maria*, identified himself and told Walker that the *Beth Dee Bob* was taking on water. He relayed the last known Loran coordinates of the *Beth Dee Bob*. Walker wrote the information on a chrono sheet, a worksheet on which the log of the day's activities would later be based. He pushed a button on the station intercom and notified Reedy. Then he pushed a button on the high site radio to inform Group Atlantic City. At the same moment, a phone that shared the cubbyhole with the high-site rang. It was Group Atlantic City. They had monitored Kirk's message and were aware of the *Beth Dee Bob*'s plight.

At about this time, Petty Officer Horace Browder, the duty officer at Group Atlantic City, got a phone call from the coast guard district office in Virginia, where a signal from the *Beth Dee Bob*'s EPIRB had been received. The EPIRB had been correctly registered, which meant that by logging its unique signal, the coast guard knew which boat was in trouble. But that did not give them a location, so they asked Browder to make radio calls to the *Beth Dee Bob* to see if the vessel could be contacted. Browder was keeping his own log of the incident and wrote in the information from Virginia. He soon discovered that Station Manasquan had been contacted by the *Danielle Maria.*

As duty officer, Browder was responsible for deciding which boats and which aircraft to assign to respond to any incident. He gave the order to have a Dolphin helicopter that was already on a training mission return to Air Station Atlantic City to pick up a dewatering pump, since his information was that the clam boat was taking on water.

Back at Station Manasquan Inlet, Reedy told Walker to radio the 41-foot patrol boat, give them the *Beth Dee Bob*'s last Loran coordinates, and tell them to head for that spot on the ocean. A 41-footer is rated for seas up to eight feet. When it left the inlet, it encountered only two-foot seas. But the farther it went to sea, the higher were the waves.

Next, Reedy took Walker's seat at the console and instructed Walker to go to a chart table that was in the middle of the communications room. There, Walker found the clam boat's location on a chart using the Loran numbers, then converted the location into latitude and longitude coordinates that could be sent to vessels using the global positioning system, or GPS.

The radio in front of Reedy came alive now with calls from other fishing vessels. A party boat, the *Jamaica,* and the *Danielle Maria* said they were heading toward the *Beth Dee Bob* to help.

When Walker had the latitude and longitude calculated, he returned to the console to handle radio transmissions. As Reedy phoned the station commanding officer, executive officer, and engineering officer to alert them to the incident, Walker got calls from the fishing vessels *Christina* and *Christian Alexa.* Those boats were also headed toward the *Beth Dee Bob*'s location to assist. The *Christina* was about four miles from the coordinates, but the captain didn't know his speed so could not say when they would arrive. In a few more minutes, the fishing vessel *Flicka* radioed that it was joining the search.

Out on the ocean, the storm was intensifying; waves were up to ten feet high, with occasional 12- to 15-foot rogues. The crew of the 41-footer was in seas well over their boat's rated ability, but they steamed ahead. Snow was blowing over the waves, and the wind whipped the froth from the wave crests, drawing it in long, white streaks across the ocean's surface. The water temperature was about 42 degrees. And somewhere in the darkness, the *Beth Dee Bob*'s EPIRB had floated free from its mounting on the wheelhouse roof. A clam boat with four men aboard was down. This much was a certainty.

ELEVEN

A FISHERMAN'S MOTHER REMEMBERS

MIKE Hager and Frank Jannicelli were in the cold bowels of the clam boat *Adriatic* that evening, continuing the work of hauling the old clam pump from its rusted mountings. As they toiled, and as the winds over the ocean increased, a parade of vessels returning from the sea steamed into Wills Hole Thoroughfare and passed before the *Adriatic*'s bow. By 6:30, several boats had made it to the clam dock, about 100 feet west of the *Adriatic*. The big, red *Christi Caroline* had unloaded its cages filled with quahogs, as had the long, low, black-and-white *Debbie & Jeanette*. The crews of those boats had already gone home. The clam dock crew had just finished unloading the *Victoria Elizabeth*, but Capt. Rodney Bart and two of his crewmen were still on board. The little red *Ellie B*, at 65 feet one of the smaller clam boats, was at one of the two clam dock cranes, and cages were still being snatched from its hold. Bill and Kathy Becica had left the clam dock office and crossed the parking lot to their home, where they were beginning dinner. They had set the office phone to forward calls. Bill picked up the phone at home when it rang. It was someone from Coast Guard Station Manasquan Inlet. They wanted to know if the *Beth Dee Bob* was at the dock. No one had been able to contact the boat, Becica was told, and the EPIRB had gone off. Sometimes that happens by accident, and they hoped that this was the case.

Becica told the coast guardsman that he had not seen the *Beth Dee Bob*. When he hung up the phone, he assumed the worst. He started thinking about the men on board and of their families ashore. He knew all of them, saw them coming and going. Ed McLaughlin and Jay Bjornestad had been back in Point Pleasant for more than a year. Roman Tkaczyk had been around the docks since he joined McLaughlin the year before. He spoke broken English, and Becica had had few long conversations with him, but he knew him well enough to say hello. Becica had known Grady Gene Coltrain for as long as the Virginian had been working in New Jersey, from back when Becica was the captain of the *John N* and sailed out of Cape May. Coltrain had come into Point Pleasant on scallop boats, as had his brother, Brady. Becica knew Brady and his girlfriend.

When he said good-bye to the coast guard, Becica dialed his boss, Daniel Cohen, owner of Point Pleasant Packing Co. Inc., which owned the clam dock and the clam boat *Enterprise,* as well as several other businesses. Then he called John Kayle, the plant manager at Surfside Products, the shucking house where the *Beth Dee Bob*'s quahogs were trucked. Kayle spoke several times a day with the clam boats that supplied his plant, and Becica hoped Kayle had better news about the *Beth Dee Bob*. But Kayle had heard nothing, not even the news about the call to the *Danielle Maria* or the EPIRB signal.

After finishing their dinner, the Becicas returned to the clam dock office and turned up the VHF radio to monitor the coast guard's communications. Rodney Bart, having heard that his friends, McLaughlin and Coltrain, were in trouble, prepared to leave. He needed another crewman, and one of the clam dock crane operators agreed to join him. As Bart steamed the *Victoria Elizabeth* back out through the inlet, he was joined by another fishing boat, the *Flicka,* a dragger that normally sailed out of Cape May.

There was little activity at the clam dock when the men on the *Adriatic* decided to call it a day. If they walked straight to their cars and trucks in the clam dock parking lot, they didn't go near the office. So George Evans and Hager and Jannicelli left unaware of the mounting concern for the *Beth Dee Bob.*

The last boat to reach the clam dock had been the *Ellie B,* whose captain, John Babbitt, lived aboard the boat between trips. Babbitt was a tough man who had quit school in his native Rhode Island, almost unnoticed, when he was about 16 to become a fisherman. He was gruff in conversation, his words coming like bursts of bullets, his comments as salty as the surf clams that filled the *Ellie B*'s hold. As the crane lifted the cages from the hold, word spread about the *Beth Dee Bob.* And as the night wore on, with a couple of newspaper reporters appearing at the dock, Babbitt sat down on the dock and cried. He couldn't remember the last winter with bad weather. *Going clamming is just like going to the bank,* he thought. *Go out and get your stuff and come back in.* But a wake-up call had been sounded, and for Babbitt and some of his friends, thoughts had to drift back to 1992 and the last time a clam boat was lost.

IF THE MEN on the clam boats had chosen to forget October 29, 1992, Rita Hutton had not. That was the day her son, Michael, was lost on the clam boat *Mae Doris,* an event that still burned in her soul even six years later.

Michael Hutton was a 31-year-old loner. He had walked out of school in the eleventh grade and joined the Marine Corps. Four years later, he was discharged and moved back to Wildwood,

New Jersey, where he became a housepainter. He got his own apartment, and when he was not working he was at the beach or on a dock, fishing, any time, day or night.

Earlier in October of 1991, Hutton had gone to Virginia to look for work. His mother had moved there the year before. But in or near her home in rural Melfa, on the peninsula that separates the Chesapeake Bay from the Atlantic Ocean, Michael Hutton found no jobs. On Sunday, October 23, he was sitting at the kitchen table of his mother's ranch house, working with her on a jigsaw puzzle—a picture of some boats on the water. He had it in his mind that he was going back to New Jersey to get a job on a fishing boat. He had never before been a deckhand, but he felt he was fit for the work.

When his mother objected and told Michael how dangerous commercial fishing was, he had a reply.

"Mom, I had all the training I need in the Marine Corps," he said.

Rita Hutton had borne five children and had lost two of them. A daughter was killed by a hit-and-run driver. A son died from alcoholism. She still had Michael, another son, and a daughter, and she wanted to keep them. But Michael was equally determined to find a fishing job. He looked at the puzzle, completed except for a patch of blue sky, and told his mother, "When I get back, I want the rest of it done."

The next day they drove north through Maryland and Delaware to the Cape May–Lewes Ferry and rode across the Delaware Bay into Cape May. They talked some more.

"You don't know how peaceful it is to be out on the water," he told his mother. "I just want to be a fisherman and live on the water."

They went to the home of Rita's daughter, Lisa, where Michael would stay for the next three days. Then, on Thursday, Lisa drove her brother to the clam docks amidst a collection of seafood businesses on a causeway just north of the Cape May harbor. That night, Michael signed onto the *Mae Doris*, an 86-foot, steel side-dredger with a recent history of minor safety infractions.

Six months earlier, the converted oil rig supply boat had been boarded by the coast guard less than three miles off of Ocean City, Maryland. The boat was cited for having its toilet plumbed to discharge in the ocean, a violation of pollution laws that the coast guard enforces. It was also found to have a high-water alarm that did not work, a ring buoy that had no line attached to it, and a first-aid kit that was empty.

Two years earlier, a marine surveyor had found, during an inspection, that the *Mae Doris* had an out-of-date battery in its EPIRB. He also noted that the lanyard connecting the life raft to the boat had no weak link, a device that allows the raft to float free if the boat sinks in water deeper than the lanyard.

The captain, Richard E. Goodwin, hired Hutton to join him and crew members William Kane and Richard Layton. Hutton told his sister he would return in two days, and the boat headed for clam beds about 50 miles southeast of Cape May. On board were 24 clam cages in the hold and eight cages on deck. Hutton was living the life of which he had dreamed.

Sometime in the next 48 hours, as the *Mae Doris* dragged its dredge along the bottom of the ocean about 170 feet below the surface, it snagged on an old communications cable, a coast guard inquiry later speculated. The boat leaned sharply to starboard. Then the dredge cable broke and the boat rolled to port. The load may have shifted, for the boat continued in its roll and capsized, dumping its cages. Then the boat sank, landing upside down, a pile of surf clams underneath its deck and the clam hose draped over its keel.

The men on the *Mae Doris* never completed a Mayday call, and the EPIRB never transmitted a signal. Six days after the boat was reported missing, an orange life ring with *Mae Doris* written on it in felt-tipped pen washed ashore on Assateague Island in Virginia on a beach where Michael Hutton had, a month before, gone surf fishing. Six days later, coast guard aircraft found an oil slick.

The four crewmen were not located, however, and Rita Hutton launched a campaign to find her son's body. The *Mae*

Doris was found where the oil slick had been, two months after it sank, by divers working for an insurance company. Due to rough seas, the divers were unable to search for victims. A group of volunteers finally dove to the boat the following spring and, although they, too, encountered seas that prevented an exhaustive search, they mounted a bronze plaque on the bottom of the boat, commemorating the lost clammers. That helped Rita Hutton in her grieving. But over those months, she had been asking questions about the clamming industry. She was disturbed by what she found and began lobbying for tighter regulation of the industry. She wanted licensing of fishing boat captains, and she wanted mandatory inspections of the vessels.

Less than a month after the *Mae Doris* sank, she received a letter from the commandant of the coast guard, who, writing on behalf of President George Bush, thanked her for her concern over the fact that commercial fishing boats were not subject to mandatory inspections. Admiral J. W. Kime informed her that a "three-tiered mandatory inspection program" had been recommended to Congress, as well as new "hull and machinery standards." Vessels 79 feet and longer would be subject to coast guard inspections and the assignment of "load lines," markings painted on the side of the vessel that should never be submerged, even when the boat had a full load, he wrote. "The coast guard is now seeking the legislative authority to implement this plan," he assured her.

At about the same time, Rita Hutton received a reply to her letter to Congressman Gerry E. Studds of Massachusetts, who expressed sadness over the loss of her son. He went on to explain: "Under current law, the coast guard has the authority to inspect only fish-processing vessels. To expand this inspection authority would require congressional action. I can assure you that my committee will take a close look at the coast guard's findings and recommendations and that we will not let this matter drop."

A year and a half after she lost her son, Hutton received a letter from a coast guard official thanking her for her support of a proposal submitted to Congress to require fishing boat captains to be licensed. He included 20 copies of a coast guard video designed to win the support of the fishing industry by explaining how the licensing plan would be implemented and how the coast guard was working with the fishing industry by cutting red tape in getting the proposed licenses. "I want to thank you for your hard work for making the fishing industry a safer place to work," he told Hutton.

Unable to reconcile herself to the loss of her son, Hutton continued her work, attending symposiums on commercial fishing safety and speaking out to the media whenever she heard that another fishing boat had been lost.

But by January 6, 1999, as the coast guard scoured the Atlantic Ocean 14 miles off the New Jersey coast in search of the *Beth Dee Bob* and its crew, little had changed. Commercial fishing boats under 200 tons—which included the entire clam fleet—still were not required to have inspections. Some captains or owners submitted to voluntary inspections by the coast guard. Many did not.

And few clam boat captains had made the effort to earn master's licenses. Congress had failed to make licensing mandatory, and there was a belief among the men already engaged in the business that that piece of paper—a license—would not make a fellow a better sailor. Only time at sea would.

Capt. Ed Platter was of this opinion. People who would require him to earn a license "have no experience. They have no idea how fast trouble can come up. It's a hands-on business. There's no book that can teach you what's going to happen in the ocean. I personally have twenty-seven years on the ocean. The coast guard retires in twenty years. So how can they classify us as inexperienced? Most of the fishermen around the Point [Pleasant] have been on the ocean for thirty to forty years."

Platter was raised in Ocean City, Maryland, where, in his teens, he was living the life of a surfer, much to the displeasure of his parents. He was about to join the military when, at age 17, he got a job on a boat, the *Billy Jo,* a former shrimp boat that was 85 feet long and had been converted to a side-rigged clammer. Four years later, he was a captain.

"I had a pretty good teacher, Harry Higbee. His teaching was the same as mine. If you ask me a question, I'll teach you. If you don't, I'll never teach you," Platter said. "He gave me a chance as soon as I asked questions. I was eager. I really wanted to run a boat."

After all his years at the helm, however, Platter's respect for what the sea can do to a boat was undiminished. "There's not a boat built to match the ocean," he said. "You can do everything in your power to keep the situation upright and safe, twenty-four hours a day, to be conscious of your survival. Never take anything for granted, and always double-check."

No, licensing is not the answer, Platter believed. Safety courses are a plus, he thought. But fines are pointless.

"Anybody that runs a boat and cares about his life should check his equipment. If you're foolish enough to go out on the ocean without the proper equipment . . . I wouldn't go out with that man. I wouldn't be nowhere near him."

FILL-IN: A DAY ON THE *DEBBIE & JEANETTE*

I HAD BEGUN asking clam boat captains to take me on their next trip the week after the *Beth Dee Bob* was lost. There were those who would not speak with a journalist out of a natural and well-placed distrust of the breed. Some others were more carefree, and one even agreed to take me along. But when he checked with the boat's owner, the deal was off.

Then one day Bill Becica caught me loitering in the clam dock office and suggested that I speak with Ed Platter. Ed is a man of about my height, which is to say five feet, nine inches. His blond hair is kept in a crew cut. He wears a small blond mustache. He says little, probably because he sees little need. But he smiled pleasantly when I met him later on the dock. "You want to go out?" he asked. "Okay." It was that simple.

I had already bought a survival suit so that I could head to sea on a moment's notice. He told me to be at the dock at eleven o'clock at night for the next trip of the *Debbie & Jeanette.* Then I looked at the boat for the first time and instantly felt some unease. It was black, with a low, white wheelhouse, and it rode very low in the water. The boat was 115 feet long. It carried a 21,000-pound dredge that, when half-full with quahogs, weighed an extra 9,000 pounds. All of that weight was high above the water, and I had little confidence that it would not topple the boat if the seas got rough.

The boat was being loaded with empty cages as I climbed the few steps to the wheelhouse. There, Platter introduced me to his first mate, Jeff Shell, 49. The deckhands, cousins Eric Matthews, 28, and Pete Matthews, 24, were up on the dredge ramp, where they were working on the clam hose. Platter went off, leaving me with Shell, a veteran of 32 years on the ocean. We talked a bit, and then I decided that it would be educational to watch the cousins repair the clam hose. Leaving Shell, I went back down the stairs through the galley and stepped out onto a walkway between the wheelhouse and the bulwark. Turning toward the rear of the boat, I was confronted with a choice: I could attempt to walk all the way to the stern on the wet and tilted steel top of the bulwark, which was no more than a foot wide. Or I could duck through two watertight doors to my left and emerge onto the deck. I had been around boats long enough to know that one should proceed slowly when on an unfamiliar vessel, so I stopped after stepping through the first watertight doorway to look back over the main deck, which was flooded with the light from the boat's rigging. Scanning the scene, looking for any dangers that might lurk there, I saw only a very flat surface that seemed to be crusted with clamshell grit. There were no hoses or pipes to step over, and the hatch covers seemed to have been drawn all the way up to the rear wall of the wheelhouse. So I stepped over the lip of the second watertight door and lowered my right foot to the deck.

Imagine my surpise when my boot failed to stop at the deck, but plunged on down into rather cold salt water, and I toppled forward.

The hold had been flooded, and what I thought were hatch covers in reality was the very still surface water. Fortunately, the hold also contained a full load of empty cages, and one of these caught my thigh, stopping my plunge before I was entirely soaked. My jeans leg was saturated, and one boot was full of water as I sheepishly hauled myself back to the galley, where a change of clothes was in my bag. What I did not know was that the crane operator who had been putting the cages in the hold had seen the entire episode. Twenty-four hours later, when the *Debbie & Jeanette* returned to the dock, I had a new nickname: Splash.

During those hours at sea—even before I discovered the nature of their sense of humor—I had begun to form some opinions about the men who go out on clam boats. They were capable of enormous amounts of work, and they had a level of self-confidence hardened by the worst the sea could throw at them. In their work, at least, they were brutally honest. And those who had been at the work for any significant amount of time shared a genuine appreciation of the sea and its beauties, along with a respect for the swiftness with which nature can unleash its deadly force. At the same time, I found it unfortunate that many, in the face of tragedies that had taken their friends, failed to look for weaknesses in their own habits but insisted that the tried ways were true. As one man said, no boat sinks without someone making a mistake. And this fellow, like so many others, believed that he would not make those same mistakes.

TWELVE

SALVATION
IN THE AIR

AT a little before six o'clock on Wednesday evening, an orange Dolphin helicopter reached the Cape May County Airport, at the southern tip of New Jersey, and the pilot, coast guard lieutenant Scott McFarland, steered for a runway, lowering the chopper's nose and then skimming above the tarmac for a touch-and-go exercise. The belly lights of the chopper flooded the ground ahead and to the sides, out to the edge of the trees, about 25 yards away. Richard Gladish, sitting behind McFarland, had been thinking small thoughts, wondering whether they would see deer this night, as so often happened. As they flew above the runway, the lights caught a small herd standing at the side. Then the chopper lifted and banked to make another pass at the runway. Gladish, a coast guard rescue swimmer, was looking for an easy night and thought, *Sure hope we don't get a call. I don't want to go in the water.*

If the need arose, however, he was prepared. He wore a waterproof, blue-and-orange neoprene dry suit with a zipper that crossed the chest diagonally. A fleece liner lay beneath the suit. On top of all, Gladish wore an inflatable vest that held a radio, knife, flares, glow sticks, a signal mirror, and a strobe. Crossing his chest was the harness to which the helicopter's cable would be attached in cases when he had to leave the aircraft. For now, the harness was tethered to the floor of the helicopter. He had dry gloves for his hands, a neoprene hood to cover his head, a swimming mask, and a snorkel. Riding in the helicopter, Gladish also wore a helmet, and he was wired to the radio so that he could listen to the pilot's conversations with the ground and converse with the rest of the crew. Inside the helicopter cabin was the litter, a wire-mesh boxlike basket about five feet long with cylindrical foam floats at each end. The litter could be shackled to the cable for lifting a victim into the chopper.

Gladish had already received orders for the next assignment in his coast guard career, and this ride in the Dolphin was, like most of the others he had taken over the last 12 years, routine. He was just biding his time until that last flight in March, after which he would become a boot camp drill instructor. Being honest with himself, he would admit that he had stuck with the life of a hotshot rescue swimmer too long. This was a young man's game, and Gladish was now 34, married, and the father of a ten-year-old daughter and an infant son. Yet here he was, flying at 120 knots through the dark as the chopper flew over the scrub oak landscape about thirty miles to the south of Air Station Atlantic City, to which the crew and chopper were assigned. Gladish saw himself as just another set of eyes looking out for air traffic.

Gladish had arrived at Air Station Atlantic City, which occu-pied a hangar at a commercial airfield in the New Jersey Pine Barrens about ten miles inland from Atlantic City's neon towers, at about two o'clock that afternoon. He had his gear ready by 3:30. At four he was on the tarmac, where McFarland briefed the crew—including copilot Lt. Edward Beale and flight mechanic James S. Bryan Jr.—on the night's work. This was a regularly scheduled training flight—one was flown every evening—and the purpose of tonight's flight was pilot training. McFarland said the flight probably would go no farther than Cape May.

There was no conversation in the chopper, whose cabin was about the size of a minivan. A man well over six feet tall, Gladish stretched his long legs from a seat at the right rear, behind McFarland. Sitting behind the copilot, a bit farther ahead in the cabin than Gladish, was Bryan. The sliding door to Gladish's right was closed, keeping out the freezing night air. As McFarland prepared to make a second touch-and-go pass at the runway, a call came in over the radio. Atlantic City had an assignment for the Dolphin. McFarland was given orders to gain altitude and head north. When the pilot had done that, the voice on the radio explained that a vessel was taking on water on the Atlantic, due east of Manasquan Inlet. McFarland was directed to return to the air station, where a couple of dewatering pumps would be ready for him to take to the stricken vessel. Gladish heard the conversation through his headset and began imagining what situation he and the crew would actually be handling. He had a habit of running through possible scenarios when an assignment came in. In the last 12 years, he had had enough experiences flying missions for his mental checklist to cover most possibilities.

A rescue swimmer's job is to leave the helicopter when it is necessary to assist boaters in distress. In some cases, he must actually enter the water and swim to the aid of victims. In other cases, the swimmer may be lowered to the deck of a vessel. The training for this work is extensive. Gladish had qualified for training when he was 22 and had been in the coast guard for four years. Three months of classroom lessons were followed by a month in the water. The instructors were Navy SEALs at the

Pensacola, Florida, Naval Aviator Training Center. Gladish learned, in one-on-one sessions, how to rescue panicked survivors, with methods of restraining the victims while keeping them and himself afloat. Some training used a complete indoor mock-up of a helicopter in a pool area, with simulated rotor wash whipping the pool. It was on a cable suspended from a winch above the pool that Gladish first felt what it was like to ride down into a boiling sea. The navy had created the school after the Vietnam War as a facility to teach methods for rescuing downed aviators behind enemy lines. Gladish started in a class of 32 students and was one of only a dozen to graduate. He felt he had accomplished something significant.

After the training, Gladish was assigned to a station in Brooklyn, New York, where the most common assignments involved looking for corpses floating in the Hudson or East rivers. He never found one. Occasionally his crew would come across a commercial fishing boat that needed help. The big event came one night in 1989 when an airliner slid off a pier at the end of a runway at LaGuardia Airport and fell into Bowery Bay. Gladish was lowered into the water, where he rescued one of the members of the plane's crew. Most of the victims were rescued by the fire and police departments. But there were coast guard boats everywhere and lots of lights. To the young swimmer, the whole job could have been more efficiently handled by a much smaller rescue team.

During the Gulf War, Gladish was assigned to Air Station Cape Cod, one of the closest bases to President George Bush's summer home in Kennebunkport, Maine. Bush, a boater, liked to spend time on the water, and helicopter crews were dispatched from Cape Cod at these times to stand by in case a crisis arose that required the president to make a quick trip to shore. That never happened, and so Gladish's time in Maine was uneventful.

Most of Gladish's duty involved search-and-rescue assignments and medevac missions. In one memorable rescue, a commercial fisherman had been stradling a cable on the deck of a scallop boat at sea. The cable snapped up, like a bowstring when the arrow is loosed, and slashed the fisherman's crotch, splitting his scrotum open and ripping out a testicle. The boat was so far offshore that by the time the helicopter arrived, there was no time to lower Gladish. Precious moments—and fuel—could be squandered. It would have to be a snatch-and-go operation. So the crew of the H-3 helicopter—the coast guard's version of the Jolly Green Giant used in Vietnam—lowered the cable to the deck of the boat, where the injured man's shipmates lifted him into the basket. They put a metal pot on his stomach and then signaled for the basket to be raised. Once they had hauled the basket through the door into the helicopter, a corpsman on board injected the man with morphine. Then he and Gladish packed the man's crotch with Vaseline, gauze, and saline solution and put him into a pair of inflatable MASH trousers to stop the flow of blood. When the man was stabilized, someone looked into the pot. It held the man's missing testicle. The man survived, but not intact.

Gladish missed the action, however, during the biggest event of his Cape Cod tour. In October 1991, the storm that spawned the book and movie *The Perfect Storm* swept over the air station. Sorties were flown from Cape Cod to the sea all day and night, and it was a helicopter from Gladish's unit that took the captain and two women crew members off the sailboat *Sartori*, against the captain's wishes. But Gladish was not in the rotation to fly, having been assigned to work on gear preparation.

During Gladish's tour on Cape Cod, he participated in about 30 medevac missions off of fishing boats from the New England fleet. The standard injuries were crushed hands, crushed heads, and chest pains. Gladish, who was trained as an emergency medical technician, felt he had done his job if he got the fisherman from his boat to the hospital still alive. As the chopper flew ashore from the boat, he would check the pulse and blood pressure of the fishermen. On enough occasions to qualify as common, he saw needle marks on the arms of the men whose lives he was saving. He asked them if they were using drugs and uniformly they said no. But Gladish and the other crewmen at Cape Cod saw the evidence of intravenous drug use so often that it was a frequent topic of conversation among them.

At Gladish's next station, drug use among commercial fishermen was not so common an issue. Commercial fishing is a major industry at Kodiak Island, Alaska, where the employment ads for crewmen state clearly, "Zero tolerance." Kodiak is home to the Alaskan halibut and salmon fleet, as well as to crab boats. It is a prosperous place where the boat owners spend the money for urinalysis tests and insist on drug-free crewmen. They loathe dependence of all sorts, and they call the coast guard for help only when the situation is critical. The coast guard at Kodiak Island is responsible not only for problems at sea but is the search-and-rescue agency responsible for serving those who live in the island's landlocked villages and who work in the dangerous timber industry.

On one summer day, Gladish's helicopter was called to a logging camp at a place called Two Moon Bay. A tree had fallen on a logger, and his neck appeared to be broken. But he was deep in the forest, with no place for a helicopter to land. That was no problem for his coworkers, who, with their chain saws and log haulers, had, in 15 minutes, cleared all the trees and made a landing site. Gladish would later recall that he had never seen so much Carhart work clothing in one place. This was another snatch-and-go operation. The man was placed in a litter and Gladish helped other loggers carry him to the chopper, which flew to a hospital in Anchorage, 40 minutes away.

The coast guard's only dry-land job in Kodiak is to conduct rescues. On the open seas, however, the agency is responsible for policing fishing and pollution regulations. As a result, Alaskan fishing boat captains are not always fond of the coast guard, and they call for help only when the situation is dire. But that was indeed the case when the agency received a distress call from the captain of a net boat—which caught fish by towing a net near the surface. As the helicopter hovered over the boat and Gladish was lowered toward the deck, the rescue swimmer could hear the screams. At the rear of the boat was mounted a huge spool for hauling the net and its catch. Somehow the captain's brother-in-law, a big man who worked as a deckhand, had become entangled in the net, which lifted him and wrapped him around the spool before anyone could stop the machinery. The captain and another crewman were supporting the man's weight, but his piercing wails rose from the boat, cutting through the chopper's roar. Both of his arms had been dislocated at the shoulders and were raised above his head and twisted together like strands of spaghetti. He had a spinal injury, as well. As his shipmates held the man in place, Gladish used his knife to cut the strands of netting that imprisoned the man. Then he and the others lowered the man to the deck.

By now the basket had been lowered from the hovering helicopter. The basket was about five feet long, and the big man would not fit in it with his arms snarled together. Gladish looked down into the man's eyes.

"Buddy, you're going to have to bite the bullet," he said. "We've got to get your arms down to put you in the basket." With that, Gladish grabbed the man's wrists and in one swift motion pulled the arms down to his sides. The solution was harsh, but Gladish was aware of the golden hour—the time between a traumatic injury and the likelihood of death. There was no time to waste getting the fisherman to a hospital. He put a collar on the man's neck to stabilize his spinal injury, then—with help—put him in the basket, which was winched up to the helicopter.

It was all in the line of duty for a rescue swimmer. There were no coast guard commendations for Gladish's efforts. But a month later he got his reward. A letter came from the captain, who said he was getting out of fishing. He thanked Gladish for his efforts and said he had had a change of heart concerning the coast guard. He would no longer hesitate to stick up for a guardsman in a bar fight.

For all of the heroic work, much of Gladish's time in Alaska seemed like a paid vacation, one that would cost civilians thousands of dollars. He rode helicopters through the jagged mountain peaks, at eye level with mountain goats and wild sheep. There were killer whales lurching out of the sea and brown bear, moose, and caribou roaming the shores and mountains.

The vacation ended in 1995, when Gladish got a new assignment, returning to Cape May, New Jersey, where he had received basic training. It was a homecoming in more than one way. Raised near Allentown, Pennsylvania, he had spent summer vacations with his family at campgrounds just inland from the New Jersey shore, a warm-water vacation spot for tourists from the East Coast and Canada. It would be ironic that in this setting, Gladish would come to face assignments more dangerous than those he had experienced in the treacherous Alaskan waters.

In September 1997, the wooden fishing boat *Eastern Shore* had punched a hole in one of its planks while at sea and was taking on water. Seven crewmen had climbed into a life raft in 40-knot winds and seas between 15 and 20 feet. The dragger—a fishing boat that drags a weighted net along the ocean floor to catch bottom-feeding fish—was 60 miles east of Cape May. Gladish clipped the helicopter's cable to his harness and, as the aircraft hovered, was lowered into the sea, where he helped the seven men into two helicopters before he was plucked from the big waves.

On a night a month later, two Air National Guard F-16 fighter jets collided over the ocean, within view of Atlantic City's casino towers. The pilots ejected and parachuted into the water, where life rafts connected to their flight suits inflated. Although they had radios, one of the pilots could not talk. He had hit his head on the canopy of his jet when he ejected, and he was in shock. At nine o'clock Gladish was lowered into the water. He swam to the injured pilot and began talking to him, as was his habit. The pilot responded, explaining he had head and hip injuries. Gladish cut him from his raft and put him in the lowered basket. When Gladish was then hauled back on board, the chopper sped for the nearest hospital, flying directly over the casinos. Gladish looked down and, through the skylights of one casino, saw crapshooters trying to beat the odds. In his own time in the air, Gladish had beaten the odds. He had been sent into the water only a dozen times in a dozen years. Sometimes it was only the tidal waters of coastal marshes. On only a handful of occasions was it into turbulent seas. Regardless of the conditions, he had always gotten the job done. He had never lost a victim. Now he had only one month left to keep his record intact.

NOW THE DOLPHIN was speeding north toward Air Station Atlantic City, and Gladish had gone through the catalog of scenarios that his memory could provide him. What he and his teammates knew was that a fishing vessel was taking on water. There was an oceanful of possibilities.

The flight to Atlantic City should take ten minutes, he knew. Manasquan Inlet would be another 15 minutes farther to the north. The flight path paralleled two highways: the Garden State Parkway, to the east, where Wednesday-night traffic would be moderate at this time, and Route 9, the old seashore highway on the mainland. About three minutes into the return flight, the chopper flew past the home on Route 9 of Patti Birchall, the big sister of *Beth Dee Bob* captain Ed McLaughlin. When the chopper reached the air station, it was within four miles of Absecon, where McLaughlin lived with Lisa and Liam.

The orange Dolphin made its approach to the air station and settled on the apron outside the coast guard hangar. A ground crew was waiting, dressed in foul-weather gear. They had two pumps on pushcarts. The crew chief opened the sliding door and Gladish told the pilot, McFarland, that he was getting out to help with the pumps. Carried in plastic boxes about three feet long, two feet wide, and two feet high, the pumps weighed about 100 pounds each. Along with the pumps, the boxes contained hoses, a gasoline container, and a flashlight. Gladish grabbed one handle of a box and a ground crewman took the other, and they lifted it into the chopper's cargo compartment, behind the passenger compartment. When both pumps were loaded, Gladish strapped them securely. Then he got back in his seat.

"Are we ready to leave?" McFarland asked.

"Yup," Gladish replied.

The Dolphin, mounted on three wheels, taxied to the runway and lifted off, on course for the coordinates the air station had provided for the *Beth Dee Bob*.

THIRTEEN

THE *BETH DEE BOB* SIGHS ITS LAST

THE men in the clam boats steaming toward the *Beth Dee Bob* knew this: if Ed McLaughlin was having trouble, he was busy trying to fix it. He had established this reputation in two prior emergencies offshore. No one—his fellow clammers or his family—doubted that he would have his hands on the problem and a solution in his mind. Trying to solve the problem himself was how he had got ten burned four years earlier in the engine room fire aboard the *Beth Dee Bob*.

Clam boats have several engines—one to push the boat, one to run the clam pump, another to pump hydraulic fluid and run one or more electrical generators. It is normally the first mate's job to take care of a fishing boat's engines. Some captains seldom if ever enter their engine rooms. But when a solenoid stuck aboard the *Beth Dee Bob*, McLaughlin accompanied his mate to make repairs. When both of them were in the engine room, a hydraulic hose split, spraying flammable fluid onto the hot engine. Flames flashed through the tight compartment, catching McLaughlin and, to a lesser degree, his mate. With second- and third-degree burns on half of his body, the captain was taken to the hospital where his sister, Patti Birchall, was a nurse. After a week, Birchall took her brother home to tend to his dressings. His convalescence lasted three months, a time during which McLaughlin proposed to Lisa and tried a lot of new recipes in Patti's kitchen.

The fire was McLaughlin's second strike, Patti thought. She wanted him to get off of the sea before he encountered his third strike. His first had come aboard another clam boat that began sinking off the coast of Maryland. He was the first mate on the vessel at the time. As the captain saw the boat settling into the sea, he decided it was time to get in the life raft, and he ordered the crew over the side. But McLaughlin did not obey. He was down in the engine room. The boat had just been fitted with two new engines, and the captain had left them running. McLaughlin was trying to stop the engines so that they would not suck in water and be destroyed as they went under. His effort was fruitless, and he climbed out of the flooding boat just before it sank. When he got ashore, he told his sister, "The son of a bitch left them running. We could have salvaged them."

Now, on the night of January 6, McLaughlin faced a similar situation. He had been in the wheelhouse at 5:40 when he told Larry Kirk aboard the *Danielle Maria* that he was taking on water and gave him his Loran coordinates. If history is an accurate guide, he then left the wheelhouse to look for or solve the problem. As he left, the boat's 1,000-horsepower diesel was throttled down to an idle. Still on autopilot, the boat made slow headway, rising and falling with the big waves but no longer pounding into them. With water flooding its hold, engine room, or both, the boat had acquired a more stable attitude in the water, a deceptive pose. Stepping outside, one could hear the wind— gusting to 40 knots—whistling through the superstructure that rose behind the wheelhouse and past the antennae mounted on it. But the water would make little sound. For a clam boat at sea, the *Beth Dee Bob* had become eerily quiet.

Bjornestad had been with McLaughlin minutes before. Only 14 miles from the dock—a little more than an hour's ride—he would not have taken to his bunk in these tossed waters. But Roman Tkaczyk was still in his bunk below the wheelhouse, recovering from the labors that had put 2,240 bushels of quahogs worth $8,960 in the boat's cages. Grady Gene Coltrain had left his bunk, and by now he may have made it up to the wheelhouse, or he may have settled at the galley table below the wheelhouse.

The big halogen lamps still lit the deck like a Broadway stage and, if one was looking through the rear windows of the wheelhouse, he now saw the sea washing across the deck and the clam-well hatch covers and sloshing back under the shaker and the A-frame and swirling around the doghouse on the port side, where the watertight door was now swung open. The pump engine, if it was on, was idling. But the valves behind the hatch covers on the starboard side were closed, and nothing was being pumped from the clam wells.

It was clear to McLaughlin that the situation was desparate. But there was no time to go back and grab the radio to issue a Mayday call. It was time to start thinking about the life raft and the EPIRB and the survival suits, stacked under the galley table.

The crew of the *Beth Dee Bob* would need all those items, but they would need more. Every safety and lifesaving device on board would be of little use if the coast guard didn't do its job. And just 12 months earlier, there had been an incident that called into question whether the agency was up to its lifesaving task.

IN THE EARLY afternoon on December 27, 1997, Michael Cornett, a 49-year-old engineer, musician, and songwriter, left the dock at Lightkeepers Marina in Little River, South Carolina, aboard *Morning Dew*, a 34-foot sailboat built in 1978 that Cornett had just purchased. With him were his sons Paul, 16, and Daniel, 13, and the boys' cousin, Bobby Lee Hurd, 14. They planned to motor the boat along the ICW to Jacksonville, Florida, a trip of about 300 miles. The boys would sleep in the vee berth, in the bow of the sailboat.

By noon of the next day, they had traveled 50 miles to Georgetown, South Carolina, near the head of the Winyah Bay. The ICW ducked behind an island about eight miles from the ocean, but Cornett missed the turn and found himself at some point passing between the ruins of jetties and into the Atlantic Ocean. He did not turn back. Heading southwest along the coast, Cornett steered over the ocean swells toward Charleston, the next big harbor, 45 miles from Winyah Bay.

As the *Morning Dew* approached Charleston, apparently sometime after midnight, the tide was low. Winds were blowing from the east at 25 knots, with higher gusts. Seas were five to six feet. The water temperature was 55 degrees. There was rain accompanied by thunderstorms, and small craft advisories had been posted.

Cornett had been sailing for 20 years. In the 1970s, he and his wife had sailed extensively in Florida and the Bahamas. He was familiar with the requirements for safety equipment. On board, Cornett had enough life vests for him and the teenagers. He also had a VHF radio, flares that he had just purchased, air horns, and a strobe light. *Morning Dew* had a depth finder, a knot meter, a magnetic compass, and an autopilot, though the previous owner said it was not functioning properly.

Cornett did not have an EPIRB or radar, each of which may have been crucial omissions.

The entrance to Charleston Harbor is protected by jetties on the north and south. The northern jetty, which extends seaward three miles from shore, rises above the water five to seven feet at low tide. Buoys between the jetties are lit by red and green lights ten feet above the water that flash at different intervals. The buoys are spaced in pairs about a mile apart. The weather may have limited Cornett's vision. The buoy lights are supposed to be visible at four miles, but on a cloudy, dark night with rain they may have been difficult to distinguish.

At some time around two in the morning, the *Morning Dew* collided with the north jetty. What happened aboard is unknown. What happened in the communications room at U.S. coast guard Group Charleston was documented by the National Transportation Safety Board (NTSB), which investigated the sinking of the *Morning Dew.*

The watchstander on duty at two that morning was a 23-year-old single man who had been in the coast guard for less than two years. He had had a slow night on the job, and he was standing at the coffeepot just outside the door of the communications room at 2:17 A.M. when a call came over channel 16. The call was weak and filled with static. He thought he heard "coast guard" spoken twice in an urgent, shouting voice. He noticed that the call came from a high-site antenna near the entrance to Charleston Harbor.

"Vessel calling coast guard, this is Coast Guard Group Charleston, over," the watchstander said into his microphone 14 seconds after hearing the call.

There was no response, so the watchstander repeated his call on all six high-site antennae, asking the caller to respond on channel 16. Four minutes later, there was what sounded like a burst of static on channel 16. Once again, 14 seconds after the call, the watchstander began the first of two calls. Neither call was answered.

The watchstander was accustomed to receiving calls from boaters who simply wanted to ask questions, so he did not play back the first call to see if he could decipher it. During the NTSB investigation, the tape was replayed and the three-second-long transmission was that of an excited adolescent male voice crying, "May . . . Mayday, U.S. coast guard, come in."

But to the watchstander, neither the time of night, the foul weather conditions, nor the excitement in the youthful voice raised any alarms. The sound of apparently excited young people talking loudly on the radio was not unusual. He figured that people calling from the water are often in a noisy environment and feel they have to shout to be heard. He thought the second burst of static could have been caused by a lightning strike.

Four hours later, at 6:20 on the morning of December 29, a ship transporting automobiles—the *Pearl Ace*—was steaming into Charleston Harbor with the boatswain on deck on the starboard side. A harbor pilot—an expert in navigating the local waters—had recently been brought to the ship, and the boatswain was securing the ladder the harbor pilot used to climb into the boat. As he completed the task, he heard cries for help coming from the water. He called the bridge and told the ship's captain, who then told the pilot. The pilot radioed the pilot boat that had dropped him off and was returning to port ahead of the ship. The skipper of the pilot boat turned around to search the waters where the boatswain had heard the cries. The harbor pilot now sent a message asking that the coast guard be notified of the incident.

The coast guard was called eight minutes after the boatswain heard the calls.

The watchstander, who was officially off duty at six o'clock, took the call from the pilot dispatcher and relayed the information to a duty officer, who had started work a half hour earlier.

The duty officer, a 37-year-old man, was a boatswain's mate first class and had been in the coast guard 17 years. When he got the watchstander's call, he had a coast guard boat at his disposal and had authority to launch it, but he didn't. In fact, he took no action as a result of the call. He explained to the NTSB: "I figured . . . if they took the time to call the pilot boat and the pilot boat called the pilot office and the pilot office called us, I was figuring, well, they couldn't be . . . too sure of the situation. . . ."

At about quarter of seven that morning, the pilot dispatcher, whose pilot boat had been searching along the jetty, called the coast guard. "Well, the pilot boat's out there, and they don't see anything and they haven't heard anything, so they're going to come on back," he told the watchstander. The watchstander called the duty officer who, again, did nothing.

A couple walking the beach later that morning saw the body of a boy floating in the surf. The water was rough and the wind was strong. A second couple helped the first couple drag the body from the water. They found no pulse and began CPR.

About 15 minutes later, another boy was found floating 100 yards away. Medical technicians already summoned to aid the first boy began CPR on the second.

Five minutes later, the coast guard duty officer received a call from a local police officer, who reported the discovery of the two boys and asked for a boat to search the area. At 11:22 A.M., the duty officer told a higher-ranking official about the call, and a search-and-rescue mission was begun. It had been nine hours since the first radio call to the coast guard from the *Morning Dew*.

Later that afternoon, the body of the third boy was found, and four weeks after the sailboat sank, Michael Cornett's body washed ashore. No one had survived the sinking of the *Morning Dew*.

The NTSB concluded that Cornett was ill-prepared for his voyage and should not have gone to sea.

But the board's major criticism was of the coast guard and its members. The training of coast guard watchstanders was inadequate, there were too few watchstanders on duty at any one time, and the 12-hour shifts stood by watchstanders were too long, the NTSB said. Moreover, "No procedures were in place at the time of the accident to provide guidance to watchstanders on actions to take when the purpose of a radio call to the coast guard could not be ascertained and when repeated callouts did not receive a response," the board said. "The coast guard does not always exercise effective oversight of its operations and communications centers," the board concluded.

As for the coast guard's communications equipment, the NTSB found it cumbersome and outdated. Direction-finding equipment was available that could accurately locate the position of a vessel through its radio signal alone, but the direction finders used by the coast guard gave only the compass bearing to the vessel, not its distance. Also, the ability of a watchstander to replay the tape of a distress call was complicated. "To be effective in the performance of their duties, communications watchstanders must be able to quickly and easily play back recorded transmissions. The emphasis should be on 'easily' because the easier the task, the more likely it will be performed," the NTSB said. The Canadian coast guard already used recording equipment that required only that one button be pushed to instantly replay the last transmission, they said.

In a speech in April 1999, more than three months after the clam boat *Danielle Maria* called the coast guard to report the *Beth Dee Bob* was taking on water, Adm. James M. Loy, commandant of the coast guard, told a meeting of the U.S. Naval Institute that he acknowledged his agency's shortcomings in general and in the *Morning Dew* incident in particular. Part of the problem, Loy said, was money.

"Budget constraints have made us cut and trim everywhere we could. *Morning Dew* tells us that further cuts would degrade public safety if our previous cuts haven't already done so. Streamlining may have gone too far. Our personnel are stretched too thin. Our people are working too hard. We have too little experience in too many crucial positions. A more experienced watchstander might have been able to pick up the word 'Mayday.' I say 'might' because I had to hear the tape several times before I could discern the distress proword, and I had the advantage of knowing precisely what I was listening for.

"Even so, a more experienced watchstander who better understood how different the world looks when you're at sea on a stormy December night than it does from a cozy operations center might have been slower to accept nondistress explanations for the two radio calls.

"I cannot rule out the possibility that our service-wide training and staffing shortages affected our response to this case,"

Loy said. And the admiral admitted that the coast guard's electronic equipment was substandard.

"There is a vast disparity between the communications capability that the public thinks we have and the communications system that we do have," he said. Lacking were the ability to enhance and replay calls on the radio. The existing direction-finding equipment was not useful, he said.

Loy said the coast guard was attempting to modernize its equipment. "But we don't expect to begin to field this system until 2001, and it is not slated to be fully operational before 2005."

ON THE NIGHT of January 6, the coast guard was not hampered by its deficiencies. It had received an accurate location for the *Beth Dee Bob* from Larry Kirk, the first mate of the *Maria Danielle*. It had been told the boat was taking on water. The watchstander had immediately notified the duty officer, who had dispatched the coast guard boat that was at his disposal and had alerted the next-higher command.

Moreover, the *Beth Dee Bob*'s EPIRB was working, transmitting a beacon that could be followed by the helicopter that was now flying toward it from Atlantic City.

But even before this had happened, McLaughlin and Bjornestad had stood in the wheelhouse and watched as, washed by the sea, the deck of the *Beth Dee Bob* began to settle below the surface.

Things were happening too fast.

Once the stern began to settle, water began rapidly pouring into the opened watertight door of the doghouse, the door that led down to the engine room. McLaughlin or Bjornestad may have made one last, desperate effort to get to the valves that could pump out the hold. But the clam pump remained either off or at idle, and the valves were never opened.

By now Coltrain had come out of the lower cabin. He may have had to wade through the water flooding the deck, or he may have come up to the wheelhouse when he heard the engines go into idle and felt the motion of the boat become calm. Neither the sound nor the motion would be welcome 14 miles from the dock, and worry would naturally follow.

At this point, there was no time to run and rouse Roman Tkaczyk. The *Beth Dee Bob* was sinking as quickly as a rock set on the surface of a pond. Water had already filled some big voids in the boat—perhaps all of the clam holds or maybe the engine room. This had occurred without being noticed by McLaughlin or Bjornestad. By the time they realized there was a problem, the boat had settled so much that the deck was flooding or already flooded, and the *Beth Dee Bob* had begun its death plunge. In seconds, the water found the openings to the cabin below the wheelhouse, and it began to pour in with the force of a waterfall. Tkaczyk and all of the survival suits were down there, and there was no way to get to them.

The water continued to rise. The *Beth Dee Bob* gave no indication of rolling. It was simply sinking, the water climbing the sides of its proud white wheelhouse which, with the top of the dredge ramp at the stern, was all that remained above the ten-foot seas.

Tkaczyk had been roused from his sleep. He headed for the stairs and the white glow of the deck lamps outside. At first, he was probably wading through the flood, but then the cold sea came slamming down the stairway like a runaway train. Tkaczyk reached the base of the steps, but he could get no farther. The water pinned him with its frigid mass, snatching his breath. The man who would quit a boat on the spur of the moment never wanted off a vessel more. But the sea settled the matter quickly. The husband and father would drown with the taste of salt on his lips, his body resting at the foot of the cabin's only escape route.

Unlike their mate from Poland, the other men had a chance. They could step out into the rising sea. The lights of the *Beth Dee Bob* may have been doused when the engine room was flooded or they may have continued to glow as the boat sighed

The clam boat *Beth Dee Bob* tows its dredge (not pictured) on a calm day on the North Atlantic. Empty cages are stacked at the rear, near the dredge ramp.
COURTESY OF THE McLAUGHLIN FAMILY.

The clam boat *Cape Fear* at the dock in New Bedford, Massachusetts, winter 1997.
COURTESY OF STEVEN NOVACK.

The clam boat *Adriatic* tied at its dock in Point Pleasant Beach, New Jersey.
COURTESY OF PATRICIA EVANS-MIZRACHI.

The *Ellie B*, one of the few remaining wooden clam boats, tied to a dock. It's unique dredge rose on a ramp built on its side.
COURTESY OF LOUIS LAGACE.

Ed McLaughlin, captain of the
Beth Dee Bob, **with his son, Liam.**
COURTESY OF THE MCLAUGHLIN FAMILY.

Steven Craig Novack,
captain of the *Cape Fear.*
AUTHOR'S COLLECTION.

John Babbit,
captain of the *Ellie B.*
COURTESY OF LOUIS LAGACE.

George Evans, captain
of the clam boat *Adriatic.*
COURTESY OF PATRICIA
EVANS-MIZRACHI.

Michael S. Hager, first mate of the clam boat *Adriatic*, who had been invited on the last voyage of the *Beth Dee Bob*.
COURTESY OF THE HAGER FAMILY.

Michael S. Hager and his son, Michael Jr., Christmas 1997 in the home of Hager's parents.
COURTESY OF THE HAGER FAMILY.

Frank Janicelli III, deck hand on the *Adriatic*, opens presents with his family in Union, New Jersey, Christmas 1998.
COURTESY OF THE JANICELLI FAMILY.

Louis Lagace (left), owner of the clam boat *Ellie B.*, and Gary Sylvia, deck hand, working on a dredge in New Bedford, Massachusetts.
COURTESY OF LOUIS LAGACE.

George Evans, captain of the *Adriatic,* checking instruments in the wheelhouse of his clam boat. COURTESY OF PATRICIA EVANS-MIZRACHI.

Richard Gladish (left), a coast guard rescue swimmer, in eight to ten-foot seas at Cape Disappointment on the Columbia River in Washington during training. COURTESY OF RICHARD GLADISH.

Coast guard rescue swimmer
Richard Gladish on the job.
COURTESY OF RICHARD GLADISH.

The first part of the author's
eight part *Philadelphia Inquirer*
serial covering the events of
January 1999. The "Lost at
Sea" series elicited hundreds of
email responses from readers.
AUTHOR'S COLLECTION.

its final gasp, air rushing from its cavities as those spaces flooded. Bjornestad had waded off of the flooding boat and was in
the water. He wore coveralls and rubber boots, and he managed to grab an orange life ring with a strobe light that had
been carried on a rack outside the wheelhouse door. He pulled
his slender body through the center of the ring and wrapped
his arms around it, gripping the rope around its circumference
with his cold hands. His body began shaking almost immediately in the icy salt water, and as the towering waves washed
over him, he struggled to catch his breath.

Once the boat disappeared, the hydrostatic release on the
life raft, mounted atop the wheelhouse, was activated and the
raft popped to the surface, fully inflated, but floating now on a
dark sea. It began to drift away in the wind and waves.

And somewhere in those waves—one minute in a deep
trough and the next raised ten feet or more—McLaughlin and
Coltrain struggled for their lives. They may have tried swimming toward the flashing of the strobe on Bjornestad's life
ring. But each wave, each ice-cold crest that washed over their
bare heads, brought a blinding pain in their skulls and drained
precious body heat. They needed to find the raft and hope that
rescue arrived soon.

FOURTEEN

ALONE IN THE BLACKENED, SLOSHING SEA

AS soon as the Dolphin helicopter gained altitude above the airfield, the Atlantic Ocean was in sight to the east. The Atlantic County Airport is about ten miles from the coast in a sandy coastal plain with no significant hills—certainly nothing as tall as the towering casino hotels in Atlantic City. If the chopper flew in a straight line to the *Beth Dee Bob,* it would have to travel nearly 70 miles, much of it over open water. The aircraft had a top speed of about 140 knots, so the trip would take a half hour. It was now about 40 minutes since the surviving crewmembers of the *Beth Dee Bob* had waded from the deck of their sinking boat into the frigid ocean. A man who was in a survival suit might last several hours in water that is 42 degrees. If he got into a life raft, he would last several days. But these men were in working clothes. If they were lucky and found the life raft, they still were wet and exposed to the 32-degree air. A canopy that popped up when the raft inflated would keep out the winds. If they were in the water, they could have less than an hour to live. The time it had taken for the Dolphin to stop and get the pump was critical time lost on the clock ticking away three men's lives. Now the chopper flew at top speed.

Rescue swimmer Richard Gladish sat in the right rear seat, a web harness around his torso strapped to the chopper's floor to keep him from falling out when they opened the sliding side door. A bag was on the floor with the rest of his gear—his fins, hood, mask, and gloves. Adrenaline pumped through his body and his mind continued to scan the possibilities. The sounds of chatter on channel 16, piped into his helmet, filled his ears. He could hear the pilot, Lieutenant McFarland, attempting to hail the *Beth Dee Bob* one moment, the air station making the same call a moment later. There was no response.

But the sound of the *Beth Dee Bob*'s EPIRB beacon was on the radio, as well. There was no way of telling whether the crew or the ocean had activated the EPIRB. It could be that the fishermen were so busy trying to save their boat that they could not answer the radio.

We definitely should be in communication range, Gladish thought. He feared the worst.

Interspersed between the calls from the coast guard on channel 16 were the voices of men steaming their fishing boats toward the *Beth Dee Bob.*

Oh, shit! This boat may have gone down, Gladish thought. *This isn't going to be a dewatering situation. Did they get in a raft?*

The rescue swimmer, the two pilots and the flight mechanic all were now talking with each other, anticipating what was to come. It was a moonless night with some clouds and some stars overhead. They were flying at between 300 and 500 feet above the water. Gladish could see the whitecaps, lit by the glow from the shore.

It seemed as if they were in the air only 15 minutes when the Dolphin approached the position they had been given by the air station. The arrow on a dial in the chopper's control panel that indicated the direction of the EPIRB signal was pointed straight ahead. And then, in the blackness, Gladish and the others saw two flashing strobe lights coming off the tops of the waves.

McFarland advised the crew that he was beginning an approach to the lights. He banked the chopper and began to circle, giving up altitude until the aircraft was 50 feet above the waves. Then he brought the chopper to a stop, hovering at that altitude. Flight mechanic James S. Bryan Jr., strapped into his seat ahead of Gladish and to the left, now slid on tracks toward the door on the right of the Dolphin. He took the door handle and slid the door back to open it. Bryan asked the pilot what their airspeed was.

Looking out his window, Gladish saw the lights of fishing boats converging on the spot where the chopper hovered. Looking down, he could see the two strobes. One was an EPIRB, attached to a line that went to a life ring. A man was inside the life ring with his hands wrapped around its lines. Gladish told McFarland what he saw.

"Rich, get ready," McFarland answered. "You're going in the water."

Gladish took off his helmet and hung it on a hook. Then he reached for his bag and, in seconds, had the rest of his gear on. Now he crawled to the door, still wearing his gunner's belt, which would keep him inside the chopper.

Bryan, using a control panel on a post inside the chopper, began to operate the hoist. Mounted on the top of the chopper was a short davit from which a hook, at the end of a cable, dangled. Bryan swung the davit out so the hook hung above the open door. Then he began to lower the hook.

By now, Gladish was sitting on the floor, his legs outside the chopper. He reached up and clipped the hook to his harness. Bryan tapped him on the shoulder, a signal to release the gunner's belt. He unhooked. Between his feet he could now see the movement of the waves.

McFarland, flying from the right front seat, could now see the man in the water, just off to his right. It was Bryan's job as flight mechanic to guide McFarland to the target. There was a hesitation in the action for Gladish as this happened. Suddenly the chopper was moving in toward the victim below and Gladish was going out the door, hanging by the cable that Bryan was lowering.

In less than a minute Gladish was floating in the ocean, unhooking the cable from his harness, swimming in the wash from the noisy helicopter hovering above. This was the first time he had been in the water during winter. From the tops of waves, he could see the man in the life ring and the strobe lights. The man was wearing coveralls, and it looked as if he was moving and conscious. Gladish began kicking with his fins and swimming up and down waves toward the man.

McFarland backed the Dolphin away, shining the two belly lights of the aircraft on Gladish and the man whom he was about to rescue. Gladish could now see that the man's face was in the water, and when he reached him, he lifted the man's head.

Jay Bjornestad's eyes were as wide open as human eyes can be. His mouth was open as wide as his jaw could extend, and seawater washed freely in and out of his mouth. Gladish checked for breathing and found none. Bjornestad's arms and legs were stiff, proof that hypothermia had seized him. Gladish saw that a long rope led from the life ring to the EPIRB, floating and flashing a few yards away. He took the knife from his vest and cut the rope from the ring so that it would not become tangled during the rescue. He left the ring around Bjornestad's waist because it saved time and the victim was slender. Then he got Bjornestad's arm across his chest and began swimming, doing the sidestroke, moving through the water with the man's head above the waves, some of which were easily ten feet high.

With the chopper in view, Gladish took a glow stick—a Day-

Glo green tube shorter and thicker than a ballpoint pen—from a retaining loop on his mask. He had started it glowing before he entered the water. Now he waved it back and forth three times, signaling to the chopper to return.

McFarland moved in, and Bryan lowered the basket litter, easing it down until it touched the tops of the waves but did not yet float. Gladish, still holding Bjornestad with one arm, swam to the litter, climbing waves until he could grab it with his free hand. Then Bryan began paying out cable, allowing the litter to float.

Bjornestad's slender frame should have allowed him to fit easily into the basket portion of the litter. But because his limbs were stiff and fully extended, Gladish had a problem. He forcefully bent the arms and legs until he could float Bjornestad over the top of the basket, placing him inside in a semiseated position. Bjornestad stayed bent.

It seemed like an eternity since Gladish had entered the water, but it was only about 45 seconds. He gave Bryan a thumbs-up signal, and the flight mechanic began raising the basket. Gladish watched as the basket reached the door and was hauled inside the hovering chopper. Then he waited for the hook and cable to return to him for his ride back to the aircraft. That did not happen, and so he reached for the radio in his vest and began shoving an earpiece under his hood, into his left ear. The radio was on, and he called the Dolphin. There was no answer. He called again. Still there was no reply as the chopper hovered above him, blowing spray off the tops of waves and lighting the ocean with its belly lamps.

Gladish's third call still failed to bring a response from above until the belly lights flashed three times, a signal that the chopper was leaving and Gladish was staying. Now, as Gladish faced out to sea with the shore at his back, the Dolphin flew over his head, gaining altitude, and McFarland's voice came over the radio. A coast guard boat was on the way, the pilot told him before signing off.

The rescue swimmer was on his own.

FILL-IN: A MATTER OF MINUTES

FOR ANYONE CAUGHT in the winter ocean, hypothermia is the enemy and time is its ally. Hypothermia is the loss of heat at the body's core.

"Whether it's air or water, the same sort of physiology happens," explained Dr. Stephen Thom, chief of hyperbaric medicine at the Hospital of the University of Pennsylvania, where he was an associate professor. "In water, the heat is conducted away very, very rapidly," Thom said in an interview after the *Beth Dee Bob* sank. "It takes less time at a given temperature [in water than in air] for a level of bad things to happen to you. At [winter ocean] temperatures, it doesn't take very long for your core temperature, your brain and heart, to drop." Studies have shown that the cause of death is usually heart failure. Fibrillation, which is the uncoordinated twitching of the heart muscle, develops. The heart fails to pump blood and, as if having a heart attack, the victim dies.

At the point of heart failure, the person's core temperature has dropped several degrees below 90. "The water temperature being thirty to forty degrees, you don't have to get near to that level before death is imminent," Thom said.

The symptoms of hypothermia proceed through several well-defined steps. Initially there is shivering. The victim feels uncomfortable. How soon this happens is determined by how fast the body's heat is being lost and its temperature is falling.

Shivering is the body's attempt to stay warm. If the motion does not generate heat quickly enough—if the body temperature continues to fall—the shivering—and all other reflex action—stops.

Now the victim becomes stuporous as body temperature falls to about 90 degrees. At this point, discomfort goes away, and any aching that the cold may have caused in the victim's muscles disappears.

"When the core temperature drops to about ninety degrees, we call that a moderate state of hypothermia," Thom said. "At that point, if you resuscitate, there's an amnesia for all that happened up to that point. You drop another five degrees, to eighty-five degrees core temperature, there's a progressive reduction in level of consciousness. The higher centers in the brain (like consciousness) just stop working. Stages of coma begin."

Now, with the core temperature falling to the mid- to low eighties, there is an increasing chance for abnormal heart rhythms developing and causing death. For each degree the temperature falls, the body loses seven percent of its metabolism.

"The nerves no longer function appropriately as they get colder. They just stop sending messages, essentially. You don't get a coordinated squeeze in the heart to move the blood. The body becomes stiff. It's not like ice, but it's stiff. There could be a coating of ice on the superficial layer of the face. The contraction of the muscles will cause the person to be stiff," the doctor said. Stiffness comes only after coma has begun.

Body fat gives some insulation. A fat victim will last longer than a skinny one. "But at those temperatures, it's still a matter of minutes."

THE HELICOPTER WAS low on fuel as it hovered above the rescue swimmer. Flight mechanic Bryan, who had already tossed the two dewatering pumps into the ocean to make space for the victim, raised the basket to the door and then hauled it inside. He checked Bjornestad for a pulse. He found none and told the pilot, McFarland, who decided he had better head for shore and the hospital, leaving Gladish in the water.

Now Bryan's job was to perform CPR on Bjornestad. He told McFarland what he was going to do, but when he tried to remove Bjornestad from the basket, the life ring around his thin waist caught on the basket. He told McFarland, who considered giving the controls to his copilot, Beale, and helping Bryan. That would not have been standard procedure. McFarland stayed at the controls and the chopper was soon at the hospital, where he began to land. By the time he had touched the ground, Bryan had Bjornestad out of the basket and had removed the life ring. But now the hospital staff was at the chopper, and they took Bjornestad out and put him on a stretcher and wheeled him away.

Jay Bjornestad was dead.

At least four other men were still in the ocean, and one of them was Richard Gladish. His face, where it was exposed, was now quite cold, and some water had seeped under the edges of his dry suit, making his body cold. The waves were chaotic, and he felt as if he were inside a washing machine. His view of oncoming waves was like that of a man lying on the floor on one side of a room with a ten foot ceiling, looking at the top of the opposite wall. His body was raised by the oncoming wave but not enough to keep his head from being dunked by the foaming crests. From the heights, he could see the lights of the commercial fishing boats. In the troughs, he could see nothing but blackness.

About the sixth time he reached the top of a wave, Gladish saw a blue flashing light, the police light on the 41-foot coast guard boat that had been sent by the coast guard station at Manasquan Inlet. He reached into his vest for his strobe light, which he turned on and attached to a Velcro patch on his hood. The boat approached, and Gladish wondered, *How are they going to get me on that boat?*

One moment, he was swimming atop a wave, looking down on the boat about 20 yards away. The next, he was looking up at it.

The boat had a three-foot freeboard, the height of the deck above the waterline.

Put it in neutral, Gladish thought, looking at the two crewmen on the rear who stood ready to grab him. He waited for his moment, and as the boat drifted toward him he swam powerfully toward it, timing his approach so that the crewmen could grab his wrists. When they did, he flopped up on the deck just as the boat reached its low point.

Once on deck, he got to his feet and went inside the cabin, where he congratulated the captain for his handling of the boat.

But the night was far from over for the skipper, who had only recently become qualified to drive this boat. The seas were well over the capability of his vessel, and returning to the inlet would be a challenge. After about ten minutes the skipper, having received instructions to head home, turned to steam into the waves, the only safe direction, but one that would take him to the southwest and would lead him to the shore far to the south of the inlet. Since the winds were blowing from the shore, he knew the water near the beach would be protected by the dunes and the waves would be smaller, giving him a chance to reverse his direction toward the inlet. The spotlight mounted atop the cabin had blown out during this mission, so the skipper had only the reflection from his flashing blue light to see the oncoming waves.

Gladish stood behind the skipper, grabbing a railing. He had experience in judging wave height, and so he called out the approach of the big ones. There were waves taller than ten feet now, and they hit the boat like an uppercut to the jaw, rocking it back. The cabin was crowded. One male crewmember was lying on the floor, vomiting out the rear door. The other crewmembers—male and female—were standing around Gladish. They steamed this way for nearly two hours until they reached a point three miles off the coast where the seas flattened. Then the skipper turned the boat north to skirt the shore.

When they reached Manasquan Inlet, the worst of Gladish's experiences this night—the boat ride—was finally over. He had thought nothing of his descent at the end of a cable from the

Dolphin or of being left alone in the dark ocean. Those were nearly routine.

Only later, when the memory of Jay Bjornestad's frozen face would return to him with its pleading eyes and the scream of its silent, gaping mouth, would the truly difficult part of the night visit him.

Maybe if we got there 30 minutes earlier . . . maybe this . . . maybe that . . .

FIFTEEN

THE PROMISE

THE *Cape Fear,* one of the mightiest boats in the clam fleet, had headed to sea from New Bedford, Massachusetts, 200 miles northeast of Point Pleasant, sometime after noon—just after the ocean began pounding the *Beth Dee Bob* on January 6, 1999, as that doomed boat steamed for New Jersey. The 112-foot-long, black-and-white stern dredger *Cape Fear* sailed past the big stone hurricane barrier across the harbor that keeps Buzzards Bay from flooding the city of New Bedford, then turned south on the bay toward the sea. But when the boat reached the mouth of the bay, its captain, Steven Novack, found exactly what he would expect from a southern gale. With no landmass to the south to protect the bay, the waves were big and steep. Novack turned the *Cape Fear* around to wait for another day when he could fill his hold with 90 cages and load

another 40 cages on his deck, a total of 4,160 bushels of quahogs worth more than $16,000 at the dock. Novack and his
four crewmembers would have to wait another day for their
share of that haul.

Back in New Bedford, the *Cape Fear* tied up at the Sea Watch
International dock in an industrial park a mile north of downtown. It was after dark when the crew heard about the *Beth Dee
Bob*. Novack was in shock. He knew Ed McLaughlin. They were
the same age and had visited the same bars in all of the clam
ports. He knew the *Beth Dee Bob*, a boat that shared with his *Cape
Fear* the reputation of being the best in the clam fleet. They
were both money boats, prized by owners and crews alike for
the income they produced.

The *Cape Fear* was more than just a money boat for Novack.
It was his home for six to eight weeks at a time. He, his first
mate, James Haley, and his second mate, Douglas Miles Kelly,
were all from Virginia's eastern shore. Novack lived in
Greenbacksville, and Haley, who was, at 35, a year younger than
Novack, lived in Oak Hall. Kelly, at 41 the oldest man on the
Cape Fear, had family in Virginia, but he had no other home
than the *Cape Fear* and used the dock in New Bedford as his
mailing address. In truth, these three men spent most of their
lives on the *Cape Fear*, dredging, unloading their cages at Sea
Watch, and heading out again, a cycle that was repeated all year
long, interrupted only by foul weather or mechanical problems. When Novack needed a break, he left Haley in charge
and returned to Virginia. When Haley wanted off the boat and
back to Oak Hall, Kelly took over. But for Novack and Haley,
their bunks below the wheelhouse were as much their true res-
idence as Kelly's was his.

The boat had only recently returned to New Bedford after
spending about six weeks sailing out of Ocean City, Maryland.
Novack was only 33 miles from home there, so he had spent
Christmas with his kids. Haley stayed on vacation when the
boat steamed north. Novack filled some of his clam cages offshore from New Jersey and brought a partial load to Atlantic

City. Next he harvested a full load off of Long Island and brought that to New Bedford.

Once the *Cape Fear* was in port in January, Haley returned. Kelly told him he had noticed a leak on the propeller shaft, and so on Tuesday, Haley repacked the shaft and stopped the leak. Then, with Novack at the helm and Kelly taking a trip off, the boat had headed to sea Wednesday, only to be pounded back by the seas.

Now they had learned that the same seas had taken the *Beth Dee Bob*. They were told that Jay Bjornestad, the mate, was dead, but the search was still going on for McLaughlin and the two deckhands. The news was unnerving, but it would not stop the *Cape Fear* from returning to work as soon as the seas settled.

The three deckhands had homes to go to, and so they left the *Cape Fear* for the night. Steven Reeves and Paul Martin, who lived in New Bedford, left together. Joseph F. Lemieux Jr., the permanent fill-in deckhand, had an apartment across the water in Fairhaven and went his own way.

Kim LaPlante, Reeves's girlfriend, had dropped him off at Sea Watch that afternoon, so he and Martin went to the factory where LaPlante ran a machine embroidering baseball caps. They found her car and were about to drive off when Kim and a friend, taking a break, appeared in the parking lot. They all talked in the car until Kim's break was over, and then Reeves drove off with Martin as she returned to work.

It wasn't until Thursday afternoon, when Steve Reeves and Kim LaPlante had to return to their jobs, that they first talked about the *Beth Dee Bob*. It was a raw day in New Bedford, the cold wind ripping up the water from Buzzards Bay. She had driven him to the Sea Watch International dock after stopping at Dunkin' Donuts for their breakfast. They were parked near the chain-link fence, facing the rambling, two-story white packing house that was separated from the dock by a concrete apron, on which clam cages were shuttled by forklift trucks. Sitting and eating their food—orange juice for him, coffee for her and muffins for both—they could see the *Cape Fear* tied to the dock and the gulls circling lazily above the boats, floating on air perfumed with the smell of fresh clams.

"Stay in," Kim said. The weather was bad, and she just had a feeling. She did not want Reeves to go.

Reeves had heard this before. She did not want him to fish. But he always told her, "It pays the bills." And he loved his work. He loved being on the ocean.

She thought something was wrong, and she pressed him to skip the trip that night.

"I need the money," he said. Then he added, "If it sinks, I'll swim." She had to be at work by three o'clock, and so they said good-bye.

"I'll be back," he said as they parted. "Don't worry."

SIXTEEN

FATHER AND SON

THE ten-o'clock news was on the television in the far corner of the living room from the couch where Dick Hager spent his life. An oxygen generator was on the floor at his side, a clear plastic tube running from it to his nose. His head was propped on pillows. He was as comfortable as a 66-year-old man with a weak heart can be. His wife, Judy, was at work on the four-to-midnight shift, packaging pharmaceuticals, and Dick was alone in their second-floor garden apartment in Brick, New Jersey, when the news reported that the *Beth Dee Bob* had sunk. Dick was seized with terror. His youngest son, Mike, was supposed to be aboard. If anything happened to Mike on the sea, Dick Hager knew he was to blame. He reached for the phone and dialed his second-oldest son, Jeff, who lived about 15 minutes from Mike's home. Jeff agreed to drive to the dock to look for

Mike. When Jeff hung up, Dick had nothing to do but turn his thoughts to his own love affair with fishing, and how he had shown the way for the last of his children to embrace the same passion.

It had been ten years since a heart attack had stranded Dick ashore. He had gone from a robust fisherman with a thick chest and strong arms to a shaky invalid whose voice came in wheezes. He moved little, and when he did his oxygen supply dragged behind him like an anchor. Sapped of energy, he seldom strayed from the apartment, but his thoughts were always of the sea, and Mike was his connection.

Dick Hager had started his life as far from salt water as you can get in New Jersey. The state is bordered by water on three sides. To the northeast, the Hudson River separates New Jersey from New York. From New York City to Cape May, the Atlantic Ocean is the border. Then the Delaware Bay forms the southwestern edge of the state for about 50 miles until it reaches the mouth of the Delaware River. The river, which is freshwater, separates New Jersey from the states of Delaware and Pennsylvania, all the way north to the New York state line. Hager was born on the banks of the river, in a town about 130 miles upstream from the ocean. His father worked in a paper mill, which used the river's water in the papermaking process. The river provided a steady income, and the steep, enveloping walls of the river valley were to some like a warm maternal hug. In 1954, when Hager, who had been a cook in the army, was discharged, he followed his father into the mill. He found the work confining, and he longed to be in the outdoors. But a month after he got home, he met a girl named Judy, and six months later he married her. Eleven months after that, Judy bore him a son. With a family to support, Dick dug in for the long haul at the mill, and by 1960 there were two boys and two girls.

Hager had gone with his father on trips to the New Jersey shore to gather clams in the bays behind the barrier islands, and he loved it there. In 1961 he found a job working on a dock on Long Beach Island, at the next inlet south of Manasquan Inlet, and moved Judy and the kids into an apartment over a service station. Within three years he had signed onto a fishing boat that sailed from Barnegat Light. He would never again choose to work on land. There were now five Hager children. The money he made on the boats was more by far than he could make on the dock. And he loved the fisherman's life.

Judy, a woman whose values were shaped in an earlier generation, never thought to question his decision to fish, nor did she share in making the decision. Within a few months, all of the boats on which her husband sailed were docking in Point Pleasant, and so they moved again.

The final child, Michael, was born within months of their arrival in Point Pleasant. With six children, the Hagers needed the income from fishing more than ever. But while the money was good, there were lean times along with the fat. The weather was bad for a stretch, or the boat needed repairs. Then the extra money in the kitty carried the family until Hager sailed again.

When Dick was at sea, peril hovered in the back of Judy's mind. Danger was not something Dick often mentioned. But he couldn't avoid the topic after a fishing boat on which he was sailing caught fire offshore. He and his crewmates were rescued from their stricken craft by the crew of a nearby fishing boat. When he got home, Judy saw that his eyelashes were singed off. He paid it no attention and went to a neighbor's house to play poker. During the game, the reality of his close call with death dawned before him, and he began shaking uncontrollably. Judy was told of this later by others. And afterward Dick talked with her as well.

But he went back to the sea, abusive as it could be. And when he had a chance, he brought his children into his world. When the boat was in port, he would take his two youngest sons, Tim and Mike, who were three years apart in age, to the boat. He would put orange caps on them so that he could keep track of them as he worked, but he allowed them to roam the boat. Before the boys were full-blown teenagers, Dick was mate on a big clam boat in Virginia. Judy and the boys would visit him there for a small vacation, and the whole family would stay on the boat rather than pay for a motel room. Each boy had his own bunk in which to dream of the day he would become a fisherman like his father.

Tim and Mike were no bookends. Where Mike was the sweet child, Tim was the terror. A skinny kid sprouting taller and taller, he could always seem to find a way to antagonize his father, who would take out a strap when it was time for discipline. The school bus would drop Tim off at the front door of school and he would walk right out the back. Dick's rule concerning school—go to school or get a job—was applied, and Tim found work.

Mike had a similar distaste for school. He quit when he was 16, and he found work as close to the water as he could. When he got a chance, he would work on a party boat sailing from Manasquan Inlet.

For Tim, the dream of becoming a commercial fisherman came true when he was 18 and his father was mate on the clam boat *Marie Kim.* The deckhands didn't want to work weekends, and Tim signed on as a fill-in. Onshore, Tim was making $300 a week working in a marine biology laboratory. On the clam boat, which sailed to the Georges Bank off New England, he could make $800 in a day. Soon he was working full-time on the *Marie Kim,* which docked at Provincetown on Cape Cod. But he got homesick and returned to Point Pleasant, where he got a job on another clam boat.

Tim Hager would follow his father's dream for another decade before yielding to his wife's demand to find work ashore. Before he left the ocean, he had two close calls. He had quit working on the original *Beth Dee Bob* shortly before it sank, and he had just left the *Mae Doris* when it went down.

Mike Hager did not get to ship out with his father in 1985 when he turned 18, but he did find a fishing job, beginning the career he had always wanted. And after Tim quit fishing in 1992, Mike became his father's lone thread connecting him to the docks. The connection probably meant as much to Mike as it did to Dick, for Mike felt he had to show his father he had become his equal as a man. He would come to visit his parents, and his father would listen to his stories and then offer advice. As the crew worked to haul out the clam pump from the bilge of the *Adriatic*, the son gave the father a play-by-play of the process. When the captain of the *Beth Dee Bob* offered him work, one of the first people Mike told was his father. Mike's enthusiasm for his work was the subject of good-natured joking for everyone in the family except, perhaps, Dick. But Mike was deadly serious. He wanted more than anything to become the captain of the *Adriatic*. He begged George Evans to let him make trips by himself, only to be denied. He was almost in tears one time when he told his best friend, Sean Domingo, "All I ever wanted to do was show my father I could run the boat."

ON THE EVENING of January 6, Domingo was lying in bed with his wife in the house they shared with his mother, watching television, when the phone rang. It was Mike Hager, and he was talking nonstop. He told Domingo to turn on channel 12. As they both watched the report in their separate homes, Hager talked about his near miss. He should have been aboard the *Beth Dee Bob*, and he was terrified. Domingo tried to soothe him. They talked for a half hour or more. And then Hager hung up and walked to a nearby convenience store.

While he was out, the phone rang in Hager's bungalow. It rang incessantly. Dick Hager was calling, and when he got no answer, dread filled him. He dialed his son Jeff and asked him to go to the clam dock.

Jeff decided to drive past Mike's home first, however, and by then Mike had returned from the store. He called his father.

"I could have used the money if they asked me to go," he told Dick. "I probably would have been on that boat."

Judy Hager knew nothing about the *Beth Dee Bob* until she got home that night and found Dick on the phone. Normally he would have been dozing on the couch, or perhaps fixing something for her to eat. Not this night. It was sometime before one o'clock in the morning, and Dick was once again talking with Mike. He filled Judy in as he listened to his son.

"I'm just so shook up," Mike told Dick. "Every time I think about it, I get chills down my spine." When Judy got on the phone, he told her: "Somebody must have been up there, watching over me."

SEVENTEEN

"THERE'S NO FUTURE IN THIS"

EARLIER on Wednesday night, at about 7:42 P.M., if he had looked out the window to his left, coast guardsman Keeven Walker, the watchstander at Station Point Pleasant, could have seen the station's 44-foot motor lifeboat speeding east through Manasquan Inlet, its floodlight shining white against rock jetties. Walker's duty officer, Colin Reedy, had taken command of the boat and was ready to join the search for the *Beth Dee Bob*. The 44-footer was rated for 30-foot seas and was built to survive being rolled over. The only coast guard boat on the scene now was the station's 41-foot boat, rated for 8-foot seas and battling 10- to 12-foot waves. By this time a second Dolphin helicopter had joined the search, and a 47-foot coast guard motor lifeboat—also built to handle 30-foot seas—was under way from Station Barnegat Light, 25 miles to the southwest. More help was to come. A full coast guard search-and-rescue operation was under way.

At his radio console, Walker received a call from Lieutenant McFarland, the pilot of the first Dolphin that had taken Jay Bjornestad to a hospital in Neptune, New Jersey. McFarland was flying to an airport to refuel before he rejoined the search.

Walker stayed by his radio as the search expanded. He and the men and women at sea knew they were looking for three men. They had no way of knowing that Roman Tkaczyk had gone down with the boat. Survivors could be in their red immersion suits or, better still, in their life raft. There was reason to hope they were alive, just as there was reason to fear that they were in imminent danger.

The coxswain of the 41-footer was by now concerned for his own crew as his boat was battered by the seas. At 7:57 P.M., an hour after the Dolphin had spotted Bjornestad in the water, he radioed Walker to say he was heading in.

Five minutes later, the second helicopter radioed Walker. The crew of the chopper had spotted a life raft. It was overturned, and there were no survivors with it. The search continued, but now the only craft on the scene were the lone helicopter and the commercial fishing boats that had steamed to the *Beth Dee Bob*'s aid.

Walker next heard from the skipper of the 47-foot motor lifeboat at 8:24, and from Reedy on the 44-footer ten minutes later. They were each about 30 minutes from the last known location of the *Beth Dee Bob*. It took McFarland until 8:45 to head his helicopter back over the ocean with a full tank of fuel. Ten minutes later, as McFarland reached the scene, so did Reedy aboard the 44-footer.

The coast guard vessels were following standard search patterns, issued by coast guard Group Atlantic City. The boats and helicopters were assigned to methodically crisscross the

heaving seas. The helicopters each flew on Victor Sierra search-
es, a pattern of three equilateral triangles flown so that one tip
of each triangle touches the same spot—for example, the last
known coordinates of the *Beth Dee Bob*.

The fishing vessels were on their own. At 9:37 P.M., the captain of the *Flicka* radioed to Walker that he was shadowing the
drifting life raft. It had traveled eight-tenths of a mile in 90
minutes. The seas were becoming ever more perilous for
McLaughlin and Coltrain, wherever they were.

By midnight, conditions had deteriorated to the point that
the two remaining coast guard boats headed for shore, leaving
only the two helicopters flying their search patterns. At two
o'clock in the morning, the coast guard district office in
Virginia dispatched a C-130 fixed-wing aircraft from Elizabeth
City, North Carolina, and took command of the search for the
Beth Dee Bob. At first light, the 44-footer and the 47-footer
returned to sea, and the coast guard cutter *Point Highland*
steamed out of Cape May Harbor to join what had become a
1,300-square-mile search.

AMY CAVANAUGH WAS walking in the door of a supermarket that
night when her beeper went off. The numerals displayed made
no sense to her—853-2628-7265. She and her roommate, clammer Frank Jannicelli, who had spent the day making repairs to
the *Adriatic*, had codes they would use to send messages using
the beeper. For example, 2255-63 corresponded to the letters
on the phone C-A-L-L M-E. She went to a pay phone on the wall
inside the supermarket door and called their apartment.
"What is it?" she asked.

"The boat sank," Jannicelli replied. He was obviously upset.
He had worked on the *Adriatic* for 18 months. The work had
been tedious, and he always knew it was dangerous. He did it for
the money. And now, on the television news, he had seen the
true wages of the sea. One man was dead; three were missing.

He knew he wanted off the *Adriatic,* even if, at almost 25 years old, he did not really know what else he wanted in this world.

Before he first reached the deck of the *Adriatic,* Jannicelli had lived a sheltered life. He was raised in a home in which, when the phone rang, the only question was which relative was calling. The house in which he was born in Irvington, New Jersey, was a twin. His cousins, Darren and Dawn Marie, lived next door. Aunts and uncles were everywhere. Everyone was Italian, and everyone was Catholic. When Christine and Frank Jannicelli thought their neighborhood was going downhill, they transferred Frank III to a Catholic school in Union, the next town in an area where, like cereal boxes on a grocer's shelf, the homes of one community blend into those in the next with little distinction. In 1984, when Frank III was ten and his brother, Jason, was six, the family moved to a detached home in Union on a nice, tree-shaded street of cozy houses. Both parents were working, so the boys spent much of their time with Christine's father, who often took them fishing. At other times, Frank III would be playing fort inside duct-taped blankets draped over the dining room chairs. His playmates would be his brother and his cousins.

Frank III was his mother's joy. At the appropriate time, he became an altar boy at Saint Michael's church. He looked like a cherub with his chubby cheeks. Sometimes he seemed less than angelic. Once he and another boy set the altar on fire by knocking over a candle. Another time he was in charge of the incense and made such a cloud of smoke that he could not be seen by the congregation.

He was, in his proud father's view, an egghead, a good student who preferred to pursue intellectual activities, like writing science-fiction stories with a friend and keeping a journal. But he lacked street smarts and was a gullible romantic. Union is within the inner layer of urban sprawl that radiates from New York City. It is a place where the natural world is far removed and where one's worth is judged in part by the names on clothing labels. Frank III had no interest in labels, and growing up, he was taunted by others for this lack of status.

As he matured, Frank became his mother's best friend. Frank Sr., employed by a heating contractor, worked nights, and Christine relied on Frank III to be her companion. They would take long walks around Union, talking about what was on their minds. The talks meant a lot to her, and they helped shape Frank III.

When he graduated from a Catholic high school in 1993, Frank III enrolled in an engineering curriculum at the New Jersey Institute of Technology and got a job waiting tables at a seafood restaurant. He hated seafood, but he needed the money.

During his first semester at college, he attended a dormitory party and met Amy Cavanaugh, who was visiting her boyfriend, Dominic Ascoli, at the school. They spent the whole evening talking. She felt completely comfortable, as though she could tell Jannicelli anything. That night he fell in love. He gave her his phone number, and they stayed in touch. When Cavanaugh and Ascoli planned a skiing trip in Vermont, they invited Jannicelli. He later told Cavanaugh that when his parents opposed the trip, he punched a hole in the wall. The tantrum paid off and he got to go skiing.

Within months of the skiing trip, Jannicelli had decided that college was not for him. He suggested to Cavanaugh, who lived in Point Pleasant, that he come live with her and share expenses. She had her own apartment, still dated Ascoli, and was earning her living working for her mother's company, handing out coupons in supermarkets. She thought his idea made good financial sense.

Jannicelli's first job after leaving school was as a dishwasher at a restaurant. Then he worked at a fast-food restaurant and a gas station. The pay was poor, and as often as not, Christine Jannicelli found herself paying rent for her son and Cavanaugh. Then one day, a credit card bill came to the home in Union. Jannicelli had decided, on the spur of the moment, that he and his friends should spend the day in Florida. He took out his credit card and charged all the airline tickets. On the way back that same day, he decided it wasn't worth it to wait four hours for coach seats, so he bought first-class tickets.

The next time Cavanaugh and Jannicelli were strapped, however, Christine was there. And Jannicelli kept his strong ties to home. He was, after all, Mama's boy. If he had an argument with Cavanaugh, he would tell her, "I'm going to call my mom!" When he was sick, he would call home. Once, when he had a tooth pulled, Christine came to Point Pleasant to buy him ice cream.

It was not the case that Jannicelli did not want to grow up. He wanted to have a relationship with Cavanaugh, and at times he would ask her why she could not be his girlfriend. She told him: "Frank, you're too good a friend. I don't want to screw it up." To her, he was her rock, the one person with whom she was completely comfortable.

His parents understood their son's relationship with Cavanaugh, and it pained them almost as much as it did him. Christine had mixed feelings. On the one hand, she thought he must be miserable because he was not getting the love that a man should. She wanted him to come home. But she also saw that he enjoyed his life with Amy and their two cats, Cinder and Patches.

Jannicelli's financial life became more bearable when he was introduced to Mike Hager, a friend of Ascoli. Hager was first mate on the *Adriatic* and, in the summer of 1997, he was looking for a deckhand. Jannicelli had been on pleasure boats but never a fishing boat. He agreed to take a trip with Hager. When he returned, he showed little enthusiasm for the trade. He simply smelled like fish and was exhausted. He just wanted to sleep. He thought he might work as a fill-in deckhand, but a career in fishing seemed doubtful. About ten days later, he made another trip and the captain, George Evans, offered him a job.

"The money's too good to say no," he told Cavanaugh when he got home. "I'll be working two or three days a week for $300 a trip."

Soon Jannicelli was making two trips a week, sailing from Monday to Wednesday and then from Thursday to Saturday. He disliked the physical nature of the work on the *Adriatic*, where the clams were shoveled into the cages. But he stayed with it. Some weeks, if they caught their surf clams quickly, they would make three trips and he would earn more than $900. Other weeks, when the catch wasn't as good, his check was as little as $180.

Every week Jannicelli saved some of his pay for taxes, because nothing was deducted from his check. The rent was $600, utilities were $150 a month, and there were entertainment expenses. Often he and Cavanaugh just stayed home to watch television or vidoes. Big nights out for the clammer and his friends involved a trip to a Point Pleasant bar where there was a band, or a visit to the gas station where Ascoli worked. Jannicelli and Cavanaugh would get in Frank's 1984 Buick—a car with whimsy that would decide to slow down on its own on an expressway—and they would drive to Toms River, about 15 minutes away, where they would spend the night in the cramped kiosk at the Amoco station where Ascoli worked the midnight shift.

Cavanaugh had visited the *Adriatic* once. Jannicelli showed her around, and although she thought it looked old, rusty, and battered, she asked Evans for a job. She was attracted by the impressive wages. Evans had dated a woman back in Virginia who worked on clam boats, but he told Cavanaugh that the work was too difficult for a woman.

Occasionally Cavanaugh would talk with Jannicelli about his future. He had no major plans. Sometimes he would think about attending a local community college, but he never followed up the talk. He seemed content to stay with what he knew was a dangerous job.

In the summer of 1998, Jannicelli faced the coming death of his grandfather, Nicholas Tirella, the man who had filled in as his father during much of his childhood and who now was succumbing to old age. The young fisherman made several trips back to North Jersey to visit Tirella in the hospital, where, with his brother, Jason, he would sit and talk with the old man. Jannicelli had had his rifts with his brother. But they were drawn together during these visits, when, as if ignited by their presence, their grandfather, a quiet man, would talk as he seldom did with others. Cavanaugh would often make the trip north when Jannicelli visited the hospital, and she saw this gentleness between grandfather and grandsons. She and Jannicelli had just returned from one of the hospital trips in August 1998 when Christine called with the news that Tirella had died. The brothers were devastated. Later, Jannicelli told his grief-stricken brother, "Don't worry. I'll always be here with you."

In fact, he was 50 miles to the south of Union most of the time, unless he was at sea. For the last month, since December 15, he had been shorebound and short on cash. George Evans had given Jannicelli a $450 Christmas bonus, but painting, maintaining, and rebuilding the *Adriatic* while it was docked earned him only a small hourly wage. Every morning Hager would pick him up at seven. At night Hager would drop him off at seven or eight o'clock. Jannicelli would end the day exhausted. In a year and a half, the physical demands of his work had transformed Jannicelli. The boy who once was rounded with fat now was a lean, strong 180 pounds. The skin on his cheeks was drawn tight, and the prominent jaw he had inherited from his father emerged from what had been the circle of his face, no longer the face of a boy.

It was that face that Cavanaugh found back in her apartment late on the night the *Beth Dee Bob* sank. But it was a face without mirth. Jannicelli was earnest in his resolve to quit clamming. "Look," he told Cavanaugh. "I'm just going to do this a couple more times. There's no future in this. It's just good money."

EIGHTEEN

A WINTER WEATHER WINDOW

AS they gathered on January 7, 1999, at the Sea Watch International dock in New Bedford, the crew of the *Cape Fear* looked forward to another profitable year. In 1998, they had made 106 trips to sea, spending 3,888 hours—or 162 full days—on the water. A worker who spends 40 hours a week on the job all 52 weeks of the year works 2,080 hours. The work done by the crew aboard the *Cape Fear* had been rewarded with a share of the catch. If the *Cape Fear* had landed a full load of 130 cages on every trip, it would have harvested 440,930 bushels of quahogs and, occasionally, surf clams. While some of the trips ended short, Steven Novack tried to fill his boat whenever he could. With quahogs at a price of $4 a bushel at the dock, the *Cape Fear* almost certainly grossed more than $1.5 million in a year. Novack got 30 cents for every bushel he landed, whether it was quahogs or surf clams, and his first mate, James Haley, got 20 cents for every bushel of quahogs and 24 cents for every bushel of surf clams. The deckhands received lesser shares. If they had worked every trip in 1998, Novack would have made $132,000 and Haley $88,000.

The biggest single beneficiary of their effort had never worked on the *Cape Fear,* although he had been a clammer for many years. Warren Alexander, a tall man with neatly trimmed dark hair, a short dark beard, and a lanky build, owned the *Cape Fear* and four other clam boats—the *Misty Dawn, Jersey Devil, Miss Merna,* and *John N.* All five boats sailed from the Sea Watch dock for most of their trips. Alexander, who had been in the seafood business for 28 years, had worked on commercial fishing boats for two decades, mostly on clam boats. Except for four years as a deckhand, he had been either a mate or a captain. He bought his first clam boat in 1985 and bought the *Cape Fear* in 1994, when he named Novack, who had worked for him on other boats, as its captain.

Alexander's approach to the clam boat business was marked by the same informality that characterized PDM's handling of the *Beth Dee Bob.* While he wrote up contracts for the crewmen and captain, he never gave formal job descriptions. It was assumed that the captain knew what he was doing and that he would tell his deckhands and mate what was expected of them. Alexander had no formal budgets, except when it was time for a major repair to a boat. He employed a port engineer whose job it was to approve or disapprove spending by the captains. Alexander himself exercised little supervision of this spending.

Nor did the owner provide written policies concerning the operation of the boats, or their maintenance or repair. He offered no formal training for the crew on his boats, and he neglected to check on the maintenance of the vessels and his boats or the lifesaving equipment on them.

Decisions of when to go to sea and when to head for the dock were left up to the captains, with their assessment of the weather as their guide. Alexander had signed a contract with Sea

Watch International agreeing to follow a fishing schedule established by the processing plant, but the contract was never enforced by Sea Watch, leaving the captains on their own.

Alexander did require his crews to round off the tops of the loaded clam cages to compensate for settling, and this was regularly done. He did not want to shortchange the processing plant, but he noted that he was not getting paid any more for extra quahogs.

Each crew member's contract specified that drugs were not allowed on the boats and required the prospective deckhand to take a drug screening test, but no new employee was ever tested.

When the boats were in port, Alexander would make a point of visiting occasionally to have coffee with anyone on board. He didn't hold formal meetings, however. The most he would get involved in his vessels' operations was to call them from time to time when they were at sea so he could tell Sea Watch when to expect their return.

The best of Alexander's boats was the *Cape Fear*. It was a dependable source of income, and the crew kept the boat going all year long. Built in 1983 in Moss Point, Mississippi, it had several owners before Alexander's corporation, Cape Fear Inc., bought it on February 22, 1994. It was about 113 feet long and 24 feet wide, with 13 feet below the waterline. The boat was cut in two in 1996 so that a 21-foot section could be welded into its middle. That operation brought the *Cape Fear* to its current length and weight, 188 gross tons, just below the 200-ton mark at which it could only have been sailed by a licensed captain. And no one on the *Cape Fear* held any such license.

THE CREW OF THE *CAPE FEAR*

STEVEN CRAIG NOVACK had no coast guard license, but his credentials as a clam boat captain were impressive. He was about 17 when he began his fishing career. He could not count the various vessels on which he had worked as a deckhand. He had been the mate or captain of the *Montauk* and the *Shinnecock*, fishing vessels of about 159 feet each, the *Little Gull*, which was between 139 and 149 feet, and the *Indian River*, which was about the same size. He had been an officer on the *John Marvin*, another 149-foot boat, and two smaller fishing boats, the *Stephanie D*, which was perhaps 70 feet long, and the *Troydon*, which Andrew Rencurrel later nearly rode to his grave.

Novack lived in a brick ranch house on three acres of land in Greenbackville, Virginia, the first waterfront town on the mainland south of the Maryland border, a place where the streets bear nautical names like Davey Jones Boulevard and Squid Circle, Pirate Drive and Shark Court, Blackbeard Road and Salty Way. Walking toward you, he rolled from side to side as if he were attempting to compensate for the tilt of a boat's deck. Thick, shoulder-length blond hair, combed back from his brow and behind his ears, swayed with each step. He was muscular, like the surfer he had been as a teen living near the northern Virginia coast, and the whole image suggested a rebel or a frontiersman. A trimmed blond mustache added a youthful, Wild Bill Hickock look. But Novack's narrow face was dominated by blue eyes under sandy eyebrows that rose and met in the center of his forehead in an expression stranded between a question and sadness.

Born the son of an electrical engineer who worked at NASA's Wallops Island, Virginia, facility, he had taken his first trip on a clam boat at age 17, at the invitation of a friend's father. After high school, Novack started studying electronics at Eastern Shore Community College. He went to classes Mondays, Wednesdays, and Fridays and caught surf clams on Tuesdays and Thursdays. An 18- to 20-hour clam boat trip earned him up to $1,500 in 1980, and soon he saw no purpose in continuing his education. He was making more than most college graduates.

He married in 1987 and his wife, Karen, bore a stillborn child a month later. Amber Lynn was born next, in September, 1991, and Lesley Lee in August 1993. When Novack was at home, there were big birthday parties and extravagant Christmas celebrations. The bills in the brick rancher mounted to $7,000 a month, but the clam boats always provided enough money to meet expenses. There were times—particularly when the weather was threatening or something broke and stopped the work—when Novack regretted having quit college with no other trade than commercial fishing. There were other times when the big-fisted man loved his work and the good times he shared with his crewmen, whom he considered friends.

Novack lived most of his life in close quarters with these men. For six to eight weeks at a stretch, the *Cape Fear* was his home, and the dock at the end of Antonio Costa Avenue along the Acushnet River estuary in New Bedford was his address.

Sailing a clam boat, Novack felt, was a matter of common sense shaped by experience. His only formal education was a 16-hour drill-conductor workshop that he had attended in Cape May four years earlier. He learned fire-fighting techniques and the use of fire extinguishers. He was taught the proper care and use of survival equipment, including life rafts and survival suits, and how to establish escape routes on the *Cape Fear.* When he was finished, he was issued a certificate that qualified him to instruct his crewmembers in these matters. At one point he had done most of the work to earn a coast guard master's license. But then he heard that being a licensed captain would relieve his boat's owner of liability, shifting all responsibility to him. He did not take the final test and never was licensed.

James Haley Jr. had worked on a number of scallop and clam boats and had spent the last nine years with Captain Novack. They had worked together for the last five years on the *Cape Fear,* on which Haley was first mate. He did not share Novack's rebel image. His hair was trimmed above his ears and he wore large-framed eyeglasses. The mustache that he kept neatly trimmed was that of a railroad conductor, not a train robber. He did speak with the same Virginia drawl as his captain, for he had been raised only a few miles from Novack's hometown. He was married and lived in a ranch house set back from the edge of a country road amidst broad fields of crops. Most of the time, he lived on the *Cape Fear*.

Haley was accustomed to having Novack call him Jimbo. He was 35, only a year younger than Novack, and had earned Novack's trust in their years working together. At times they seemed to think the same thoughts, so that no words had to be exchanged to get the work done.

As mate of the *Cape Fear*, Haley understood his job to be supervision of maintenance of the engines and the deck equipment. He was the one who oversaw the filling of the various tanks aboard the boat—fuel, ballast, hydraulic, and freshwater—and the filling of the clam cages. He had no training other than his 15 years of experience at sea. Nor did he hold any coast guard licenses.

Steven Mark Reeves , a deckhand on the *Cape Fear*, was generic New Bedford: a white man who had dropped out of school and was accustomed to a life of poverty, who had found his way to the docks because fishing offered a financial foothold that little else in the city of 100,000 did. Nearly half of New Bedford's adults have no high school diploma, and even in the best of times, the unemployment rate is about double the rate for the rest of Massachusetts. More than half of the households had annual incomes in 1990 of less than $25,000, and more than 15 percent of the residents received some form of cash assistance.

The lower stratum of the city embraced Reeves when he was born in 1969. His mother, Sue Allen, raised him in a public housing project, along with a brother and two half brothers. He was independent, even at the early age of two, when he would slip out of the apartment looking for adventure. Just as the sea would tug at him when he became a teen, he was drawn with some other tots to a small pond in the woods behind the project. He went with a purpose—to catch fish. Every trip he would return empty-handed. Then one day he caught a snake, which he proudly hauled back to the apartment building, only to lose it in the cellar.

The project grew progressively rougher as Reeves grew older. He survived, able to find his own path, but also always surrounded by his friends. Like many of them, Reeves lost interest in school and dropped out when he was 15. He got a job at Elvira's, a local restaurant, and worked as a dishwasher. He knew this was not his calling. He was just biding his time. He moved out of his mother's apartment, and he waited for the day when he could become a commercial fisherman, the job for kids who lacked formal education but were risk takers. Reeves qualified on both counts. He and his friends called themselves the Lost Boys, after their favorite movie video about a band of hell-raising youthful vampires, and Reeves impressed the adults who met him as a fearless young man. He had the body to match—sinewy and very strong.

Sue Allen had worked on the waterfront for years. When there were jobs, she labored in a factory that made the cheesecloth bags in which scallopers package their catch. She also tended bar in a tavern near the docks where the scallopers and draggers tied their boats. When Steve was old enough to become a commercial fisherman, he asked his mother to help him find a job, and she did. A friend of hers, Hans Davidson, who at one time worked with her making the scallop bags, had moved on to become a scalloper. He agreed to take Reeves with him.

For the poor city kid, it was like hitting the jackpot. Reeves could spend ten or eleven days at sea and come home to a $5,000 paycheck. He would stay in port for five days and then head back to sea. He worked with Davidson for a while, then switched to other boats. Eventually he returned to work with Davidson on the scallop boat *Edgartown* and remained until the scallop industry went into decline.

Scalloping is backbreaking work. The crew spends long hours at sea on a rocking deck, bent over, culling scallops from the trash dredged from the sea bottom, shucking them, and putting the meat in bags. The crews are large—eight to ten men on deck—and the work is as dangerous as any in commercial fishing. Reeves did not complain. He was as at home at sea as any man, and when he was ashore, he had a pocketful of cash, a Jeep, a hot Camaro, lots of friends, and a girlfriend, Robin Lima, who, in 1995, bore him a son, Tyler. The baby gave Reeves something to spend his money on besides a good time. Tyler had all the toys a poor child never could have had. Still, Reeves had his own toys. He spent his time riding dirt bikes with friends, and he paid a mechanic to rebuild the Camaro.

His relationship with Lima had ended by 1997, and Reeves had left the *Edgartown* to work on the clam dredger *John N.* Clamming was a step above scalloping, with more sophisticated machinery and less manual labor. The opportunities to make big money aboard scallop boats had disappeared because federal regulations severely limited where the boats could work. There simply were fewer jobs available. Working on the *John N* kept Reeves in the money. He was making about $40,000 a year. And because the boats made two-day trips instead of the longer scallop runs, he had more frequent nights ashore to be with his friends. On one of these nights, in August 1997, he met Kim LaPlante. Reeves was 28; she was 22. She was a dark-haired beauty, slender, with dark eyes and a welcoming smile. He asked her to go four-wheeling with him in an industrial park.

For LaPlante, it was love at first sight. Reeves was about five feet, seven inches tall, a little shorter than she. He had light brown eyes, fine, shoulder-length brown hair, a tiny goatee, a powerful build, and a tattoo of the Grim Reaper on his right biceps. He made jokes, he was independent, and, although he wouldn't back down from a fight, he was sensitive. In short, he took her breath away. A week later she moved into his apartment. It was not at all the wretched place she would have expected of a bachelor. She touched it up with curtains, but she did not have to clean. She was very happy, and so was Reeves.

Not long after he met LaPlante, Reeves moved up to Warren Alexander's top vessel, the *Cape Fear*. The money was better, and everyone on the boat was a hard worker. He confided in LaPlante that there was another reason he left the *John N.* A member of the crew on the boat was doing hard drugs, and he did not want the added risk of being aboard a boat with an addict, he said.

Reeves was no puritan. People on the waterfront who knew him said that he dabbled in drugs. And he loved the life in the taverns. He and Kim spent a good deal of their time together at Shenanigans, a bar in New Bedford's north end. He was always surrounded by friends, always had Kim on his arm. As she got to know him, she found he was not like some fellows, who out of insecurity ignore their women when they are with the guys.

Together, LaPlante and Reeves began making plans. They wanted to have a house, and Reeves had an idea for a business. He took ordinary strings of Christmas lights and put two halves of scallop shells around the bulbs. The shells were scraped clean and painted with polyurethane. They glowed in pastels, and Reeves believed he could make some money with these seashell lights. He found a source of shells, and he set LaPlante to work scraping and painting them.

LaPlante had her own desires. She wanted to have a child with Reeves. They had not agreed on this, but a couple of times when she thought she might be pregnant, she found him to be accepting if not enthusiastic. "We'll deal with it," he said.

In October 1998, they took a ten-day vacation to Florida. It was Bike Week at Daytona, and Reeves had acquired a craving for his own Harley-Davidson motorcycle. The trip was one long party. The couple rode Jet Skis, took snapshots, and attended a Mardi Gras–type celebration. The weather was gorgeous. They felt like staying. But they returned to New Bedford in early November, just before the *Cape Fear* cast off for its long trip to Maryland. On Thanksgiving, Reeves called LaPlante from the boat. He said he would be home for Christmas. She went shopping for his presents—lots of thermal underwear—and at his request, she decorated a Christmas tree in the apartment. When they opened presents, hers were negligees from Victoria's Secret.

LaPlante kept her own secret. She had a wish he could fulfill. She did not ask him yet, but she would in March, when her birth-control pills were finished. She felt they could handle a baby. They had Tyler with them most days when Reeves did not sail. And Reeves had so much going for him, unlike some fishermen she had seen who blew their money on drugs and booze. Reeves had something to show for his work. He had a nice apartment, a couple of fine cars, and, when he went back to sea in January, he would come home with the money to buy the sparkling blue-and-chrome Harley.

Joseph Lemieux Jr. was, at 28, the youngest man aboard the *Cape Fear*. He had worked on clam boats for 15 months, mostly as one of Novack's deckhands, although he had filled in on other clam boats as well. He was the regular fill-in hand, which meant that he worked about two weeks out of every four, taking the place of another crewmember who wanted time off. He was a solidly built man, with a dark goatee and his hair drawn back in a ponytail.

Paul Martin was a 35-year-old who had been a fisherman for the last five years. He had first worked for Warren Alexander in 1995 when he was hired by the captain of the *Miss Merna* as a deckhand. He had moved from that boat to the *Cape Fear* in October 1998, and had made several trips with Novack since then. Martin had an extended family in the New Bedford area, including his parents, Anthony and Mary Martin, and brothers, cousins, and a score of nieces, nephews, and other young relatives. He, like Reeves, loved motorcycles and cars.

Douglas Kelly, 41, was the oldest member of the *Cape Fear*'s crew. He called himself second mate of the vessel. Kelly was a natural descendant of all the sailors who had called New Bedford their home port, for he had no other home than the city's docks. He had earned some time off in January 1999, and he was about to take it. Where he would stay when the *Cape Fear* sailed was his choice to make. His home would head back to sea.

WHILE THERE WAS a coast guard regulation requiring that safety drills, including practice putting on survival suits, be conducted on clam boats and all other commercial fishing boats once a month, Novack had his own approach to this training. He would talk about survival issues on occasion, but he never required his employees to actually practice. He had a similar seat-of-the-pants method of assuring the stability of the *Cape Fear*. Alexander had paid a naval architect to produce a stability letter, actually a book of many pages that gave detailed instructions on how to operate the boat safely. The book was kept in the wheelhouse, and it outlined in bold letters a dozen things that the captain should do aboard the *Cape Fear* and nine items that he should not do.

Most of the items on the DO list were common sense to an experienced captain.

DO restrain all dunnage, stores and spare gear in such a manner to prevent shifting in a seaway.

DO keep cross connections between port and starboard tank pairs closed at all times.

DO use fuel and other consumables in a sequence such as to minimize trim and list.

DO keep watertight doors, ice scuttles, and access hatches closed at all times except when in actual use.

DO maintain freshwater and hydraulic oil tanks forward as full as possible to minimize trim.

DO make every effort to determine the cause of any list in the vessel before taking corrective action.

The DON'T list was similarly a matter, in most cases, of common sense.

DON'T restrain dunnage or deck cargo by attaching to hatch or door handles.

DON'T move heavy gear on deck during bad weather.

DON'T flood holds, especially with empty or no cages.

DON'T operate in bad weather unnecessarily with flooded holds. Heavy following seas are particularly bad with
flooded holds.

The naval architect who wrote the stability letter assumed,
for the purposes of his calculations, that the *Cape Fear* would
carry 120 clam cages, although he did not place an enforceable
limit on the number of cages that could be carried.

Steven Novack had glanced at the front of the stability letter
when it was first brought aboard the boat. He never got to the
DOs and DON'Ts. He calculated how many clam cages to load
aboard the boat by its feel, working up from 115 cages to 130.
He had, he believed, lived and worked on the water long
enough to trust that feel.

First Mate James Haley used habit as his guide to stability. He
loaded the *Cape Fear* the way it had always been done. He did
not consult the stability book.

ON THE AFTERNOON of Thursday, January 7, Novack and Haley
were on the boat when the crew started to arrive. Steve Reeves
had parked by the fence for a while with his girlfriend. Paul
Martin and Joseph Lemieux were on hand, too. Novack, sitting
in the wheelhouse, checked the weather on the VHF radio.

"Small-craft advisory," the radio reported. "Buzzards Bay, this
afternoon, northwest twenty-five to thirty knots diminishing to
twenty to twenty-five knots late. Seas four to eight feet. Light
freezing spray developing."

The good news was that the wind was from the northwest,
meaning the seas had a landmass blocking the development of
waves. The report continued:

"Rhode Island Sound, this afternoon, northwest wind twenty
to twenty-five knots, diminishing to fifteen to twenty knots late,

seas three to six feet. Buzzards Bay and Rhode Island Sound tonight, northwest wind fifteen to twenty knots early, then diminishing to ten to fifteen knots. Seas subsiding two to four feet. Friday, variable wind less than ten knots becoming southeast fifteen to twenty knots in the afternoon. Seas two to four feet."

The report concluded and Novack made his decision: the *Cape Fear* would go clamming.

Everyone was on board at 3:15 when Novack pushed the throttle forward and steered the *Cape Fear* out onto the Acushnet River. The sky was overcast, and the water, whipped by a strong breeze, was gray as granite as the clam boat passed through the drawn Fairhaven Bridge a quarter mile south of the Sea Watch dock. Next, the boat passed through the opening in the hurricane barrier and then crossed Buzzards Bay, moving toward the open ocean.

Once past the hurricane barrier, Novack lowered the outriggers. It was Novack's intention to steam the boat to the clamming beds, about four hours from the dock, and then to run the boat until he needed sleep. Haley could use these hours to sleep, as could the deckhands. There would be no work for the hands until the boat neared the clam beds and it was time to prepare the equipment for dredging. Novack let the hands decide among themselves when each of them would work and when they would sleep. They all worked hard, in the captain's estimation. There were no complaints about anyone slacking.

All of the crewmen aspired to work on the *Cape Fear* because of the money they could make compared with lesser boats. The *Cape Fear* was not aesthetically beautiful. Its wheelhouse was atop the crew quarters and galley, and this little two-story building was crammed all the way forward on the long deck to make room for six huge clam tanks that held 90 clam cages. The bow of the boat was nearly plumb, and the other lines of the vessel were straight and stark. If the boat had all the gracefulness of rock-crushing machinery, it also could haul quahogs and surf clams quicker than most other boats.

A unique feature of the *Cape Fear* added to its attractiveness for clammers. Unlike almost all of the other clam boats in the fleet, it had a means to keep its catch cold, even in the summer. A system had been installed to pump seawater, cool it, and spray it over the tops of the loaded clam cages. Insulation had been sprayed on the underside of the hatch covers to keep the coolness inside the holds. While on another clam boat, a crewman would have to work short, less lucrative summer trips to keep the catch from spoiling, on the *Cape Fear* there were no such limitations.

On this Thursday afternoon, with the temperature near freezing, the refrigeration system was not in use. The crew knew that, weather permitting, they could expect to dredge 130 cages and, when they returned to port, have a good chunk of money to begin their 1999 season.

That money still drew them to sea, even with thoughts about the loss less than a day before of another state-of-the-art clam boat, the *Beth Dee Bob*. As the *Cape Fear* headed out, the coast guard was issuing a second press release on the fate of that boat. A flotilla of vessels had conducted 19 search patterns covering 2,680 miles but had not yet located the three missing crewmembers. Survival in an immersion suit was still possible this long after a person entered 42-degree water. But the limit was quickly approaching.

NINETEEN

LOVE AND DEATH

THE only good news as the search for the crew of the *Beth Dee Bob* spread farther across the Atlantic on Thursday was that no bodies or empty immersion suits had been found. Those familiar with the sea knew not to be hopeful, however. Bill Becica, the clam dock manager in Point Pleasant Beach, had long since concluded that his friends, Ed McLaughlin and Gene Coltrain, and their shipmate, Roman Tkaczyk, were lost. Still, the coast guard continued the search. Information on currents and winds had been entered into a computer, and the agency's aircraft and vessels followed a plan based on that information.

Lisa McLaughlin waited for news, holding on to her memories of the last touch from Ed. It was Monday night, and Ed had given Liam his bath, just before his eight-o'clock bedtime.

Then Ed had held Liam and his wife in that group hug at the door of the condo.

"Will you be home before the weekend?" she asked.

"Definitely," he said. And then Jay Bjornestad had arrived to drive Ed to the dock.

On Wednesday, not two full days later, McLaughlin left a message on the answering machine at home. The storm in which the *Beth Dee Bob* was steaming would make clamming impossible for at least another day, and he wanted to grab some time with his family. He told Lisa he would be home late at night. That meant, *When you hear the key in the door, don't be startled.* Lisa now waited and hoped, against the odds.

The rest of McLaughlin's family prayed the same prayers as Lisa. Ed's sister, Patti Birchall, had always shuddered at the name of his boat and the tragedy it represented.

"Ed," Patti had told her brother once a year or two before, "three strikes are coming up. When are you going to get off?"

Now Patti and the rest of the McLaughlins knew the answer to that question. But the most dreadful question remained unanswered as Thursday night came and went and Ed and his crew were still lost. The family clung to what they knew about the captain, a man who had repeatedly put himself on the line for the underdog, who was always there to back you up when you needed him and who seemed, as a result, incapable of losing a battle for his own survival.

GEORGE EVANS, THE captain of the *Adriatic*, knew the survival statistics for clam boats that were lost. He had been fishing for nearly 30 years, mostly on clam boats. With the loss of the *Beth Dee Bob* fresh in his mind, he tried to explain the reality of his life to Joan Nowicky, his new girlfriend. He told her his was the most dangerous work in the nation. He said that a clam boat in a bad sea, fully loaded, could sink in 15 seconds. She was incredulous and challenged him: "What about police and fire-men? It can't be more dangerous than those jobs." He did not attempt to persuade her. It was too early in their relationship and she knew nothing about his industry. In reality, she knew little at all about him, other than the pull that they both seemed to exert on each other.

She cringed at how it all began on December 30, barely a week before. Moby Dick's Tavern was not chic, and she had not gone there looking for a man. She and a friend had taken a coworker out for a going-away dinner, and when that was over, they had looked for a place to have some drinks. They came through the door under the red BUDWEISER BLVD. sign at about ten that night and found a seat near the south end of the nine-sided, amoeba-shaped bar. Beside her was the MICKEY MANTLE DR. sign, and on the far side of the bar was the loud jukebox. She ordered a drink, set it on the pale green Formica bar, and, as her friend began talking with a man, she took in the scene—seven wall-mounted televisions, each showing a sports program; men and women talking loudly; and the karaoke singers doing their thing in the corner. Suddenly a man was beside her. He was dark, handsome. His blue eyes revealed a gentleness, and he was well dressed. She felt it necessary to explain to him why she happened to be in this particular bar, and so did he. He said he was looking for a place close to his apartment so he would not have to drive after drink-ing on New Year's Eve. She said she had gone to a more upscale bar with her friend, but it was too crowded. Having justified their presence, they let their conversation flow, and it was easy.

Nowicky considered herself a very strong woman. She did not need to be taken care of. She was a registered nurse, work-ing in the field of medical appliances. She worked hard, owned her own town house, was well-spoken and undaunted by the business world. Men, she believed, were intimidated by her strength. They seemed to be comfortable only with some-one who was weaker, with whom they did not have to deal on an emotional basis. If a man was like that, Nowicky was not interested.

But almost instantly, she was interested in George Evans. Nowicky's friend left with the man with whom she had been talking. Nowicky and Evans kept talking. Then it was closing time, so they went outside and decided to continue their conversation in his Jeep Cherokee. They talked, and then that moment came when the magnetism between them took over. They kissed and discovered in each other the passion that had been politely waiting. By three o'clock in the morning, Nowicky thought, *Okay, I've got to get out of here.* Although it was now Thursday, New Year's Eve day, they both had to be at work in a few short hours. So they said good-bye and she gave her phone number to Evans.

The sea captain called the nurse at her office the next day. She was happy if tired from the late night. She got out of work at three o'clock and went home for a nap. The phone rang at seven, rousing her. She took a shower and at nine Evans arrived, a bottle and a half of champagne in his hands.

She had a message for him, and she delivered it up front.

"Things got a little crazy last night," she said. "I don't want you to think you're in like Flynn."

He smiled a gentleman's smile, and they left for the restaurant.

The next night, Friday, New Year's Day, they met again and tried another restaurant. Point Pleasant had a number of good places: Harpoon Willie's, the Ark, the Mongolian Barbecue, Frankie's. Like most fishermen in town, Evans held dear to his heart the Broadway Bar & Grille, two blocks from the beach, about the same distance from the Manasquan Inlet and just across the street from the nearest commercial fishing boats.

Saturday was normally a workday for Evans and his crew, now that the *Adriatic* was undergoing repairs. Nowicky invited him to her place for dinner after work. She prepared a special chicken dish, and the town house—spotless as a furniture boutique—glowed with candles. They ate at the dining room table, sharing a bottle of wine. If fishermen were supposed to be lowlifes, who was this man? She had asked him to respect her and, by his restraint, it was clear that he did. He was wonderful. But enough was enough. After all the years of dating, she just knew this was right. She pushed her chair back from the table.

"I can't help myself, honey," she said.

IN THE DAYS that followed, Nowicky set about the task of establishing her boundaries with Evans. She was doing laundry one day when he visited her home and he asked if he could throw his shirt and trousers in the wash. "I'll do your pants, but I'm only doing dark clothes," she said. She did not want him to think of her as a maid service. She was impressed; he was not affronted. He just took his shirt back. Later she washed it without telling him. Another time, he accompanied her when she went shopping for a new clothes dryer and stepped aside while she negotiated with the salesman, whom she caught attempting to overcharge her. Evans seemed to appreciate her self-reliance, and she interpreted his reaction as a strength, one that she admired. When the dryer was delivered, she was quite happy to let Evans install it. He was there when she needed him, but he was not overbearing.

By early the next week, Evans had invited Nowicky to see his apartment. Every night she rode with him to the dock, where he put on a dirty jacket and went aboard the *Adriatic* to check the heater and the temperature inside the boat. One night they drove to the Beacon Garden Apartments, a complex of two-story, beige brick buildings about two blocks from the Moby Dick Tavern. Evans's second-story apartment was at the rear of the complex. In the living room was an oil painting by his grandmother, a still life. In the bedroom was another. There was a framed photo of sailboat masts at sunset. Nowicky's critical eye scanned the rest of the apartment. The bathroom was clean. The office was neat. He put on the music and they sat down at his computer and logged on to the Internet. She discovered that he had always wanted to go to Belize. She had, too, and already knew which resort she wanted to visit. They searched for the Web site for Mata Chica resort on Ambergris Caye, an island off of Central America. There were photos of pure, white sand and green-blue water, of cottages with thatched grass roofs and bedroom walls painted in bright Latin colors, of palms and hammocks, a paradise with a price tag of between $3,000 and $6,000 a week. They began making plans for their vacation there together. In Nowicky's heart, the plans were not that simple. George Evans was the first person with whom she had ever felt she wanted a lasting relationship. She thought she understood him, even to the point of knowing how he saw himself.

If he were to describe himself, Nowicky guessed, Evans would have said he had reached a point of maturity. He admitted that he still had feelings for his ex-wife. He had been through a number of relationships, and he knew how the sea could come between a man and a woman. He had fathered one daughter and adopted his wife's son and daughter. They were all in Virginia and he was here, 300 miles away.

Evans talked about the *Adriatic*, explaining to Nowicky that he had mapped the ocean floor to know where to go clamming and where to find all the rubbish and wrecks on which a dredge could become snagged. He told her he never over-loaded his boat and that he never went out with a short crew. If his crew showed up drunk or with hangovers, he would require them to sleep it off before they worked, he said, because it was too dangerous a job to start with. Evans told Nowicky about Mike Hager, his first mate, a man in whom he had faith. Hager was a work in progress for Evans, who was training the mate to be captain. He told her about the two waterfront properties he owned near Virginia Beach and how, soon, he hoped to retire there, supported by his income from the *Adriatic* but with the leisure to enjoy the fruits of his hard work.

For now, Evans would be home every night. But once the *Adriatic* was ready for sea, he would be gone more than half the week. And when he came ashore, it would be in Atlantic City because the packing house that bought his clams wanted his load delivered there. Nowicky understood this and, in fact, did a lot of business traveling herself.

For now, they made their plans day by day. Among other things, they hoped to meet with his sister, his only sibling, in New York City to see a Broadway play. It would be George's first chance to introduce Joan to her.

And Evans told Nowicky he was going to help her stop her pack-a-day smoking habit. He would kiss her every time she wanted a smoke.

She could live with that.

TWENTY

THE MANY WAYS TO
SINK A BOAT

NIGHT had pulled itself over the quahog dredger *Cape Fear* and the surrounding Atlantic like a heavy blanket. The last, faint light of day disappeared over the western horizon an hour before the boat reached its destination 14 miles southwest of Buzzards Bay. The wind was easing, and the lights of communities along the shore to the northwest began to color the sky. To the southwest, the lights of Block Island did the same.

But the brightest glow on the darkened sea was from the deck lights of the *Cape Fear* as it plowed through the ocean at about nine knots, a slow-moving comet crossing the black expanse. At about 6:30, the hands gathered on the deck from where they had been waiting—the wheelhouse or, perhaps, the galley below, where they could take a final meal before the 24 hours of labor they now faced. For the next 20 minutes, the deckhands worked at letting out the eight-inch clam hose. When that floated behind the boat, the men uncoiled the towline and tossed it into the streaming sea to be drawn back with the hose.

Someone by now had turned on the clam pump engine, which was warming up under the deck. And the birds had been lowered from the ends of the outriggers and were being drawn through the sea like huge fishing lures. The hatch covers on the first two clam tanks, up near the main cabin, had been drawn back, exposing 15 empty cages in each tank. Deckhands placed the chutes on the sides of the conveyor belt, running up the center of the deck, aiming them to fill the appropriate cages.

The *Cape Fear* was ready to harvest quahogs. It was seven o'clock at night. The workday had already begun, and now the dredging began as one of the hands removed a pin that held the dredge in place and Novack flipped a lever, letting the dredge slide down the ramp and slip silently into the ocean.

Novack had found a good spot. The quahogs were thick here on the bottom, and every 20 to 28 minutes, he hauled the dredge to find it held enough clams to fill two to three cages. With two men on deck and one sleeping, the crew worked fast, squeezing two dredges into every hour, including the time it took to haul the dredge and return it to the bottom. They began by filling three cages in one of the forward holds and then three in the other—port, starboard; port, starboard—until, sometime between one and two o'clock in the morning, the cages in both forward tanks were filled. Novack had been told by Warren Alexander—and the crew had been told by Novack and James Haley, the mate—that the cages should be rounded up, which meant shoveling extra quahogs on top of already filled cages, up to 18 inches high. The deckhands knew from experience that you loaded one side of the boat as much as the other to prevent the boat from listing—or tilting—to one side or the other. A list could affect the stability of the boat, and an unstable boat, the crew knew, is an unsafe boat.

THERE ARE MANY ways, below the deck and above it, in which a clam boat—even the best in the fleet—can be made to sink. Uneven loading of the quahogs is only one consideration, because a clam boat is a collection of components, each potentially lethal in the hands of a crew whose seamanship is lacking.

When the *Cape Fear* left the dock in New Bedford, it had aboard 2,900 gallons of freshwater in a tank wedged into the bow of the boat. Behind that, there was a 2,400-gallon tank of hydraulic oil, followed by four tanks of diesel fuel, totaling 18,900 gallons. Then there was another tank almost full of hydraulic oil and two ballast tanks filled with 7,800 gallons of seawater.

The quantity of fluid in each tank directly affects how the boat sits in the water. If the tanks in the front of the boat are empty, the rear of the boat will settle in the water. In nautical terms, the boat would be trimmed aft. If the tanks on the starboard side have less than those on the port, the boat will list to port. A conscientious seaman will alternate the use of fuel between tanks to keep the list and the trim even. The *Cape Fear* would burn about 1,400 gallons of diesel fuel during this trip, enough to heat an average southern Massachusetts home most of the winter. If it all came from one tank, the boat's equilibrium would be affected. The stability letter in the wheelhouse instructed: "DO use fuel and other consumables in a sequence such as to minimize trim and list." But Novack and Haley had not read the stability letter.

While improper loading of the clams or the various tanks can imperil the boat, a more direct and likely cause of sinking is by water filling the various chambers in the boat that hold mostly air. A boat is like a cup with a little water in it, floating in the kitchen sink. You can add more water up to a certain point and the cup will continue to float. Add one drop too much, however, and the cup will sink.

For a boat to sink, that one extra drop has to get in. This can happen through doors, hatches, vents, valves, or by a hole being made in the hull.

The *Cape Fear* had four watertight doors. One led from outside the main cabin's rear wall to the engine room, which was under the cabin. Another led from the engine room to the "shaft alley," the space below the clam tanks through which the shaft that drove the propeller traveled. The third watertight door, leading into the galley, was beside the door to the engine room. And the fourth was in the doghouse, the small structure on the starboard side that allowed access to the aft hydraulic room, in which machinery that controlled the dredge and the shaker was located.

Of these watertight doors, three were permanently held open while the *Cape Fear* was at sea. The engine room door was tied open to prevent it from banging. The door between the engine room and the shaft alley was kept open so someone sitting in the wheelhouse looking at a television screen could see, through pictures transmitted by a television camera mounted on the engine room ceiling, what was happening in the shaft alley without going there. The galley watertight door was also left open so crewmen could easily travel between the cabin and the deck. The door on the doghouse, the one most directly exposed to seas washing across the deck, was held shut by two of its six "dogs," sturdy bars that pivoted in the middle, with a handle on one end and a latch on the other that pulled against the door frame to keep the door from swinging open.

The stability letter that was kept in the cabin of the Cape Fear instructed the crew: "DO keep watertight doors, ice scuttles, and access hatches closed at all times except when in use."

Each clam boat has its own style of hatch covers protecting its hold, if it has any. The hatch covers that covered the clam holds on the *Cape Fear* were huge steel lids that rode on steel tracks, held on only by their own weight. They were weathertight, meaning that they kept out most of the spray that would cross the boat's deck. They were not watertight, nor were they meant to be.

To keep water from building up in the holds, the *Cape Fear* had individual pipes connected to the system that pumped water to the clam hose. By turning valves, located on the deck behind the last clam hold, the crew could pump water from any of the six clam holds or from the engine room and discharge it directly into the sea. Smaller electric pumps were installed for each of the six clam holds primarily to pump out water that built up during the summer, when the quahogs were sprayed with refrigerated water. These pumps discharged their water directly overboard through pipes with one-way gates on them.

Novack and his crew had several ways to learn when water was getting inside their boat. There was a second television camera in the hydraulic room, next to the engine room, that constantly relayed a picture of that space. And there were bilge alarms. If water got into the engine room, the shaft alley, or the aft hydraulic room, these alarms would be activated by floating switches. Then lights would flash and horns would sound in the wheelhouse. If water got where it was not welcome, someone in the wheelhouse would be able to see it on the two television monitors, see the flashing bilge alarm lights, hear the alarms, or all three.

But there was a danger that could not be seen or heard, and it lay in wait below the clam holds, in the tanks holding 4,800 gallons of hydraulic oil and 18,900 gallons of diesel fuel. Fire is a distinct possibility on any fishing vessel.

In both the engine room and the hydraulic room, there are hydraulic hoses under high pressure and fuel lines for the engine. Tremendous heat is being generated. In short, there are the elements for fire should something break or wear out.

But if disaster struck, the *Cape Fear* was equipped with all of the equipment it should have for its men to survive, from ring buoys to the life raft, mounted on the wheelhouse roof, to the EPIRB, which Novack had tied to its bracket with a tether.

To get to some of the survival suits, the crew had only to pass through the door from the deck into the main cabin. The door led into a vestibule that also served as the boat's laundry room. Four suits were in bags stored on a shelf above the washer and dryer, just inside the door. There were four more suits on board the *Cape Fear*, two in the crew quarters and two in the wheelhouse.

The crew quarters occupied the forward portion of the main cabin, which extended from the bow back 25 feet and from the bulwarks on the port side to the bulwarks on the starboard. The vestibule and laundry facility was on the starboard side of the cabin. Inside the vestibule, there was a door that led into the galley. The galley counter, sink, and range were mounted against the rear wall of the cabin. Forward and to port was a U-shaped dinette. Directly to starboard of the dinette was the door to the lavatory, or head, and between that door and the dinette were the stairs up to the wheelhouse. Forward of the galley, dinette, and head were a five-person bunkroom and a one-bunk stateroom. Haley's personal survival suit was stored atop a locker on the starboard side of the five-bunk room. One of the deckhands had a suit stored on a shelf in the one-bunk room.

The final two survival suits were stored in the wheelhouse, under a desk.

The suits had been inspected by the crew in the fall. The batteries in the strobe lights attached to each suit had been replaced. It had been about five months, however, since the waterproof zippers on the suits had been waxed, not the three-month interval recommended by the manufacturer.

NOVACK HAD BEEN at the helm about 14 hours when, at five o'clock in the morning, Haley took command. The crew had filled a few less than half of the 130 cages, but the boat was still bringing up two to three cages worth of quahogs each time the hydraulic engine whined and the dredge, showering the deck with seawater, climbed the ramp. The clattering racket of shells spilling into the hopper was as welcome as the jingle of coins falling from a slot machine.

The National Weather Service had issued a forecast about 90 minutes earlier for Buzzards Bay and Rhode Island Sound that was substantially different from the one Novack had listened to the day before in New Bedford.

"Today: Northwest wind ten knots or less this morning . . . GALE WARNING . . . This afternoon . . . wind becoming south-east fifteen to twenty knots. Seas two to four feet. Visibility lowering to under one mile in snow. Tonight: Southeast winds twenty to twenty-five knots becoming southwest and increasing to twenty-five to thirty-five knots. Seas building four to eight feet. Snow changing to rain early with visibility below three miles and locally below one mile."

Novack still wanted to load 130 cages.

At about noon, the 90 cages in the six holds were heaped with quahogs. Haley stepped out onto the walkway behind the wheelhouse—actually the roof of the main cabin—and, using a line run through a winch there, closed the hatch cover on the rear starboard clam hold. He heard it slam shut against its coaming. Later, a deckhand, using the same rope the mate had used, closed the cover over the rear port hold. A knot in the end of the rope got caught between the cover and the coaming, so that the cover could not close completely, leaving a gap of three to six inches.

Haley directed Joe Lemieux to pump out each of the clam holds, using the valves behind the rear port hold. As Lemieux carried out his orders, Haley stood on the walkway and watched, assuring himself that the deckhand turned the valves correctly and that the valves were closed when the pumping was finished.

There were still 40 more cages sitting on the deck waiting to be filled, and the crew set about this chore, first filling four cages on one side of the boat and then four on the other side.

Then they filled cages they had placed on the forward hatch covers.

Novack relieved Haley in the wheelhouse sometime before five o'clock, and when the deckhands had about ten cages left to fill, he asked them to begin pumping all of the clam holds dry and to watch the discharge to assure that the holds were empty of water. Lemieux began the pumping but then switched to the job of loading the remaining cages. Reeves took over the pumping and left the pump running to suck water from the rear port hold, the one on which the hatch cover was slightly open.

Novack had been told about the open hatch cover. He decided to have the crew use a come-along, a system of pulleys and cables, to close it. Before he issued the order, however, he went on to other business. The day was nearly over, the weather had turned snotty, and the *Cape Fear* was ready to drive for home ahead of the gale, with a full load.

FILL-IN: DOOMED BY DESIGN

THERE WERE FEW in the clam industry who would have ridiculed Novack or his mate for their disregard of the stability letter carried in their boat. Many clam boat captains were either ignorant of the contents of these documents or held them in disdain. They had been on the ocean for years, and the ocean had taught them lessons. There was little that a so-called expert could tell these men that they had not already learned through their daily lives on the water. One such man was William Parlett, captain of the clam boat *Richard M.* Parlett was a 25-year veteran of commercial fishing, 20 of them as a skipper. At one time, he had filled in as captain of the *Beth Dee Bob*. He knew that boat had a stability letter. Several years later he could recall precisely where it was kept on the boat. When asked if he had ever read it, he replied stiffly, "No, sir." Asked why, he explained, as if it were obvious, "Didn't need to." But why? "If I felt she was unsafe, I'd get off it."

An example of Parlett's attitude toward the stability of a boat is found in his approach to the presence of water in the clam holds. How much water in the hold was okay? That amount, Parlett said, that would "keep (the boat) on a level keel."

"You could flood the holds completely if you wanted to," the captain said. "All it did was make it more stable."

According to naval architects, however, water in the hold is one of several factors that can quickly destabilize a fishing boat. Sloshing from side to side, the water can tip the balance from being stable to being on the verge of capsizing—without any warning.

I was aware only after I began writing this book that I, too, had little real understanding of vessel stability. When I asked the Society of Naval Architects and Marine Engineers (SNAME) for the name of an expert on fishing vessel stability, they directed me to Bruce Johnson. Johnson is a retired professor of naval architecture at the United States Naval Academy, and he is coauthor of a textbook on the subject. He is also a member of an ad hoc committee created by SNAME in 2000 to look into the alarming rate of loss among commercial fishing boats. John Womack, a naval architect with an office in Cambridge, Maryland, is another member of that committee, along with his business associates, David Wallace and Ricks Savage.

"To most fishing boat crews, the determination of their boat's stability is a lot of black magic by the naval architect," said Womack. "Often, the stability instructions run counter to how they believe the boats should be loaded. Over many generations, fishing boat crews have developed many misconceptions about how stability works. The crews really only worry about how the boat 'feels' at low angles of roll that they typically encounter during routine trips. The naval architect, on the other hand, worries more about the worst case conditions during storms and large angles of rolling caused by large waves and high winds," Womack said. A boat's stability at low angles of rolling tells you nothing about its stability when the seas get kicked up, "and in some cases may actually give the crew a false sense of security by masking a lack of overall stability," he said.

The conflict between the views of fishermen and those of naval architects is set aside on the boats by captains and crewmen who rely on their own experiences, Womack said. Working mostly in good weather when they have succeeded in carrying larger loads than those allowed by their stability letter, the fishermen learn to ignore the limits. Then, when a major storm and its wind and waves are encountered, "the boat's stability is now deficient and there is very little the crew can do to remedy the problem."

Stability, according to Womack, is "the measure of any floating object's ability to right itself to its correct, upright position after being disturbed." A stable boat is not motionless, although to one unaccustomed to the movement of a vessel, that might appear to suggest stability. In its natural environment, any stable vessel must roll with the punches of the ocean environment. There is wind—either steady or gusting—that pushes against every part of a boat above the water. Waves push at the submerged part of the boat as well as its exposed surfaces. They can be rhythmical, sloppy—sailors call these seas confused—or extraordinarily large, often referred to as rogue waves. Other forces that act to tip a boat to one side or the other are off-balanced loading; the weight of fishing gear such as dredges, nets, and hauling devices; and the sudden shifting of unsecured loads.

A properly loaded boat will always be stable, according to Womack and his colleague Bruce Johnson. They give as an example a canoe in which a person is sitting on the bottom. That vessel can handle wind and waves, whereas a canoe in which the person is standing is unstable and, with little force, can be tipped over.

It is possible to build a boat that will always return to its upright position. Single-hulled sailboats with heavy ballast low in their keels are one example. Another is a rescue boat built for the coast guard that, after being completely rolled, will always return to its upright position. Most other boats, including commercial fishing boats, are stable to a point, beyond which they will continue to roll until they assume a new position of stability—by capsizing. "A boat when capsized, if it remains afloat, is actually stable again even though it is upside down," Womack said. "When a boat is unstable, it is at the exact point when it will either capsize or return to its upright original condition," he said.

Any boat or any object will float in water if it weighs no more than the amount of water it displaces. If, for example, a block of wood is placed in water, it will sink into the water up to a point, but it will float. The amount of the block that is below the water has a certain volume. That same volume of water, were it to be measured, would weigh precisely the same as the block of wood. In other words, a one-pound block of wood would displace one pound of water.

A one-pound block of solid steel would sink in water because it weighs more than the same volume of water. But a one-pound steel box, if it contains enough air, can float because the box displaces its weight in water before it reaches the point where it is submerged.

Most clam boat captains understand the law of water displacement intuitively. But intuition is lethally deceptive when it comes to understanding what keeps a boat stable. Womack and Johnson said that even the coast guard, in a pamphlet designed to explain stability to sea captains, got the principles wrong.

A boat's stability is a complex interaction between the weight of the boat pushing it down into the water and the force of the water pushing up on the boat, or its buoyancy. On a fishing boat, this interaction is affected by both fixed and variable items. Fixed items include the shape of the hull, the layout of the superstructure, and the arrangement of tanks, holds, and fishing gear. Variable elements include wind and waves and the way the crew operates the boat's machinery, the way they pilot the boat, load it with fluids and catch, and whether they keep watertight doors and hatches closed.

Two terms are helpful in understanding how a naval architect determines whether a boat is stable. A boat's *lightship weight* is the total of all the fixed weights—the hull, deckhouse, engines, and masts, for example. Its *deadweight* is the total of its variable weights—the fuel on board, the clams caught, and the crew.

At any given moment, the total of the lightship weight and the deadweight is exactly equal to the weight of the water the boat is displacing. The displacement varies during a fishing trip as fuel is consumed and clams are caught.

When a naval architect calculates a boat's stability, he or she calculates the vessel's center of gravity and its center of buoyancy, which is the center of all of its underwater volume. The weight of the boat can be viewed as a force pushing down through the center of gravity. Its buoyancy is a force pushing up through the center of buoyancy. Sitting at a dock, with the center of gravity directly above the center of buoyancy, the boat is actually unstable. But it does not tip over. It just rocks to one side and then back to the other. This rocking is a symptom of how the forces through the two centers keep a boat upright.

Womack and Johnson explained that as a boat tips to one side, the shape of its underwater volume changes (one side dips deeper into the water while the other lifts out of the water), and the center of buoyancy shifts to the submerged side. Thus the force of buoyancy also shifts to that side, attempting to push the boat back to upright. The center of gravity, while it has moved a small amount in the same direction, has not moved as far. With the weight of the boat still pushing down near the center of the vessel and buoyancy pushing up farther out toward the side, the boat rotates back toward its upright position.

Most of the work done by a naval architect is accomplished through the use of computers, out of view of the boat's crew. First, an accurate set of drawings of the hull's shape and the location and shape of tanks, cargo holds, and other items is made. This is necessary to calculate the center of buoyancy and to measure the effect of loads in various tanks and holds.

The next step brings the architect to the dock, where he or she meets the captain and crew and conducts an inclining test, "a relatively simple process that on the surface appears somewhat crude but produces very accurate results," Womack said. The architect sets up three pendulums and then moves weights known distances across the deck to measure the resulting angles of heel. The same test is used on the smallest fishing boats and the largest tank ships. The architect also measures the amount of freeboard—the height of the deck above the water—to determine the location of the boat's waterline. Since the waterline is dependent on deadweight, the architect also measures the level of liquids in various tanks. And the architect walks through the boat to record any missing weights. On a clam boat, for example, the dredge might have been removed from the boat, or clam cages may be missing.

When the architect returns to a computer, there are numerous calculations to be made to determine under which conditions the boat will right itself and under which it will capsize—essentially when the center of gravity is farther toward the side of the boat than the center of buoyancy. The architect makes these calculations for various angles of heel. There is also a calculation for the angle of downflooding, the heel angle at which uncontrolled flooding into the hull or superstructure occurs. Water might enter through an exhaust stack or vent mounted high on the boat, for example.

Fishing boats with a registered length of less than 79 feet are not required to meet any stability standards. Since 1991, those over 79 feet have been required to meet federal standards designed to allow them to survive "normal" storms.

Whether a boat that meets these standards can survive or whether it capsizes depends on a number of factors. The seamanship skills of the crew are vital, as are the practices of keeping watertight doors and hatch covers closed, maintaining the various openings through the hull, such as the clam pump intake, in a watertight condition, and keeping the rudder post and propeller shafts from leaking.

An otherwise stable boat can capsize if its engine or steering mechanism fails, leaving the crew unable to handle the boat to fend off heavy seas. A stable boat may also capsize if water is allowed to leak through the hatches or watertight doors or if the bilge pumping system fails.

"Free surface effect is a very deadly problem," Womack said. Free surface is the sloshing of a liquid in the boat to one side or the other, creating an off-center weight that heels the boat. This could be a small amount of water in the bilge, fuel in tanks that are not properly balanced, or even a small amount of water on the deck that concentrates on one side of the boat. "Water must be able to quickly drain from decks when it is shipped on board during a storm," the architect said. "Successive waves breaking on deck without the water being shed between waves will quickly overwhelm a boat." Clam boats are typical of American-designed commercial fishing boats because they often have low freeboard. In rough weather, the deck of the boat can actually dip below the waves as the boat rocks. This water on the deck adds to the weight available to capsize the boat.

Similarly, overloading a boat can make it unstable. At low angles of heel, the boat may feel comfortable. But in heavy seas, as the angle of heel increases, the overloaded boat suddenly has a center of gravity that has moved too far toward the side, and in an instant, the boat is gone.

Flooding from improperly secured watertight doors and hatches "causes the most deadly reduction in the boat's overall stability," Womack said. The flooding creates a free surface effect inside the boat, and the weight of the flooded water overloads the boat.

The very design of many fishing boats in the United States is suspect, according to the naval architects. "Commercial fishing boat design in the U.S. has a history of being a trial and error process of development for many of the fisheries," Womack said. Moreover, "Many fishing boats, though originally safe when designed and built by a qualified designer and yard, are modified by their crews as fishing methods change or the boat changes fisheries. These modifications are made many times without checking their effect on a boat's stability. Since most of these changes occur high on a boat, additional winches, net reels, et cetera, typically degrade a boat's stability."

As a result, fishing boats capsize for the same reason sport utility vehicles roll over, both naval architects agreed.

There are problems associated with vessel stability that go far beyond the willingness of captains and crew members to follow instructions, Womack and Johnson said.

"Within the [coast guard stability] regulations, there are three different versions of what is the correct stability criteria," said Johnson. "Our question is: Which one is the best? You can use any one as far as the rules are concerned.

"Also, the [standards were created] in the 1930s, when boats were built totally different. Go back and look at boats that were being used then. They were old schooner hulls with good qualities. Now you have big, flat boats. Are the configurations still valid? The rules don't take that into account," said Johnson. "The rule we have now is a one size rule which [supposedly] fits everything."

"Most naval architects don't really understand what's going on behind the rules," Womack charged.

Johnson asked insurance executives why, when it was clear a boat was loaded in violation of its stability letter when it sank, they agreed to pay claims. He said the response was that the boat owner "will just go to the next insurance company. Nobody enforces the rule anyway."

With the insurance companies failing to enforce their own requirements for stability letters, the potential for stability tests to save lives is undermined.

That same insurance company sentiment was expressed during a coast guard inquiry into the sinking of one of the boats in January 1999. Robert William O'Sullivan, executive vice president of Flagship Group Ltd., of Norfolk, Virginia, said his company insured a boat even though no stability test had ever been performed on it. Asked why, he replied in defense, "Let me make it really, perfectly clear that the company that we're speaking of is the only one, to my knowledge, that requires stability tests for all clammers. There are and have been a number of other underwriters that never required stability tests. We did, and as a matter of fact, in many cases that was used against us because it's not an inexpensive thing to have performed, and if the premiums are approximately the same and we require something that is going to cost five to ten thousand dollars and the other company doesn't, you don't have to be a rocket scientist to determine which way the insured probably is going to lean in placement of that coverage."

TWENTY-ONE

DEATH ROLL

IT was January 8, 1999, a day cluttered for Steve Novack with dark memories. It had been 11 years to the day since his first child, a son, was stillborn. As the weather deteriorated, the *Cape Fear* headed northeast for New Bedford with 90 loaded clam cages in its hold. Another 12 cages were on each side of the deck, or waist, wedged between the bulwarks to the outside and the hatch covers to the inside. And 16 more cages were loaded atop the forward hatch covers, on either side of the conveyor belt, pushed up against the back of the main cabin and held in place on either side by the cages on the waist. Water was washing across the steel deck from the building southeast seas. There was snow and rain in the air, but fortunately for the deckhands, there was no ice underfoot or gathering on the rigging, as sometimes happens.

Joe Lemieux and Paul Martin finished loading the last few cages, and Steve Reeves took care of pumping the holds dry a second time. Because the rear hatch cover on the port side was slightly open, Reeves left the pump engaged and the valve open to draw any water that might wash into that hold.

Earlier, when the dredge had come up for good, one of the hands—Martin or Reeves—had slipped the pin in place to keep it from falling. Now Reeves, with his mates filling the final cages, opened the door on the doghouse by the starboard bulwark and descended into the hydraulic room to turn on an air compressor. When he returned to the deck, he walked to the stern, where the piping from the clam pump was joined to the clam hose, which dragged behind the *Cape Fear* in a long loop. He turned a valve, and pressurized air shot through the clam hose. The seawater was forced through the hose, racing around the loop and back to the dredge, where it sprayed from the nozzles and rained down onto the hopper and deck. When the last of the water sputtered from the nozzles, the black hose floated on the surface of the sea, trailing 200 feet behind the *Cape Fear.* Novack decided to leave it there rather than risk the safety of a deckhand, who would have to climb atop the dredge to tie the hose in place while another retrieved it.

All three hands gathered at the stern to haul in the towline as Novack idled the boat, and then the captain put the throttle "in the corner" and headed in earnest for the dock. Novack checked with Reeves, asking how he had left the valves for draining the holds. Reeves said he had left the rear port tank valve open and ready to suck from the hold, the hatch cover of which was slightly open. Novack suggested it might be better to leave the rear starboard valve open, since the seas were washing on deck from that side. The captain knew water could get under the hatch covers. But Reeves noted that the boat already had a port list, so Novack decided to leave the valves as they were and the pump engine running. He would need that engine in operation later, in any case. When they reached protected waters inside Buzzards Bay and were ready to haul the clam hose, that engine would power the winch that did the hauling. Novack was happy with the list to port. It raised the starboard side against the waves advancing from the southeast, giving the deck some protection.

When all the deck work was done, one of the hands turned off some of the deck lights, and then they all went inside the cabin to shed their foul-weather gear and shake the fatigue from their bodies. The last man in shut the watertight door but did not turn the handles to secure it.

It was about seven o'clock, and James Haley was sleeping by now. Reeves, Martin, and Lemieux were not ready for slumber, so they climbed the stairs in the center of the cabin and emerged in the wheelhouse, where Novack sat at the helm, on the starboard side, facing toward the center of the boat. The autopilot was steering the *Cape Fear*, and from his seat Novack had a view of the radar screen and the two television monitors. To his left, he could look across the stairwell and see the rear windows of the wheelhouse. Beyond, the dredge ramp and deck were lit by the remaining deck lights.

As they arrived in the cabin, the deckhands took seats. Reeves hopped onto a table on the starboard side, facing Novack, and Lemieux and Martin settled into chairs on the port side, also facing the captain. A television was playing, and there was nothing left to do until they were inside the shelter of Cutty Hunk Island, when they would haul the clam hose. Reeves, like a man in the grip of a new love, was filled with anticipation for the silver-and-blue Harley-Davidson motorcycle that would become his when he got home. His share of the income from 4,160 bushels of quahogs that rode behind the wheelhouse would seal the deal. He had several snapshots in his apartment of him sitting on the machine or standing by it.

The *Cape Fear* had nearly three hours left to the dock and about 90 minutes until it reached protected water, and so Novack and his hands settled into a comfortable, male jocularity. With the throttle set at three-quarters, the boat rolled from side to side, but the motion was slowed because Novack had decided to leave the birds in the water to compensate for the rough weather. The wind was now blowing 20 to 30 knots and the seas had built to six to eight feet. Water washed constantly through the scuppers along the starboard bulwark. At times, sets of two to four waves—all green water with no foam—broke over the bulwark, splashed on the deck, and washed forward before sliding out through the port and stern scuppers. Some of the waves splashed across the rear clam hold hatch covers before flowing overboard. Novack and his crew had seen this many times. The *Cape Fear* was a wet boat that rode low in the water. Snotty weather often sent waves across the deck.

About 45 minutes into the return trip, Novack sent Reeves back to the clam hold valves. The captain could not see the discharge from the pump, and, wanting to be assured the rear port clam tank was being drained, he had Reeves backflush the system to clear any debris from it. Novack, Martin, and Lemieux could see Reeves through the rear wheelhouse windows, and they saw by the way he was turning the valves that the pump was working. Novack looked at a water pressure gauge in the wheelhouse and confirmed that Reeves was turning the correct valves.

When Reeves was finished, he looked over the port side to see if the pump was discharging. Then he walked up to where the cages were stacked on the waist, against the bulwark, and he leaned over the side and looked again. Then he crossed to the starboard side and entered the main cabin, grabbing something to eat before he climbed to the wheelhouse.

"What did you see?" Novack asked Reeves.

"I can't actually really see," the hand replied. "The way it sounds, everything sounds fine." If the hold was being pumped dry, there would be a gargling sound, with foam spitting out from the port side of the boat. "You know what it sounds like," Reeves told his skipper.

"So what are you telling me?" Novack asked.

"Everything's fine and calm."

As the boat came within view of the beacon of Cutty Hunk lighthouse, near the entrance to Buzzards Bay, an alarm sounded in the wheelhouse, indicating there was water in the hydraulic room at the stern. No one was particularly disturbed, since only a few gallons of water sloshing about in the stern would set off the alarm. It happened on almost every trip. But as a precaution, Novack climbed down into the roar of the engine room and turned a couple of valves to activate a bilge pump in the hydraulic room. While he was there, he bent over to look along the shaft alley. He saw no problems and so he went up to the deck, where he glanced over the side to assure himself that the bilge pump was shooting water overboard. It was. He returned to the wheelhouse and his crew.

All four of Warren Alexander's boats had been dredging this day, and two were now returning to the dock with the *Cape Fear*. A few minutes earlier, the *Misty Dawn* had overtaken the *Cape Fear*. It was now about two miles closer to the Sea Watch dock than its sister vessel. The *Miss Merna* had made its last drag about two hours before Novack stopped dredging. The *John N* was still clamming a dozen or so miles farther south than the beds Novack had worked.

At about eight o'clock, even as the seas seemed to be settling, the crew felt a couple of waves hit the rear of the boat with particular force. The water washed away, but Novack was sufficiently impressed that he picked up the VHF microphone and radioed John Mathis III, the mate aboard the *Misty Dawn*, to tell him about the waves. "She rolled hard two times," he told Mathis.

As he looked out the rear wheelhouse windows, Novack could see the water wash partway up the rear hatch covers and then recede, wave after wave. Each time, when the water had drained, the deck was again visible.

And then one wave advanced as had the others, but the water remained on deck.

Novack stood confused. What he saw under the glare of the deck lights was nothing like any sea he had ever experienced.

He looked up at the two television monitors. Everything was fine below deck. The engine room was dry. So was the hydraulic room.

No. It's going to wash back off, he thought. He could see the same thought in the eyes of Reeves, Martin, and Lemieux.

But the water stayed on the deck.

Novack reached to his right and pulled back on the throttle, leaving the boat in gear but the engine idling. A boat's propeller tends to dig a hole in the water as it pushes the boat forward, and the rear of the boat settles into that hole. Novack's experience told him that by slowing the boat, he could cause the stern to rise and the water to slip off.

That did not happen. Instead, in a matter of seconds, the line of water began advancing *up* the deck, toward the main cabin, and the stern of the boat—which was still level—began to sink.

Novack's stoicism comforted his crew. He could have been teetering on the edge of panic here in the storm-tossed black of night a dozen miles at sea, yet his practiced expression revealed nothing but calm. In fact, he was perplexed. He knew that in six- to eight-foot seas, the big, black clam boat could not be sinking; not this, the queen of the clam boat fleet. He had been shown the proof.

Only a year before, the *Cape Fear* had survived much worse. Novack and his crew had been dredging for quahogs in the ocean south of Martha's Vineyard, Massachusetts, and had not yet taken their full load when the wind, blowing from the northeast, stiffened and then became a gale, with gusts up to 70 miles per hour. The *Cape Fear* could work in a 15-foot, rolling ocean swell, but these were "wind waves" six to eight feet high, and work was no longer possible. The bow hammered into the steep walls of water, which stopped the boat dead, and so Novack told his crew to prepare for the trip home. He steered close to the Vineyard where, blocked by the land, the seas were more docile. But to make it back to New Bedford, the *Cape Fear* had to leave the protection of the island and steam northeast, directly into even more ferocious waves, before cutting between smaller islands and making the final seven- to eight-mile dash across Buzzards Bay.

Novack trained the boat's floodlights on the seas ahead, and he cut the throttle to zero when the biggest waves loomed. But he could not see beyond these foaming mounds to steer, and so he kept his face close to the radar screen while steering his course.

Suddenly he found himself looking up at the biggest wave he had ever seen, a mound of green water that slammed over the wheelhouse, obliterating the outside world from view. The *Cape Fear* seemed to be lifted and moved to the left, as easily as a child moves a toy boat. Just as quickly, another mammoth wave pounded the boat and there was an awful crashing sound. Novack, now keeping his eyes on the radar alone, called to his crewmen to look to the rear. He suspected one of the boat's outriggers—long poles that extend from the side of the boat to give it stability—had been ripped away. But when they looked aft, the crewmen saw only that the entire rear of the *Cape Fear* was submerged. More than 80 feet of steel boat was underwater. The deck and the outriggers were nowhere to be seen.

And then, like a submarine surfacing in an emergency, the clam boat surged up through the water and over the next wave, escaping the sea with its outriggers intact and almost no damage.

Now, on this January night when the sea was snotty but not monstrous, Novack thought back to that experience and was certain the *Cape Fear* and its 230 tons of clams could not sink. But if he was not yet alarmed, he was puzzled and concerned. Why *was* the water that only a moment before had flooded the deck now advancing toward the wheelhouse?

Novack told Martin to go down to the bunkroom and wake Haley. The first mate could be grouchy if his sleep was unnecessarily interrupted, but it was Novack's habit to have all hands on deck when he was unsure what was happening on the boat.

"It looks like we might have a problem," the captain told his crew.

Reeves went with Martin down the stairs, and Novack and Lemieux kept watch out the rear wheelhouse window. The water continued to advance, and Lemieux, on his own, scurried down the stairs to the galley. He knew the situation was serious, and he wanted to make sure the rest of the crew hurried. He saw they were all moving, so he ran back up the steps, where Novack yelled for everyone to get into their survival suits. The captain ordered Lemieux to take one of the two survival suits from under the table where Reeves had been sitting and get into it. He knew Lemieux did not know how to swim. Novack grabbed the other suit.

Haley, dressed in his sweatsuit and glasses, by this time had run up the galley stairs behind Lemieux. He had been working with Novack long enough to know that what he saw was bad news. Novack had a survival suit pulled up around his waist and Reeves had his half-on. Without a word, Haley ran back down the steps and turned left, toward the vestibule and laundry, where four other survival suits were stored. Paul Martin was already there, grabbing a suit, so Haley held the door open for him to leave. Then the mate stepped in and grabbed a bagged suit. But Martin had chosen to put his suit on just inside the galley door, blocking that exit, so Haley turned around and opened the watertight door to the deck, stepping out through it onto the same deck where the sea was flooding.

Up in the wheelhouse, things seemed to be happening in slow motion. But in fact precious seconds were flying past. The sea now covered the rear hatch covers and was beginning to flood over the middle hatches. Novack had started to put his arms in his survival suit sleeves but stopped. He grabbed the VHF microphone. The radio was still tuned to channel 8, the frequency on which he had talked with John Mathis on the *Misty Dawn*. A thousand things were going through Novack's mind. He decided a call to Mathis was his best bet for a speedy response.

"Hey, Jack, I think we have got a problem here," Novack yelled into the microphone. "If you get a chance, can you turn around and come check on us?"

Novack still could not pinpoint the problem from the television monitors. He pulled back the throttle lever for the clam pump to idle, thinking that somehow the 6,000-gallon-per-minute pump might be sinking his boat. Nothing changed. The water, now covering half of the hatch covers over the second clam hold, continued its advance.

Mathis called back from the *Misty Dawn*, asking what the trouble was.

"I think you need to call the coast guard. You need to call me a Mayday; we are taking on water fast!" he yelled into the radio.

Under Novack's feet, the boat was beginning to lean to port. He turned to Reeves and Lemieux.

"We have got to get out of the wheelhouse now!" he yelled, throwing down the microphone.

Novack headed for the door at the rear of the wheelhouse, leading Reeves and Lemieux outside. The deck was tilting faster to port as they scrambled up toward the starboard side of the boat. Novack hollered to Reeves and Lemieux to grab the life raft, but then recanted.

"Forget the life raft!" he screamed. "We don't have time for the life raft!"

With the two men following him, Novack scrambled to the bulwark beside the wheelhouse, but the motion of the boat threw all three back against the wheelhouse. Now they climbed up over the edge of the bulwark, Reeves with his survival suit still only up to his waist, Lemieux fully inside his suit, and Novack with his arms in the sleeves but his head still outside the suit's integral hood. The captain was still struggling with his zipper, which was stuck halfway down his chest.

"We've got to get off this boat now!" he yelled as the roll of the boat gained speed. "I mean now!"

With Reeves beside him, his suit half-on, Novack began to slide down the side of the hull. The two men could now see the bottom of the boat, risen out of the water.

Less than five minutes had passed since Novack first noticed the sea flooding the deck of the *Cape Fear*.

The roll came too fast for Lemieux. He had not yet started to slide when the bottom of the boat rose higher than his feet, and he was thrown backward toward the sea.

Reeves and Novack hit the cold water beside each other and immediately were plunged under the dark waves. When they came up, they were in nearly total darkness. They began yelling for each other, calling for anyone. The lights of the boat, which seemed to glow underwater for a moment, were quickly gone. The engine rumbled somewhere in the darkness. There was a hissing of air escaping the hull in geysers of spray. But nothing was visible. Novack then heard Reeves's voice calling, 20 or 30 feet away.

"Do you have your suit on?" the captain called.

"No, I don't," Reeves answered. "I need help."

"Remember, man! Try to be calm," the captain called.

But in the six-foot seas, Novack was getting dunked by each passing wave, and the cold water was giving him blinding headaches, as if jolts of electricity were piercing his skull. He could be of little help to his deckhand unless he could get his hood on and get his suit zipped. He was losing body heat with each new wave. From his surfing days, he knew the next step toward hypothermia was to get disoriented, and he began to wonder if he could survive. At the same time, he thought about Reeves with no suit on. As he rose to the top of a wave, he looked for lights. There was one on the horizon, perhaps the lighthouse at Cutty Hunk. Novack's own strobe light, attached to his survival suit, was dark. When he tried to turn it on, nothing happened. Maybe his hands were frozen, he thought.

JAMES HALEY HAD been on the deck when the *Cape Fear* began its death roll. He had managed to get fully inside his survival suit, and he jumped over the starboard bulwark. He was too late, and the side of the ship came up to meet him. At the same moment, a chain from the starboard outrigger whipped past, hitting his face and tearing away his glasses. As he was thrown from the boat, he saw the cages beside him on the starboard waist begin to topple in the water like dominoes. And then he was under the water.

Haley had struggled for several frightening seconds before he finally surfaced and caught his breath. He could hear air jetting from the boat, and he smelled diesel. He began swimming—he didn't know which direction to go; he just swam—for fear the sinking boat would suck him down with it. Now he could hear Lemieux hollering. He heard Novack's voice farther away. He turned on his strobe light and set out in the direction of Lemieux, the nonswimmer. In the flash of his strobe, the mate saw a large plank. The deckhands had used it to make a platform across the hopper when they needed to work there. He grabbed the plank and floated it toward Lemieux.

"Just keep calm," Haley told Lemieux. "I have a board. I am going to come over to you."

As he swam closer, the mate asked, "You are going to be calm, right? You are not going to freak out or anything, because if you do, you are going to sink us with this board."

"No, I am doing all right," Lemieux answered.

When Haley reached Lemieux, the deckhand grabbed one end of the board. Then the mate began swimming the board toward the sound of Novack's voice, calling to him, his strobe lighting the way. When they reached the captain, Novack, who had been swimming toward the strobe with one hand holding the neck of his suit shut, took the other end of the board. Haley was in the middle.

Minutes had already passed since the men had entered the water, and they began questioning each other about Martin and Reeves. Novack told the others he had been talking with Reeves in the water. But no one had heard Martin's voice, and they assumed the worst.

Novack told Haley he couldn't get his hood on or his suit zipped, so the mate grabbed the captain's hood and yanked it over his head and pulled his zipper closed. The hood was on cockeyed, and Novack was unable to see, so he eased the zipper slightly. Then Haley tried to turn Novack's strobe on, but it was dead.

Now, without warning, Reeves's voice came out of the black, not more than five feet away, faint but pleading.

"Oh, God!" Reeves cried.

The three men began swimming with their plank toward the voice. Inside their survival suits, they were ineffective swimmers. They thrashed, and they reached for a piece of Reeves.

There were no more cries, however, and everyone paused to look around. The tossing sea was nearly silent, and the darkness was broken only by Haley's strobe. Once Novack or Lemieux glanced at the light, their vision was dotted with spots and they could see nothing.

TWENTY-TWO

A SEARCH AND
SOME ANSWERS

AS soon as Steven Novack had dropped the microphone in the wheelhouse of the *Cape Fear*, John Mathis, the first mate of the *Misty Dawn*, had radioed the coast guard on channel 16. The message was simple.

"We're right here at Buzzards Bay Tower. We got another clammer right here alongside of us. It's the *Cape Fear*, taking on water." The *Misty Dawn* was headed to help, Mathis said.

It was 8:15 P.M. Friday night when coast guard Group Woods Hole, at the northern end of Buzzards Bay, received the call. Group Woods Hole, an administrative unit, was responsible for search-and-rescue missions, and a petty officer on duty coordinated the search that followed, briefing the group's operation officer by telephone.

Two minutes after he got the call, the petty officer contacted

Station Woods Hole, the coast guard unit with the boats, letting the station know the *Cape Fear* was taking on water.

At 8:19 P.M., the petty officer issued an "urgent marine information broadcast," alerting all vessels at sea in the vicinity of the *Cape Fear* as to the clam boat's troubles and asking those vessels to keep a lookout for the boat, assist if possible, and report any findings to the coast guard. Five minutes later, the coast guard cutter *Juniper* radioed Group Woods Hole that it was about 20 miles south of the Cape Fear. It would take the *Juniper* about 90 minutes to arrive on scene if it was needed. The cutter moored at the U.S. Naval Station in Newport, Rhode Island, and waited for instructions.

At 8:33 P.M., Mathis called the coast guard again. He could see strobe lights ahead, but he did not see the *Cape Fear*. With this information, the petty officer ordered the launching of a 44-foot motor lifeboat from coast guard Station Menemsha. Then he notified the coast guard district in Boston of the emerging situation. The motor lifeboat was under way by 8:37 P.M.

HALEY STILL HELD on to the middle of the plank, facing Novack and Lemieux on the other side holding on to the ends. Except for the wash of the six-foot waves, the sea was silent. Haley was facing north, the other two south, so Novack and Lemieux did not see the lights of the approaching *Misty Dawn*. Then the waves turned the plank and Novack saw the lights.

"Hey, man, here comes Jack," Novack told his mate.

"Yes, I know that. He's been coming for a while," Haley replied.

"Well, thanks a lot for telling me," Novack said. He could see that Mathis was searching with a spotlight. It shone directly on the captain, mate, and hand and then it swung away. Novack was worried.

"He doesn't see us," he told Haley.

"Yes, he does," Haley said.

"Look, if he doesn't see us, we'd better come up with another plan, because we are going to get run over here. Look! He's moving the light again," Novack shouted. All three men began yelling at the boat and waving their arms inside their survival suits.

When the boat got closer, they could hear the crew of the *Misty Dawn* yelling back, and Novack's worries eased.

Mathis edged closer, keeping the three men on his starboard side, and deckhands tossed two life rings to them. Mathis took the engine out of gear, but momentum kept the boat moving. Haley grabbed one life ring and Lemieux caught the other. Novack reached for Lemieux's ring and found himself being towed slowly through the water like a water-skier. As the men flopped in the water, their motion steered the life ring away from the boat and back to it. Novack and Lemieux, in their effort to keep their hold on the ring, were dunking each other. *Well, one of us has got to let go,* Novack thought. *Next time it swings to the boat, I'll grab the scupper hole.*

The line swung out and then returned to the side of the *Misty Dawn,* and Novack reached for a scupper and let go of the ring. Lemieux's grip on the ring was permanent.

A crewman appeared above Novack and grabbed his suit.

"Man, don't let me go!" Novack said. His suit was filled with water and the weight prevented him from pulling himself up to the deck.

"Don't worry. You're as good as being on the boat," the crewman said, pulling Novack over the bulwark. When Novack was on the deck, the crewman asked if he was all right.

"I'm fine. Help the other guys," the captain said.

By now, Haley had climbed onto the deck unassisted. He had properly donned his survival suit before he entered the sea and, as a result, there was no water inside the suit. He helped another crewman haul Lemieux aboard and then he lay down on the *Misty Dawn*'s conveyor belt, exhausted. The crew herded the three survivors into the galley and had them get out of their gear. As Novack peeled off his survival suit, he realized for the first time how cold he had become. Hot coffee and blankets were handed out, and the men drew closer to the cabin heater.

In the wheelhouse, John Mathis Jr., the captain and the mate's father, was crisscrossing Buzzards Bay, his spotlight sweeping the water as he and his crew looked for flashing strobes, the life raft, or any debris. Suddenly there was an awful screeching of metal on metal as the *Misty Dawn* rode completely over the upturned belly of the *Cape Fear*. Captain Mathis sent a crewman to the engine room to check for damage. When he returned, the news was not good: a pipe had snapped and water was flooding into the boat. It was about nine o'clock when the *Misty Dawn* radioed the coast guard, reporting that they were leaving the scene and that the clam boats *John N* and *Miss Merna* were there, continuing to search for Martin and Reeves.

By now, the coast guard had ordered a helicopter launched from Air Station Cape Cod and had diverted the cutter *Point Francis* from elsewhere on Buzzards Bay. The cutter would take two hours to reach the scene. The cutter *Hammerhead* was also launched, and a little after nine o'clock, a 44-foot motor lifeboat was dispatched from Woods Hole.

The helicopter was kept on the ground until 9:24 P.M. due to poor weather conditions. It arrived on the scene of the *Cape Fear* sinking 24 minutes later, the first piece of coast guard equipment engaged in the search. At 10:15, the helicopter located a strobe light attached to a life ring, raising hope that there was a survivor nearby. The pilot of the chopper tried several different search patterns, but he found nothing.

All of the coast guard vessels had reached the search area by midnight, but a half hour later, the helicopter returned to its base due to renewed bad weather while the boat crews continued to search.

THE *MISTY DAWN* reached the Sea Watch clam dock sometime after ten o'clock. Red flashing lights swept the dock as ambulance crews waited to ferry the survivors to a hospital. A small crowd of friends and fellow clammers had gathered, as well. Warren Alexander and his boat manager, Tom Becica, greeted the boat, and boarded to talk with the survivors. Then Novack, Haley, and Lemieux were taken by ambulance to a New Bedford hospital, where between eleven o'clock and midnight they were admitted and examined.

Kim LaPlante had just left work at the baseball hat factory. She called her parents' home and asked her sister, Tina, whether Reeves had called. He had not, and an unease that had settled in her earlier in the night grew deeper. About halfway through her shift at the factory, she had told two of her friends that she felt something was wrong. In truth, she had been unsettled since the day before, when she had talked with Reeves about the sinking of the *Beth Dee Bob*. After making her call home, she went with two girlfriends to a café. One of the friends, Dawn Bergeron, had a beeper, and she was repeatedly paged. As the women entered the café, Bergeron found a pay phone and called the number. LaPlante and the other woman stood by as Bergeron made a connection, and they heard her response.

"She's going to flip," Bergeron said, and she handed the phone to LaPlante. "Your sister."

LaPlante's worst dread was realized when she took the phone and heard her sister's voice, telling her the *Cape Fear* had sunk and Reeves was missing. LaPlante left the café and drove to Reeves's apartment in the north end of New Bedford, not far from her parents' home. She called the girlfriend of Reeves's best friend. She was praying for a miracle.

It was a few minutes before midnight when Reeves's mother, Sue Allen, was awakened by the ringing of her telephone. She had gone to bed as she usually did without seeing the news on the television. The call was from one of Reeves's friends. He told her that the *Cape Fear* was down and her son was missing. Searchers were looking in the vicinity of Horseneck Beach, about ten miles southwest of New Bedford. She got dressed and went to the home of her son, Scott, who was a year younger than Steve, and she waited to see if there was any news. She couldn't sit still, and by one o'clock in the morning she was at the bar where she worked. She thought the bar owner might have a VHF radio on which she could monitor the coast guard's search. All he had was a handheld radio, and it was too weak to receive the communications between the search vessels out on the bay. She returned home at 4:30 on Saturday morning with no news, and at seven she went back to the bar to begin work.

THERE EXISTS a coast guard regulation that requires the owner and captain of a vessel involved in a casualty at sea to undergo drug testing. Warren Alexander was aware of the regulation, and Novack was vaguely aware of it, as well, although he later said he did not know the details. But no effort was made while the captain, his mate, and his deckhand were at the hospital to gather samples for that testing, and sometime after midnight, all three were released. With the *Cape Fear* down, Novack and Haley had no home in New Bedford and no possessions. An attorney for Cape Fear Inc. drove the three men from the hospital to Lemieux's waterfront apartment in a pleasant neighborhood of old single family homes in Fairhaven, directly across the Acushnet River from the Sea Watch dock. The men opened some beers and began to unwind as best they could. The phone rang, and Novack answered. It was Lt. Lisa Campbell from the coast guard. She told Novack that he and the other men had to be tested for drugs. An arrangement was made to do the testing later in the morning. Until then, the three survivors would stay in Lemieux's apartment.

OUT ON Buzzards Bay, the coast guard cutters *Point Francis* and *Hammerhead* had been searching through the night, the only vessels involved after the weather grounded the helicopter, and the crews of the 44-foot motor lifeboats were sent to shore due to fatigue.

By seven o'clock, as Sue Allen was arriving at the bar for another day of work, the helicopter was back in the air, and when it arrived in the search area the crew immediately spotted the *Cape Fear*'s life raft. It was tethered to the sunken clam boat. The helicopter crew reported its find, and the crew of the *Hammerhead* launched an inflatable boat and inspected the life raft. Once the *Hammerhead* arrived at the life raft, the helicopter continued the search, flying east to Cutty Hunk, an island south of Cape Cod, and then west across Buzzards Bay to the western shore. Just after nine o'clock, the helicopter crew spotted an empty survival suit floating in the water off Slocums Neck. The Massachusetts Environmental Police were notified, and an MEP officer retrieved the suit.

Ten minutes later, the helicopter crew saw a body in a survival suit off of Gooseberry Island, part of Horseneck Beach. An MEP officer and a local police officer waded into the water and brought the body of Paul Martin back through the surf.

Low on fuel, the helicopter returned to its base, replaced by another helicopter that arrived on the bay at noon. The crew of this chopper spotted a life vest and a leather jacket on the beach between where Martin's body and the empty survival suit were found. The chopper continued to search until two in the afternoon, when wind gusts of up to 70 knots grounded it. At 5:45 P.M., the coast guard suspended the search. The water temperature in Buzzards Bay was 36 degrees. A slim person like Steve

Reeves could survive in that water without a survival suit for only 45 to 90 minutes. It had now been more than 21 hours since Reeves had entered the bay with his survival suit clutched about his waist, and only slightly less time since his mates had heard his last pleading cry.

Later, when a coast guard inspector tried to move the zipper on the empty survival suit, he was unable to budge it. A consultant hired by Warren Alexander was able to move it. The strobe light on Reeves's suit was inoperable when it was found, as it was filled with water.

An autopsy performed on Paul Martin found that he died of hypothermia and drowning. The zipper on his survival suit was partially open when the police pulled his body from the water. The police were unable to move the zipper, nor was a coast guard inspector able to close it. Again, however, Alexander's consultant moved the zipper.

Martin's face was scraped, but the medical examiner found no evidence of head trauma. The last person to see Paul Martin alive was James Haley, the mate, who left him in the galley, where he was getting into his immersion suit. A short time later, the *Cape Fear* capsized.

The medical examiner reported one other item as a result of the autopsy on Martin. In a blood sample taken from the body, the examiner found the presence of benzoylecgonine, an indication Martin had used cocaine before he died. The substance was found at nearly four times the level that triggers an official report of its presence.

At 11:20 A.M. on Saturday, more than 12 hours after the *Misty Dawn* reached the dock, Steven Novack gave a urine sample at the Metromedic Walk-In Medical Center in New Bedford. When the sample was analyzed in a New Jersey laboratory, there was evidence of cocaine. When he was interviewed four days later, Novack told a physician that he had used coke after he got off the *Misty Dawn*.

James Haley gave a urine sample ten minutes after Novack at the same clinic. The same laboratory found evidence of cocaine and marijuana. Haley declined to be interviewed by the physician who had spoken with Novack, and he invoked his constitutional right against self-incrimination when he was questioned in a formal coast guard inquiry.

At 11:45, Joseph Lemieux gave a urine sample. When it was tested, there was no evidence of drugs. When he was questioned during the coast guard inquiry about possible drug use at his home after the sinking, he said he, Novack, and Haley had a few beers. He made no further comment on drug use after lawyers representing Novack and Alexander objected to the questions.

TWENTY-THREE

SECURING THE
FUTURE

TWO boats down in two days. So much had happened so suddenly in George Evans's world: so much that was frightening, so much that was exhilarating. Since Christmas, he had been on the phone every day with his little sister, Patricia, who lived on Long Island with her husband. Their home had, in the past, become his refuge, and Patricia had become his confidante.

Patricia Evans-Mizrachi was a school psychologist, and George had a lot of emotionally charged questions for her to consider. Most of them were about relations with women. Though the sea captain had dated several women, Patricia had more dating experience than George, so he began picking her brain. Although he had been living with a woman in Point Pleasant until recently, that was over and he had considered taking a Club Med trip as a way to meet someone. Evans wanted a relationship and he wanted stability. He had not found that with the women in his past. But this Joan, she was different, and he wanted to tell his sister everything—what Joan did for a living, what they talked about, how pretty he thought she was.

At the same time, Evans needed to talk to someone about the clam boats that had sunk. Two of them had gone down in two days, and both were better equipped than the *Adriatic*, with its rust-stained white sides and its antique machinery. When the *Beth Dee Bob* sank, a concerned friend asked Patricia the name of her brother's boat. Alarmed that a clam boat had sunk, she called him to make certain it was not his boat. He told her about survival suits and the short amount of time it takes the cold water to kill a fisherman. When she asked if anyone would know to call her if he had trouble, he said no. He said that if he was in trouble, his EPIRB would notify authorities. He said that if he did not arrive at the dock when he was expected, that would also trigger a search.

Although some other clammers at one time called Evans "Crazy George" because of his willingness to go to sea when others wouldn't, Patricia knew her brother to be a cautious man. When he visited her home, he spent an unusual amount of time watching the weather station. He would call his first mate, Mike Hager, or Hager would call and leave messages for Evans about the weather. Owning a boat had been a dream of his, and he handled the *Adriatic* as if he were already the owner. He had taught himself computer skills and he programmed the computer in his apartment to serve as the *Adriatic*'s home office. This allowed Evans to do his own accounting, hire employees and manage a payroll just as any small businessman would. George had, in a sense, become the man his father had imagined he would.

George and Patricia were both born in Norfolk, Virginia. The family moved to Virginia Beach when they were small and, as children, they watched their father build a home for the family near the beach. Their father owned a company that sold typewriters and other office machinery, and he instilled in his children the importance of an education. He promised George that when he was old enough, he would either send him to college or set him up in business.

But as a child, George's only thoughts were of the beach near their summer home on the Chesapeake Bay, near Virginia Beach. All summer long, George and his best friend, Richard Freeman, would swim and sunbathe and explore in the dunes. Patricia would try to follow them, and they made every effort to shed the little sister who always seemed to get hurt and get them in trouble.

George and Richard were inseparable. As teenagers, they decided they wanted to become surfers, but they could not afford a new board. George persuaded Richard that they could build one, and so they did. It was distinctive in its resemblance to an éclair.

It was remarkable to Richard the freedom that George enjoyed. He lived on the first floor of his parents' house and had his own entrance, allowing him to come and go at will. But he repaid that trust with a quiet conscientiousness. Throughout high school, he earned an income delivering newspapers and he maintained good grades. When he graduated, he was accepted at Virginia Polytechnic Institute to study engineering.

College was not what Evans wanted, however, and after a couple of years he quit, bought a van, and went surfing. He traveled to Florida and then California. He was 20 and enjoying the surfing life. But it was a life without Freeman, who was in the army in Vietnam, where he would fight in the gruesome battle of Hamburger Hill.

Then Evans's draft notice arrived in the mail. His freedom at an end, he joined the Marine Corps and went to basic training at Paris Island. His military career was cut short when he contracted pneumonia and was sent home. When he recovered, he returned to the sea, but this time to the fishing docks, where he got a job on a clam boat. Having spent so much time riding his board on the seas, now he found he could make a good income out there. His wanderlust evaporated, for he had found a career. He was making about $25,000 for working half a year, an impressive amount in 1970.

Once Freeman was discharged from the military, he returned to Virginia and would join Evans every time the young fisherman was in from the sea. They would cruise the bars and nightspots of Virginia Beach, where Evans had no difficulty attracting women. Freeman found this ironic, since Evans was shy and had never been one to use first-rate pickup lines. He spoke softly, with that refined Southern accent. If he was asked a question, he might ponder for what seemed an interminable time before answering. But he had a nice way of letting other people talk without interruption, and he had a great smile.

Cruising the bars ended in the mid 1970s, when Evans started dating a woman who had been a high school classmate and who also had been Richard Freeman's first date. Now in her twenties, Marilyn Barnes had two children, and Evans embraced the little boy and girl as if they were his own. He married Marilyn on February 21, 1976, and adopted her children, and then they had a girl of their own, Shelly. Although at times he thought he would like to do other things, now Evans had a purpose for all the money he could make on clam boats. And with an attitude, instilled by his father, that he should be the best at what he did, he focused on his fishing career. He would be a captain and, in time, own his own boat.

The fisherman's dream lasted into the 1980s, when the fisherman's nightmare replaced it. Commercial fishing is a hard life in many ways, including the toll it takes on fishermen's families. A man is at sea for days on end. If the weather is suitable, his boat will dock only to unload and then it will head back to sea. Relationships become strained. Many wives of fishermen eventually demand that their husbands find other work and share more than just the financial burden of raising a family.

Evans, who had been sailing out of Chincoteague, two hours to the north of Virginia Beach on Virginia's eastern shore, was crushed when his marriage ended in the summer of 1987. When he was in port, he would sit in the office at the clam plant where he unloaded, clearly distraught. His was not an unfamiliar story to those around him, and they sympathized with him. The office manager, Thelma Hill, would tell him, "George, the water takes a lot of marriages off the wayside."

Evans decided that the only solution to his misery was to take himself off the water. He found a job repairing video game machines in arcades. The pay was a fraction of what he had been making, but he was at least able to come home every night. Still, the move did not heal the wounds in the marriage, and Evans found himself divorced, the final decree coming in 1991.

Perhaps the demands of the sea were not entirely to blame, for Evans could be demanding in his own quiet way. In the months that followed his separation from his wife, Evans, who was now 39, was living in his parents' cottage, within yards of the Chesapeake Bay and within view of the Chesapeake Bay Bridge Tunnel. Across the small street that ran by the cottage was a waterfront home owned by the parents of a woman who was also recently separated. Evans met her and they began dating. Teresa Gower was seven years younger than Evans. They wind-surfed together and went dancing. Her parents loved Evans, and the fisherman—who sometimes would be gone for a week at a time—thought he had found what he wanted: a woman willing to wait for him onshore. But Gower liked her freedom, and Evans's expectation that she would give him her undivided attention was a burden to her. The relationship ended in 1989 when, without consulting with Evans, she decided to go to North Carolina with some male friends for a weekend.

By that time, Evans was back on the water. While he was working fixing arcade games, he told Gower that he could not stand being indoors all the time. Her impression was that he loved the sea and longed for it. He gave his friend Richard Freeman another view, that of a man who was tormented by his lack of financial success, who saw his friends with their big cars and houses and growing families, who worried about the future for his three children and who, eventually, had no choice but to return to fishing. It was the only place he knew where he could get the money that for him symbolized a successful life. Indeed, when he told Freeman of his decision to head back to sea, he seemed disheartened. But his focus was now clear. George Evans would own a boat and master his fate. In the late 1980s, the clam fleet was migrating north in search of more clams. The quota system had not yet been mandated, and southern clams were becoming scarcer. Evans moved from Chincoteague to Ocean City, Maryland, and later to Cape May, working on several different boats. As his work pulled him farther from Virginia, he saved his money and invested in Virginia property. The pull of his home was not only exerted by a connection to the land. His children were there as well. When his daughter, Shelly, was small, he had brought her to the dock with him when he checked on his boat. And now that he was working farther from home, he still made time to get back to Virginia to visit Shelly and her brother and sister. For a time beginning in 1991, he dated Thelma Hill's daughter, Christi Patrick, a woman 16 years his junior. She was a diver and had been hired at times by Evans to make underwater repairs on his boats when he worked closer to his home. She had also worked on clam boats, becoming first mate on one. She understood the sea, and she saw the way Evans was being pulled in different directions by his work, his children, and her. As he moved farther north, she sat him down and ended their relationship. He needed more time with his kids, she told Evans.

In 1992, Evans's boss, Bernard Rubin, bought the clam boat *Adriatic,* and he made Evans its captain. Two years later, Evans signed a contract agreeing to lease the *Adriatic* from Rubin with the option to buy the boat. On January 1, 1995, he made his first $3,569.26 monthly payment to Rubin. He finally was approaching his goal. He could count the years—six—before he would own his own clam boat. But he was not yet entirely his own boss. After the first payment, Rubin directed Evans to move the boat to Point Pleasant, New Jersey, 100 miles farther from Virginia than Cape May. Evans rented an apartment. With no intention of permanently moving away from Virginia and his children, Evans cemented his ties to home by continuing to invest in Virginia real estate, buying a shorefront property that stood between his cottage and the Chesapeake Bay. And, as he worked out of Point Pleasant, he began investing in equipment to modernize the *Adriatic*. The new equipment was temporarily stored on land. Evans did not have the money or time to install it on the boat yet, so the deckhands still managed to load their cages with shovels.

The one advantage of Evans's new location was that he traveled less than two hours by parkway to be at the home of his sister, Patricia, whom he had walked down the aisle in her 1992 wedding. Their parents were both gone now, and the wedding strengthened their bond. Patricia's new husband, Shim Mizrachi, embraced Evans. As time passed, the Mizrachis decided that when they retired, they would move to Virginia Beach to be close to Evans.

It was clear where Evans's heart lay. He returned to Virginia as often as clamming would allow. In the summer of 1998, he had invited his old friend Richard Freeman to his cottage, and he was filled with pride when he showed him the two-story waterfront home he had bought. He showed Freeman a video and snapshots of the *Adriatic*. His dreams were finally being realized. His worries over his financial future were beginning to be conquered. Still, he admitted that his career was hazardous. As he walked Freeman to his car, he started talking about the perils of the sea.

"It's dangerous out there," he told his oldest friend. "I just have to do my best to do everything right."

Freeman had survived the slaughter at Hamburger Hill. He always assumed it was a miracle, and nothing else in the world impressed him as coming close to the nightmare he had seen. But now he realized his friend's life every day hung in just as delicate a balance as had his in Vietnam. He turned to Evans. "I hope you're going to be careful out there, George, because I would hate to have anything happen to you."

"It's okay, Dicky," Evans replied. "I'll be careful."

At Thanksgiving 1998, Evans again returned to Virginia for a family gathering, with about 30 uncles and aunts and cousins and Patricia and Shim. Conscious of the few extra pounds he had gained, Evans had started to work out at a gym. He was renting his parents' house and the beach house, and he had three storage units to keep all the junk he always saved. Recently, the sea captain had begun to talk about how he hoped he would make it to his retirement and a life of leisure at the beach.

At Christmas he went to Long Island, where he picked up Patricia's old Toyota and drove it to Virginia as a Christmas present for Shelly, who was now in college. Then he returned to Point Pleasant and met Joan Nowicky, and the pieces of his life seemed, in an instant, to click into place.

TWENTY-FOUR

GEORGE'S AMERICAN DREAM

LOUIS Lagace knew where George Evans was headed. He had already followed the same course and arrived at the sought-after place.

Lagace owned the *Ellie B*, a 65-foot wooden clam boat. It had dredged a steady stream of dollars for him in the 12 years since he had bought it. He had worked aboard the boat as captain for seven years before it became his. When he purchased the *Ellie B*, he worked another year before he hired John Babbitt as alternate skipper. In time, Lagace stayed ashore and simply waited for the money to arrive in his bank account. Lagace was 47, a whimsical man with a droll wit. It was he whose matter-of-fact message on his answering machine advised callers, "I'm not here right now. I'm currently on a three-state killing spree." When he made a video of life on the *Ellie B*—one that evolved over several years—he interrupted the scenes of work with a command to his crew: "Dance!" They dropped their work and, with the herky-jerky movements of marionettes, obliged their boss, laughing hysterically or deadpanning commentary about the joys of life aboard a clam boat.

Lagace saw life this way: "Fishermen are like one of the last truly American-type pursuits. Whereas a man without even an education—he could still be intelligent, but even not—a man could start working on a fishing boat, he's learning mechanics, the ocean, the weather. He can work himself up. If he's a good deckhand, somebody will take him. If he works hard, he can become the mate. Then captain. Then, if he saves his money and doesn't drink it or use it on drugs, he can get his own boat.

"This is the American dream."

Lagace began dreaming the dream as a young man when he wandered down to the waterfront in his hometown, Fall River, Massachusetts. Fall River is a mill town a dozen miles west of New Bedford, on the Mount Hope Bay. It lacks the renown as a fishing port shared by New Bedford and Gloucester. And Lagace did not come from a fishing family. Neither circumstance impeded his movement toward the sea.

Lagace graduated from high school in 1969 and entered the University of Massachusetts in Amherst, at the western end of the state, far from salt water. He enrolled as a civil engineering student, paying his way through jobs and loans. He, like George Evans, had doubts about his future in his chosen profession, but he stayed in school for three years. Then, in the summer of 1973, he got a job in a mill that finished curtain material, and when September arrived he simply kept working, leaving school behind.

A mill job was a Fall River boy's destiny. He stayed for six years, choosing to work the third shift so that he could have a nightlife.

"I came to the realization that if you're going to do anything in life, either become good at what you're doing or do something else," Lagace recalled. But work at the mill, though he was good at it, just wasn't fulfilling. He considered returning to school, but then asked some friends for a summer job working on their small clamming boat.

"This was April. I just really liked it. I was thrilled to be working outside on a boat. After growing up in a city—Fall River[, that] didn't have a fishing industry per se—I was thrilled to death. I just never thought about going back to school. I still lived with my parents. They were old and needed me around. I wasn't married. I didn't have a family to deal with." The boat broke down a lot, and Lagace made little money. Then it broke down so badly that it was hauled out of the water for a long period of time, and he got a job with another boat.

He was "on the deck, picking clams and shoveling crap overboard. The lowest of the low, but I was thrilled. I was a deckhand." When the first boat on which he worked was fixed, Lagace was offered the job of captain. He became obsessed with catching clams, and the owners were impressed. Although he was more successful with this particular boat than were others who had captained it, he still made little money because the boat was not very efficient. But he was happy.

After he was married in 1980, Lagace continued to work on the boat until a winter of thick ice kept it from leaving port. At that same time, Roger Brayton, who had commissioned the building of the *Ellie B*, needed a captain. He hired Lagace in January 1981. The *Ellie B* was a bigger boat and was almost new. Lagace made good money for Brayton and for himself, catching surf clams in shoal waters southeast of Nantucket Island. And he saved his money. When, in the summer of 1987, Brayton offered to sell the *Ellie B* to him, Lagace felt confident he could succeed, and, with a mortgage, he bought the boat.

A year later he hired John Babbitt, a local captain, diver, and welder, to run the boat part-time. On one of Babbitt's first trips, as he returned to Point Judith, Rhode Island, fire broke out in the engine room an hour from the dock. Babbitt had his diving equipment on the boat. He put on his mask and air tank and went into the engine room with fire extinguishers. His efforts were not enough to put out the flames, and when the coast guard arrived, they ordered Babbitt off the boat. The coast guard crew fought the fire and were able to keep the *Ellie B* afloat and tow it to the dock.

Lagace had been in New Hampshire on a hiking trip with friends at the time, and he had decided not to check in with the boat every day, as had been his practice. He returned to find a charred and gutted wreck that would take six months and thousands of insurance company dollars to repair. Once the work was done, however, the *Ellie B* was like new, with several improvements. The hold had been expanded to carry up to 25 cages instead of the 19 it had once held. It had a rebuilt engine, and the wheelhouse was completely refinished, from a new stainless-steel helm up front to a new galley along the port wall and double bunks along the rear wall. The controls had been modernized, with new electronics and, along the starboard wall on a low shelf under the windows, new dredge controls that were at the captain's fingertips. Just aft of the dredge controls, a door led back to the deck. Another door was in the rear wall, on the port side near the galley counter.

Outside, the *Ellie B* looked about the same. Its dredge was hauled up the starboard side on a steel ramp and emptied into a hopper there. One conveyor lifted the clams from the hopper and spilled them onto another conveyor that led to a shaker—a new piece of equipment.

Two men could operate the *Ellie B* now, although a crew of three was normally aboard. There was an extra bunk below the forward deck, and there was a working shower in a closet in the wheelhouse. When Lagace was nearly done with the restoration, but before he had plumbed a toilet, the boat made its first voyage to the clam beds off Nantucket. It was an extremely successful trip, and, because the thrill of clamming was back and nobody wanted to take the time off, the toilet never was installed. A bucket sufficed.

Back when Lagace bought the *Ellie B,* she was a boat that had always caught surf clams and had always fished in New England waters. The surf clam population there was spotty, unlike the New Jersey coastal waters, where surf clams came up with every haul of the dredge and a captain knew how long it would take to fill the clam holds.

There were a lot of problems associated with clamming off the Nantucket coast. It was an eight- to ten-hour steam from Point Judith to the clam beds. Also, the currents were strong, running two to three knots at times. When the wind rose to oppose the currents, severe waves built over the shoals. And the bottom was irregular. The dredge would be 100 feet deep in one spot, while a mile away, the bottom could be six feet down.

But Lagace loved his native waters for one reason: you could hit a sweet spot where the clams were knee-deep. If you struck one of these shellfish bonanzas, you could dredge in one spot all day and fill your hold.

In New Jersey, the work was slow but steady, and in 1990 Lagace took the *Ellie B* south. The boat would leave the dock in Atlantic City with 14 cages in its hold, enough to fill one trailer, steam an hour offshore, and catch that many clams in six or eight hours. When the new quota system was enacted later that year, Lagace got only a surf clam quota. If he wanted to fish for quahogs, he had to lease or buy someone else's quota. So he stayed with the surf clam business, and he stuck with John Babbitt as the alternate captain of the *Ellie B.*

By now, Lagace had learned that he could make his money without being on the boat, and although he traded trips with Babbitt for a while, as time went on Babbitt became the full-time captain and Lagace worked from shore. He might make one trip a year, but except for working on the boat when it was in port, he had little contact with his vessel or its crew. There was still a part of him that wanted to be at sea. The piece of him that harbored pride was not entirely satisfied with life onshore.

"A boat owner has to have some accounting skills, mechanical, electrical, welding skills. He may have to deal with politicians and councils. It's like a jack-of-all-trades thing," he explained. "A lot of times, you'll be out there and you're getting your ass kicked. Everything in the galley is flying around. You tough it out. You get your trip. You're coming home. You clean up. You pick everything up. Everything's all spick-and-span. Nobody sees that you're catching fifty percent shit with the clams. The wheelhouse is all tidy and people think that's what it's like, and nobody has a clue what was happening a few hours before.

"I grew up in Fall River, Mass. Working in the mill, people think, is dangerous. Got to look out, they've got all that heavy machinery in there. You take a boat and essentially it's a factory.

"I've heard of guys who fell overboard on boats and were never found. [They were] pulling in the hose or leaning over the stern of the boat when it's really rough. [The question is] whether you're going to drown or freeze to death first. What overcomes me is an overwhelming loneliness. I haven't been in that situation. I have climbed out on the dredge when the boat's on autopilot. Imagine the feeling of watching the boat's lights getting smaller and smaller and knowing you're not going to see your family again. It just has to be the worst feeling in the world, knowing it's over. No sign. The person just disappears."

It was more than just the working life of clammers that people didn't understand, Lagace believed. It was their very work.

"I had a beef on how the perception of fishermen has been changed over the past few years," he would say with little provocation. "Years ago, even then, fishermen were looked upon as independent, hardworking people. There are some real jerks and some real intelligent and decent people. There are cheaters and there are hardworking people. But in general, it was looked on as being like the American cowboy and the farmer.

"But since it's only near the coast, it was probably in people's mind some old guy with a corncob pipe and sou'wester on. Even then, the perception wasn't quite there. I would put up a fisherman against any other type of employment. The cowboy and oil derrick worker, get them out on a fishing boat in the winter and rough weather and see how they do.

"Now, with the consciousness on environmentalism so much in the forefront—the mind-set of: Whatever's there, don't touch it—it's like we're rapers of the oceans and killers of dolphins and whales, a bunch of greedy exploiters.

"There's pseudoscience or half-baked statements made by influential people, whether they be celebrities, who alter people's perceptions. I'm all for environmentalism, but some of the radical aspects of it really get me. It's not like clear-cutting forests. I liken it [clam dredging] to plowing a field, in my mind. That's not very scientific. It's like anything on Earth. You need raw materials and you need food. Can you do it responsibly?"

What really irked Lagace was high-profile criticism of the fishing industry. "There's a lot of money behind it, and there's maybe a lot of well-meaning people behind it," he said. "If you don't agree with these people, you're a money-grubbing raper of the Earth in some people's mind.

"*National Geographic,* I like," Lagace said, no hint of sarcasm in his voice. [But] "they did an article on marine sanctuaries. There's different marine sanctuaries around the country. There's one in the [Florida] Keys. He [the reporter] interviews some guy who's a fisherman. He puts a statement in how dragging these heavy nets over the bottom damages the bottom." Lagace was concerned about how people would extrapolate this criticism of the net draggers to apply it to clammers, because he knew that a steel clam dredge appears to be a more formidable weapon of ocean-floor destruction than a weighted net. "Even the dragger guys look at a clam boat and are afraid of what clammers are doing," Lagace said. In Lagace's view, clam dredges were towed in narrow paths through broad expanses of mud and sand, making their furrows in tiny strips but leaving most of the vast ocean floor undisturbed. "Now this statement in *National Geographic,* people might not even pick up on it, but the thing is, it's there. It affects their consciousness. It's just one more [antifishing] thing they get bombarded with.

"As far as politicians go, they're the ones who make the laws. Outside of special interests, they're going to follow what the people want them to do. If there's a groundswell against commercial fishing, they'll jump on the bandwagon even if they don't know anything about it."

Lagace said he had seen actors Ted Danson and Mary Tyler Moore making public comments opposed to commercial fishing interests.

"Somebody like Ted Danson or Mary Tyler Moore, they're good actors, I'll give them that. But their opinion is not worth any more" than any other average person. "But because of their celebrity, they carry a lot of influence.

"Celebrity doesn't mean jack crap.

"It's just a little thing I have because it affects my livelihood," Lagace said, somewhat apologetically, as if to say, Mine is just one man's opinion. "There's enough blame to go around. The fishermen blame the regulators and the regulators blame the fishermen and they'll both blame somebody else."

TWENTY-FIVE

TOUGH MEN, TREACHEROUS SEAS

A full week had passed since the *Cape Fear* sank when John Babbitt steered the *Ellie B* out through Manasquan Inlet on Saturday, January 16, 1999. The captain had had time to think about the perils of his trade, and he had a plan for dealing with them. As with most of his plans, he had not shared it with his deckhands, Gary Sylvia, 45, and Jason Wilson, 24.

The seas were choppy just before sunrise when the red boat with the broad white stripe along each bulwark and the white wheelhouse passed the end of the stone jetties and lowered its outriggers. It was a trip like any other, except for the memories floating around Babbitt's mind of the men who had been lost. Their dying had taught him something.

"Man your stations!" Babbitt barked from the helm, then, "Jason, get the survival suits!"

It was the first time Wilson had heard that command in the 18 months he had worked with Babbitt. He knew what it meant, however. The captain had assigned him to be in charge of the suits, which were stored in a cabinet on deck just outside the galley door or were used as pillows on the double bunks along the back wall. But the crew had never actually put the suits on. When he heard Babbitt's order, Wilson tossed a suit to Babbitt and another to Sylvia. All three men got into their suits in less than a minute, and Babbitt's cheeks bunched up in a grin. They had passed the test, and Babbitt was pleased with his men.

THE CREW OF THE *ELLIE B*

JOHN BABBITT STOOD out, even in the community of strong individual personalities that is the clamming industry. He was a boistrous 43-year-old, stood just under six feet tall, and weighed about 200 pounds. Babbitt's hair was short and receding. His eyes were the brilliant shade of light blue found in marbles and were set under brows that gathered like storm clouds even when he smiled. He had a confrontational manner and his grin was often skeptical if not an outright sneer. The captain had strong opinions, and his opinions were law on the *Ellie B*. No one doubted that.

Being a tough man did not single Babbitt out. Being a coast guard–licensed captain did. He had been injured one winter and decided to study for a master's exam during his recovery. His courses familiarized him with the notion of vessel stability, and he learned about weather systems as well. Until that time, Babbitt had learned everything he knew the traditional fisherman's way: on the job.

His lessons began when he was 13 during a summer job fishing for quahogs. For the next three years he worked on boats when he was not in school in his hometown of Little Compton, Rhode Island. Then one day when he was about 16, he walked out of school and went to work on a fishing boat. He noticed that no one came after him to force him back to school, and so he kept working on the boat. A few years later, Babbitt took a job as a machinist, and he stayed onshore for six years. Then, during a lunch break, he walked out of the machine shop and down to the nearby waterfront and thought, *What the frig am I doing here?* He had to get back on the water, and so he did, never returning to his machinist job.

Babbitt had run a couple of clam boats and, between those assignments, was always able to find work around the water, diving or welding. Then Louis Lagace offered him a job as part-time captain of the *Ellie B.* When Lagace sent the boat to Atlantic City, Babbitt went with it, clamming on weekends and making two or three trips before returning to Rhode Island. He slept on the boat when it was at the dock, but most of the time he was working. In time, he became full-time captain. He had a wife and four children at home, so during the week he found jobs as a commercial diver and welder to earn enough money to support them well. Anything that involved the ocean was part of his life. The ocean had been good to him. It had more than fed him. He owned a large, modern house secluded in the boulder-strewn woods of Little Compton. In most ways, he was his own master.

Babbitt believed that a man could not be a clammer for the money alone. He would fail to learn the things he must know to survive. "If you're going to risk your life, you'd damn well better love what you're doing," he would say. "Why risk your neck for money? It comes and it goes." His rule was: Use your knowledge to stay safe. In the winter, cover every inch of your body that you can with your oil gear, the heavy rubberized overalls, jacket, and gloves that are the fisherman's uniform. And always check the bilge alarms before leaving the dock, a simple task, since the alarms are activated by a float switch that can be moved by hand.

There were some things that could sink a boat that knowledge and care could not prevent, Babbitt knew. A steel boat could have a welded seam split. A wooden boat like the *Ellie B* could break a plank. But, he believed, if you have been on a boat long enough and you know every inch of it, you can *feel* if something is wrong. In Babbitt's ten years with the *Ellie B*, he had reached that level of comfort with her. He and his sea mistress had gone a lot of places together, and she had always taken care of him. Babbitt knew that he pushed the envelope, but to some extent, it was a case of *Me against the pond*. Babbitt and his faithful *Ellie B*, that is.

If he trusted his boat, Babbitt was more circumspect about potential crewmembers. In a decade as captain, he had been through 28 crewmen. If they showed up at the boat with a hangover or stoned, he fired them on the spot. He had kept the same crew for the last 18 months, however. He had known both of them most of their lives and knew their families. If he knew their personal flaws, he also knew their strengths.

Gary Sylvia was 45, just two years older than Babbitt. He was single but the father of two teenage children. Sylvia had been fishing since he dropped out of school in the tenth grade to go net fishing. In his career, he had done everything from lobstering to clamming. He was of average height, wore a mustache and glasses, and cut his brown hair longer than his bosses, giving him a more youthful appearance. He had been on the *Ellie B*, off and on, since Babbitt became captain. In Sylvia's mind, Babbitt was a "pissy" captain, a hard, tough man who shared little with his crew and demanded complete obedience. It could grate on Sylvia, this domineering attitude, but in the end, when you worked with John Babbitt, you made money. So when he had had enough, Sylvia would get a job on another boat, only to come back to the *Ellie B* for a financial boost.

Jason Wilson was, at age 24, young enough to be the son of Sylvia or Babbitt, who were already experienced hands when he was a toddler. Wilson had left another boat and signed on to the *Ellie B* around the last time that Sylvia returned. He had worked once before with Sylvia, in 1991, when the two of them arrived in Gloucester and boarded the long-liner *Andrea Gail.* Wilson had just celebrated his eighteenth birthday. They stepped on board on June 21 and headed for the Grand Banks to catch swordfish. But the skipper had trouble finding fish, and the boat worked farther and farther east. The weather was spectacular—sunny and calm—and they finally filled their hold and returned to port on August 4 after 44 days at sea. Sylvia and Wilson got off the *Andrea Gail* and did not return for the next trip. Two months later, the boat was lost with all hands in the Halloween gale that was the subject of the book *The Perfect Storm.*

THE MEN ON the *Ellie B* were pleased with their survival suit drill. It was reassuring to them as the boat plowed east for a couple of hours in growing seas, spray dotting the windows that wrapped around the curved prow of the wheelhouse. The tip of the bow, which obliterated the view dead ahead, rose above the horizon and plunged below it, and the Detroit Diesel engine below the floorboards roared flawlessly as the autopilot steered for a spot Babbitt had chosen as a likely moneymaker.

The money that the crew would get from this trip was determined by Lagace via Babbitt. Lagace gave Babbitt 30 percent of the amount paid at the dock for surf clams, which now was about $11 per bushel. The *Ellie B* had 25 cages in the hold and another three on deck, for a total of 896 bushels. The load would bring about $9,800 at the dock, of which almost $3,000 would go to the crew, not a bad payoff for a 24-hour day. It was not evenly divided, however. Babbitt, true to his nature, took the lion's share, giving Sylvia and Wilson each 70 cents a bushel, or about $625 for the trip. No one complained. In a two-day weekend, each hand was making about $1,250. And Lagace reasoned that Babbitt was more than a captain. Whenever the *Ellie B* needed the services of a diver or welder, Babbitt did the work without any extra pay.

THE CREW ASSUMED that this Saturday trip would be the first of two or three they would make, nonstop, if the weather held. Babbitt had not detailed his plans. He never did. The crewmembers knew to be ready each weekend to drive from their hometown, Little Compton, Rhode Island, to Point Pleasant. Beyond that, they were in the dark. If they didn't trust Babbitt, they could get off his boat. On a typical weekend, Wilson drove himself to New Jersey and Sylvia rode in Babbitt's truck. They would arrive on Friday expecting to head immediately to sea and to return to Rhode Island on Sunday night. That was Babbitt's way.

By ten o'clock, the *Ellie B* had reached its destination about 25 miles from the Point Pleasant clam dock. It was the job of Sylvia and Wilson to couple the clam hose to the standpipe at the stern of the boat and then put it in the water. The hose, kinked like a cheap garden hose but eight inches in diameter, was stored on the starboard deck, to the rear of the dredge ramp and the shaker, between the bulwark and the clam hold. Wrapping their arms around the hose, the two men horsed one loop after another over the bulwark across the stern until the motion of the sea behind the moving boat dragged the remaining loops from the deck. When Babbitt saw that all the hose and the towline were in the water, he steered the boat in a long arc to starboard until he was lined up with the course along which he wanted to dredge. Then, reaching down to the counter below the wheelhouse windows to his right, he flipped a lever, releasing the dredge from its ramp. The dredge slipped into the water and, pulling the end of the towrope and the hose with it, sank to the bottom.

When the towline was taut, Babbitt dragged the dredge along the bottom for about five minutes. Then, with the winch engine whining, he hauled the dredge. Wilson was standing between the hopper and the sorter, watching for the dredge to surface. As it did, he turned a hydraulic valve that swung an arm out from the ramp to guide the dredge onto its track. Sylvia, standing near the rail, watched from the rear of the sorter. He could remember when there was no hydraulic arm to guide the dredge. Indeed, it could be said he was the reason the mechanism was invented. In those days a man, often Sylvia, stood on the side of the ramp, holding on with one hand and leaning out over the water while shoving the dredge into place with his right foot. Once, about ten years earlier off Nantucket Island, Sylvia was lining up the dredge when it settled its several tons onto the piece of steel where his hand happened to be. No bones were broken, but his hand swelled until the blood burst from the skin.

Now, in the January cold off the New Jersey coast, Sylvia stood between the rail and the conveyor that carried the surf clams down into the cages in the hold. After the dredge emptied its first load into the hopper, he began culling the debris from the clams that had passed through the shaker. The boat rolled with the tossing seas, and although little trash came up with the dredge, there were also few clams. If the dredge was dragging through a hot spot, the *Ellie B* could load three to four cages an hour. But at this rate it would take two hours to load three cages. There were 25 cages in the hold and another three on the deck, so it would take 18 hours to fill all the cages with surf clams. And almost nothing stopped John Babbitt from completing his trip.

Once the hopper was empty, there was enough time for Sylvia and Wilson to duck into the wheelhouse and catnap for four or five minutes. Then the boat tilted to starboard and the engine strained, signaling that the dredge was about to rise once more. It would be a long day and night before anyone could get some genuine rest.

TWENTY-SIX

READY TO SAIL
THE *ADRIATIC*

WORK on the *Adriatic* was almost finished that Saturday afternoon, January 16. The clam pump was installed and had been tested. The dredge, which had been placed ashore to make room for the pump installation, had been hoisted back on deck. All that remained was to paint the new steel that had been welded to the belly of the boat, and George Evans insisted that Mike Hager and Frank Jannicelli finish the job before they went home for the night. In the morning, they would sail for the first time in 34 days, and he wanted everything to be in order. Besides, he had no reason to rush home. Joan Nowicky was in California on a business trip and would not return until the morning. Hager and Jannicelli finally left the *Adriatic* after seven o'clock, their clothes spattered with yellowish orange primer paint.

Hager went directly to his parents' apartment, where he had left his son, Mikey, in the morning. He found Mikey on a couch, sleeping near his father, Dick, and his mother in the kitchen, starting to heat his dinner.

"Well, Mom, I've got to get one guy," he told Judy Hager. The *Adriatic* was short one crewman, and he had three slips of paper with names on them. He took the top slip of paper and went into another room to make a phone call. When he returned, he told his parents, "I've got my man." The crew that began the deadly year of 1999 making repairs to its boat was now complete and ready to go to sea.

Hager's man was Douglas Oland, a 21-year-old college student, home on semester break and hoping to make some quick money. It was natural for Oland to look to the sea. He had helped form a surfing team at his high school, and in high school essays he wrote that in the ocean he saw the beauty of God. He told his parents that when he looked at the ocean, he drew from it a sense of peace that could last all day.

Oland was big, over six feet tall with broad shoulders, the kind of build that earned him the nickname Teddy Bear from the girls in his Catholic high school. Despite his size, Oland was known among his friends not as a roughneck but as a peacemaker. If they needed words to describe him, they would choose *gentle* and *generous*. These qualities were typified by his approach to competitive surfing, which he viewed less as a contest than as a way for people to connect with nature. Riding the waves, he felt, was like playing with Mother Nature.

Oland lived within a few miles of the New Jersey coast, and his first choice for college was a school in another seaside state—Florida—where he continued surfing. He became certified in SCUBA diving and thought he might make a career of diving. A few months earlier, Oland had transferred to Keene State College in New Hampshire, and he was studying sports management with an emphasis on scuba diving. For odd jobs when he was home, he had gone on party boats, and he had given his name to someone at the Point Pleasant clam dock, hoping he would be called as a fill-in deckhand. He had made one other trip aboard a clam boat before Hager drew his name from the top of the pile.

◈

DOUGLAS OLAND HAD never met the crew of the *Adriatic* when he got Hager's call. But he was available, and that was what counted to Hager, who ate his dinner, gave his father and mother hugs, and then gathered little Mikey to head back to his house. He had friends coming for the evening.

In another part of town, Frank Jannicelli was preparing himself for his return to the sea. It was a reluctant return, one made dreadful with his own mental images of the *Beth Dee Bob* and *Cape Fear* going under. He had filled out an application to become a lineman for a cable television company. The application was sitting on a table in the apartment, ready to be turned in after the *Adriatic* unloaded its surf clams in Atlantic City on Monday.

In five days, Jannicelli would celebrate his twenty-fifth birthday, and his friends and family had the occasion planned. His parents would take him and his friends out to dinner at a restaurant with a medieval theme. His friends were also getting him tickets to a rock concert.

After Jannicelli got home Saturday night, his mother called. They talked at length about a television program they both enjoyed and about his coming birthday. They were on good terms, despite what had happened only six days before.

Christine Jannicelli had driven the 50 miles from Union, New Jersey, to Point Pleasant on that day, Sunday, January 10, to visit with her son. If her dreams could come true, he would have moved back into his room in her home with a view of the Garden State Parkway, four blocks away; in her home where she could hear him engaged in deep, philosophical conversations with his father, Frank Jr., and his brother, Jason; where she could see him playing with Max, the chunky five-year-old half rottweiler, half shepherd who at times seemed like his other brother. She would have him cut off the ponytail he had grown, as well.

But if her son would not do as she wished, then she at least would visit him. On this Sunday, she had arrived with a plan to take him shopping. They drove to a nearby discount super-market. Frank III, dressed like a kid in a black shirt, jeans, and no shoes, rode on the shopping cart, flying down the aisles, his ponytail bobbing as they loaded up on more than $200 worth of items. After grocery shopping, Christine Jannicelli planned to take her son and Amy Cavanaugh out to dinner. But after they returned to the apartment and unpacked the groceries, Amy said she wanted to stay home. When Frank told his moth-er he wanted to stay home, too, she was hurt and, showing it, took her leave.

"Ma!" he called after her. "You forgot something."

She returned and they hugged.

Now it was the following Saturday night, and when his phone call with his mother was finished, Jannicelli still had a whole night ahead of him. He and Cavanaugh were headed to the Amoco station 15 minutes away, where Amy's boyfriend, Dominic Ascoli, worked. Motorists are not permitted to pump their own gasoline in New Jersey, so if a car arrived between midnight and eight in the morning, Ascoli was there to serve them. Normally, five cars would be a busy night.

Jannicelli and Cavanaugh brought a television, a VCR, and two videos. On the night before he would return to the sea, the clam boat crewman watched *Lethal Weapon 4* and *Blade* with his friends until five o'clock in the morning. Then he and Cavanaugh drove to their apartment and slept until it was time for him to ship out.

The smell of kids' food—hamburgers or hot dogs—usually filled the kitchen in Michael Hager's little home, as it did on

Saturday night. Hager's closest friends, Sean and Christina Domingo, had brought their son and daughter and planned to spend the night. The Domingos lived with Sean's mother, and their weekend visits with Hager gave them some breathing room. The arrangement also gave Hager's son some playmates.

With dinner cooked, they all gathered in the living room next door to the kitchen and put a video—*Lethal Weapon 4*—in the VCR.

Hager and Domingo had met in the seventh grade at Point Pleasant Memorial School. Before they had met, they had mutual friends. Domingo knew that Hager had a nickname that only his closest friends used, and one day at school he called him by it.

"Hey, Ginger!"

Hager's reply was a punch in Domingo's stomach.

By the next day, the eleven-year-olds were best friends. They roller skated together and went fishing near the docks. As teenagers, when one stopped dating a girl, the other would start dating the same girl. Their friendship continued when Hager quit high school and Domingo stayed on to graduate. At one time, they lived in the same house for six months. Then Domingo married Christina and they moved out of state. When they returned to Point Pleasant in 1996, the young men resumed their friendship, and soon Domingo signed on the *Adriatic* as a fill-in deckhand. Hager, who was first mate on the *Adriatic*, was happy to have his friend aboard. And Domingo liked the money. He had moved his family in with his mother, but when he saw what he could make in clamming—at least $700 a week—he and his wife found their own place.

On board the *Adriatic*, there were distinct lines of communications, and they all ran through Hager. George Evans was quiet, seldom speaking with the deckhands. He always seemed either to be in the wheelhouse or sleeping in his stateroom. His visits on deck were infrequent. If he wanted something done, he told Hager. If the deckhands wanted something from Evans, they also spoke with Hager.

In those days, the *Adriatic* ran smoothly, if not flawlessly. On one trip, the boat was steaming back to port and had entered the Manasquan Inlet when a hydraulic line broke and the steering was lost. The boat swerved toward a jetty, but Evans threw the transmission in reverse and stopped the boat. The coast guard boarded the boat and inspected, finding that a hydraulic hose had been painted, masking the deterioration of the hose. Another time, a pinhole leak was found in the hull and the boat was hauled out of the water the next day.

The big problem aboard the *Adriatic* was the clam pump. It repeatedly fell out of alignment, and it failed to provide enough pressure to adequately stir the clams from their hiding places in the ocean floor. There were times when the *Adriatic* would dredge only eight cages in 24 to 30 hours at sea. There was always talk about replacing the pump, but until Evans docked the boat in December, no one aboard actually believed it would happen. And although a hydraulic system had been installed that could run conveyor belts and sorters, no one thought Evans would ever mechanize the *Adriatic.* It would always be a shovel boat.

While Hager seemed to thrive on the hard work, Domingo stayed on for the money alone. Then in the fall of 1998, Evans went directly to Domingo and accused him of taking his paycheck out of Evans's stateroom, a major offense, since the captain did not want the crew in his room. He did not believe Domingo, who said the checks had been lying on the galley table. Domingo did not like being called a liar, and since for him the only nonmonetary rewards of the job included back pains and exhaustion, he quit the boat.

Hager was disappointed to lose Domingo as a hand, and as of this Saturday night, he had not yet given up on getting him back. But he had a fill-in for the Sunday trip, and he was eager to head back to sea.

It was not unusual for Hager to talk all night with his companions about the boat, since the *Adriatic* and Mikey were always the topics of his conversation. He began talking about survival suits, explaining how they worked and how a man had to be able to get into his suit in one minute if he was going to survive. He surprised the Domingos when he went to the end of a short hall off the living room and pulled down the trap-door ladder from the ceiling. He disappeared into the attic and returned with an orange bag the size of a sleeping bag with a zipper on one side. It was the survival suit that his brother, Tim, had given him when he quit fishing, a suit that he had been given by a friend when Tim worked on the doomed *Mae Doris*.

"Get your watches ready!" Hager announced. The Domingos checked their watches. "Now, go!" he commanded, and he grabbed the zipper and yanked. It would not budge, and he pulled some more. As the second hands ticked toward one minute, Hager struggled. The zipper was frozen in place. The minute was up. Hager laughed.

"I'd be dead now!" he told his friends.

TWENTY-SEVEN

SLEEPWALKING

IT was about two o'clock in the black of night when the last of the 25 cages in the *Ellie B*'s hold was filled with surf clams. The seas had built through the afternoon and stayed mean into the night. But though the seas never quit, seldom was the time that John Babbitt would turn for shore with a partial load. The dredge would go down and the deckhands would catch a nap. Then the winch engine would strain, Babbitt would turn the wheel to starboard, the weight of the dredge would tilt the boat, and Sylvia and Wilson would get back on deck. Wilson, standing inboard and higher than his mate, would guide the dredge on board. Sylvia would take his place by the rail. Sometimes the boat tipped so far to starboard that the water washed over the bulwark and flooded Sylvia's boots. He would flinch, angry with his captain, but he would not skip a beat in his deck work. The waves were big breakers, foam hissing along their tops, their leading edge a wall of water. Some were greater than others, and when one of the big ones smacked the boat as it was hauling the dredge, it would feel as though the *Ellie B* were going over.

Every successful fisherman must be of two minds. One, which is closer to the surface of the brain, contains his good thoughts—those of the beauties he has seen at sea and the money he has made. The other, deeper compartment harbors his terror. On this night, Gary Sylvia was filling the deeper of these two. Some people might have said it was time to quit. Sylvia could not say. He kept working. All decisions were the skipper's to make.

With 25 cages in the hold, the *Ellie B* had three left to fill. Two were on the deck beside the holds and another was at the stern. So at two o'clock, Wilson and Sylvia began the process of removing filled cages from the hold, positioning them on deck, and replacing them in the hold with the empty cages. As the boat rocked from one side to the other, they attached a cable to a cage and winched it from the hold to the deck or from the deck to the hold.

By four in the morning, the wind had subsided but there remained a big surge of waves as the final empty cage was placed in the hold and loaded. With a three-hour steam ahead of them before they reached the dock, the deckhands blew air through the clam hose, hauled the towrope, and then dragged the hose back onto the starboard deck. When they had washed down the deck and had all the gear secured, they entered the wheelhouse to shed their oilskins. Both men had been working 18 hours straight on deck. Babbitt had been at the helm for 21 hours. It was time for someone to rest.

The *Ellie B* was on autopilot, and Wilson took the first watch, sitting in the white vinyl captain's seat. An alarm in the wheelhouse was set to go off in seven minutes to make certain Wilson was awake. Babbitt took the top bunk along the rear wall of the wheelhouse and Sylvia took the lower bunk. In their exhaustion, they fell quickly asleep.

Every seven minutes the alarm sounded and Wilson reached to turn it off. The men at the back of the wheelhouse were undisturbed. When Wilson had been on watch for about 90 minutes, he roused Sylvia from his bunk and they exchanged places.

The first light appeared on the eastern horizon about a half hour later, at six o'clock. They were crossing the north-south shipping lanes a dozen miles from the coast, and Sylvia's lookout had to be sharp. In the early flat light, which offers no horizon between sea and sky, a ship and its running lights could blend easily into the background, although it would appear on the radar screen regardless of the time of day or the weather conditions. Once the shipping lanes were crossed, the tops of tall objects on the shore—the water towers and other structures—began to appear on the western horizon like dots floating on an unbroken sea. As the *Ellie B* drew closer and there was less curve to the earth between the boat and the shore, more and more of the New Jersey coast and its necklace of lights became visible, and the sea slowly turned from shades of gray to a faint pink blush. The water grew calmer nearer the shore, and it was one languid pool when, about seven minutes away from Manasquan Inlet, Sylvia got out of the captain's chair and walked back to the bunks. Babbitt always drove the boat in from here. It was his job to turn off the autopilot, raise the outriggers, and steer between the stone jetties. When Sylvia spoke to him, Babbitt got down from his bunk and headed for the helm.

"You all right, John?" Sylvia asked as the captain climbed into his seat. It was 6:35 and the sun was just coming up, its light coming through the starboard door behind Babbitt's right shoulder. In front of him, on the far side of the boat's pointed bow, was the inlet, the huge boulders in its jetties now individually distinguishable.

"Yup, yup, yup," Babbitt replied.

Sylvia was so tired he could have fallen asleep standing, but he chose to sit down at the galley table, with his back to Babbitt.

A catnap would be rest enough. He would get back up in a minute and talk with the captain. Work was not done once they were inside the inlet. There were 28 cages to unload, two truck-loads, and then they might well head back out for a Sunday run.

As dreams swept briefly into Sylvia's mind, something similar was happening up at the helm. Babbitt's feet had moved him to the helm, but nothing could drag his mind from the sleep that total exhaustion had demanded.

The autopilot steered a true course right across the mouth of the inlet, and it was the sound of splintering wood that awak-ened all three men aboard the *Ellie B.*

"Oh, shit!" Babbitt yelped. He looked down at his feet at the trapdoor that led to the engine room and saw water squirting up around its edges. He reached down and lifted the door, and the wooden engine room ladder popped up into the wheel-house, buoyed by the seawater already inside the boat. Babbitt shoved the throttle full ahead to keep the engine revved, driv-ing the *Ellie B* into the rocks. At the same time he called out to Wilson to get the survival suits.

Wilson threw suits to Babbitt and Sylvia, just as he had done 24 hours before. As Babbit was pulling his suit up his legs, he grabbed the VHF radio microphone and called the coast guard station a quarter mile to the west.

"Mayday! We hit the wall! We're going down!"

The water was around the captain's knees as he pulled his suit up the rest of the way and stepped out the starboard door. The water was waist-deep there on the deck, and he began swim-ming. Wilson was by now in his suit and stepping out the door by the galley, followed by Sylvia. As the boat rolled to starboard, Sylvia swam in that direction after Wilson, then back-paddled to avoid getting hit by the boat's mast.

Because it was dawn, several commercial fishing boats were just heading out to sea. When they saw the *Ellie B* crash into the rocks, they turned to rescue the survivors. Sylvia saw a boat coming toward him and he relaxed. In that instant, exhaustion overcame him and he began to fall asleep, floating on the surface beneath which 28 cages' worth of surf clams were returning to the sea.

Within minutes, all three men had been hauled aboard boats, unharmed. The *Ellie B* was a total loss, its planks shattered, its engine full of seawater. The men had lost their personal property—wallets, car keys, and a few clothes. But, luckily, that was the extent of their losses. Their lives had been spared, and their reputations as clammers would go untarnished. Louis Lagace would stand by Babbitt, dismissing the wreck of his boat as an understandable by-product of aggressive fishing. At most, the men had lost their payday and their workplace. There were always boats in need of seasoned fishermen, and the jobs would be there when they decided to return to the sea.

TWENTY-EIGHT

SORROWFUL SEA DOLLARS

WHEN the dollars and sorrow produced by clam boats during the past two weeks were tallied by the men of the *Adriatic*, the money still motivated them to get out of bed that Sunday morning. They had spent a lean month with their boat tied to the pilings in Point Pleasant. Thin wallets demanded a return to the sea.

George Evans was already looking at a stack of bills. The workers at Laurelton Welding had put more than 200 hours into the *Adriatic*. Evans told Thomas Gallagher, the owner of Laurelton, to hold off on billing him. He would return in a couple of weeks for more work on his boat. Evans knew he would have to catch a bunch of surf clams just to pay that tab.

Things were no better financially for the *Adriatic*'s crew. Hager's support payments for Susan Cornell had continued even though his income was cut by two-thirds. And Jannicelli had been relying on his mother for groceries. That, he knew, could not go on indefinitely.

EVANS WAS ALONE in his apartment on Sunday morning when the phone rang. Joan Nowicky had taken a red-eye flight from California and had just arrived at her town house. He had rescheduled the *Adriatic*'s departure from midnight to noon because foul weather was predicted to arrive late Monday night, and he wanted to be off the water by then. He had time only for a short visit with his girlfriend, but short was better than none. He got in his truck and drove west.

Michael Hager still had a house full of guests when he stirred at about nine o'clock. Soon he had the bungalow filled with the smells of bacon, eggs, and toast, and everyone—the Domingos and their children and Hager's son, Mikey, who seemed a little cranky this morning—gathered in the kitchen. When they finished breakfast, the Domingos headed home and Hager drove Mikey to his parents' apartment. It was about eleven o'clock, and Hager could not stay. He told his parents he had to buy grub for the boat. He hugged his mother and father and said good-bye to Mikey.

"Oh, Daddy, don't go," the boy whimpered. Hager thought his son might be ill, but staying onshore and nursing him was not an option. His father called to him as he stepped out of the apartment door: "Have a safe trip."

Hager's first stop was the nearby Food Town supermarket, where he bought provisions—soda, bread, milk, Delmonico steaks, bacon, eggs, cigarettes. The bill came to $50 or $60. His share—one quarter of the bill — would come out of his pay. Evans would reimburse Hager for the rest.

Jannicelli, having fallen asleep at the late hour of five o'clock, was up at 11:30, waiting for Hager and his ride. Amy Cavanaugh was up with him, and her concern was evident. He had told her he was nervous about the trip and that Hager was as well. Hager arrived just before noon, and Cavanaugh hugged Jannicelli.

"God, Frank, if anything happens, make sure you get that suit on and get into that life raft," she said.

"No shit, Aim," he replied.

George Evans said his good-byes to Joan Nowicky at noon. She was feeling the effects of jet lag and decided not to follow him to the dock. She saw him leave and then began unpacking from her trip.

When Evans got to the dock, his crew had already arrived: Hager, Jannicelli, and Doug Oland, an eager, fresh face. The weather was perfect, with little breeze and almost no clouds in the sky. The news of the *Ellie B* had spread along the dock, and everyone knew the moral of the story. John Babbitt had been sleeping at the helm. It wasn't a case like the *Beth Dee Bob* or the *Cape Fear*. It was a story of human error, not the treacherous sea, and that had to be soothing. By one o'clock, Evans put the *Adriatic* in gear and eased the boat forward between the pilings until it was clear and in the channel of Wills Hole Thoroughfare. Then he steered sharply to starboard and followed the S-shaped course around the red and green buoys until he was in the inlet. The water straight ahead on the open sea was calm, and sunlight filled the wheelhouse. The outriggers came down, and as the *Adriatic* neared the end of the jetties, Evans looked to the left. There in the water were the remains of the *Ellie B*, and up on the rocks he recognized John Babbitt, who had come with his deckhands to see their boat. Evans waved, and Babbitt and his crew returned the salute. When the *Adriatic* reached the sea buoy a half mile offshore, the captain steered south toward his usual fishing grounds. In 24 hours, when he had his load, Evans would steam even farther south, to Atlantic City, where two trucks would be waiting. For now, if this was going to be a typical trip, it was time to turn the watch over to the first mate and grab some sleep. Hager would normally man the wheelhouse until they reached the clam beds.

Then he would dredge while Evans finished his nap. When Evans returned to the helm, Hager would either relieve one of the deckhands or would go to his own bunk. Someone would be sleeping at all times while the rest of the crew worked, and the work would be nonstop.

THE *ADRIATIC*, ONCE white as a wedding dress but now streaked with rust, was, as Hager stood watch, as primitive as any clam boat afloat. Its clam hose hung from the sides and stern in lazy loops that dragged along the surface. Its dredge was chained on the deck, overhanging the starboard bulwark. There were six clam cages riding on the deck and another 24 in the four holds, under hatch covers into which 18 circular holes had been cut to allow the cages to be loaded without the covers moved. Now, when Hager looked out the rear wheelhouse windows, he saw sheets of scrap steel covering the holes. What he did not see were conveyor belts or a hopper or shaker, which were common on the more modern boats.

Hager had a good view from the wheelhouse, which sat high and near the middle of the boat. It was a simple structure, with windows on all four sides. The doors—one on each side—had brass knobs, simple but elegant against the wood paneling, stained dark walnut. The stairs down to the galley and the crew quarters, where Jannicelli and Oland now slept in one cabin and Evans in another, descended near the rear wall.

On the lower deck, the galley was toward the rear, where the boat's motion was felt the least, and the crew quarters were forward. There was one watertight door on the port side of the galley. There were two other means of escape should something go wrong. Inside the forepeak—a space forward of the bunk rooms—was a ladder leading to a hatch in the deck in front of the wheelhouse. There were also doors leading aft from the forepeak to side decks that ran between the main cabin and the bulwarks.

The *Adriatic* carried modern navigational electronics in the wheelhouse and the standard safety items, including a life raft and an EPIRB, both mounted on the wheelhouse roof. Each was in its own canister that was held in place by a hydrostatic release. Evans had replaced the hydrostatic release on the EPIRB at the recommended interval. He had not replaced another critical component of the EPIRB's case, however—a nylon rod that held the case shut and that was designed to be sliced in two by a razor automatically if the unit was submerged in water. Once the rod was sliced, the lid of the case would disengage and the EPIRB would float free, triggered to signal for help. Evans kept the old, white rod in the device instead of replacing it with a new black rod.

The boat's survival suits were all on the top bunk, except for Evans's, which was in his stateroom. The captain had never held a drill aboard the *Adriatic*, but Hager had decided on his own that he would try on a suit during this 90-minute trip to the clam beds. The stuck zipper on Saturday night had frightened him.

EVANS WAS AT the helm at eight o'clock Sunday night and the *Adriatic* was slowly catching clams. He picked up his cell phone and dialed Nowicky's number. When she answered, he asked her to call him back to test the reception of his phone. It was a harmless ruse. He just wanted to hear her voice. All she could hear was the noise from the boat's engine, as if Evans were calling from a factory floor. But his words assured her it was a peaceful night at sea.

"It's just beautiful out here," Evans told Nowicky. The moon was out; the sea was calm. Everything seemed to be working well. "What a gorgeous night," he exclaimed.

"Be careful," she said as they spoke their farewells for the evening. "Call me when you get in."

Evans's leisurely telephone call contrasted with the sweaty work that Hager, Jannicelli, and Oland were performing behind him, on the deck. As one of them, probably Hager, ran a winch mounted on the boat's boom, the dredge was dragged from the sea on the starboard side and swung over the deck. At the rear end of the dredge was a chain bag. Jannicelli grabbed a rope that, like a drawstring, held the bag together, and he yanked, knocking loose a brass wedge that had held the drawstring tight. The bag opened and the surf clams fell out, clattering on the deck like a pile of ceramic saucers. Once the dredge was returned to the water, all three deckhands bent from the hips and began picking through the heap of clams, tossing out anything that was not a clam. When part of the pile was culled, they tossed the good clams between their legs toward the holes in the hatch covers, or they grabbed large, scooplike shovels to pitch the clams into the holds, which were pumped full of seawater to keep the clams from breaking.

The noise on deck was deafening. The engines made their bulldozer roars. The shovels scraped loudly against the steel deck. Conversation was held only when necessary and required strong lungs.

The noise and the shoveling were the constants on deck on the *Adriatic*, along with the diesel fumes, the cigarette smoke, and the backaches.

The crew worked on through the night, far enough at sea that the glow of the sky over the lights onshore simply hinted where the horizon lay. Then the moon yielded to sunrise and, at 9:30 in the morning, Evans's cell phone rang. It was Everett "Bub" Giverson, the dock manager at Barney's Dock in Atlantic City. It was a brief call. Giverson had a habit of checking with clam boats that unloaded their catch at his dock. Evans told Giverson that he was working and should have 30 cages filled by noon. He promised to call then and let Giverson know when he would arrive at the dock.

What Evans failed to mention was that despite the new clam pump in the *Adriatic*, he was not catching clams any faster than before. In December, when he quit clamming to replace the pump, he was catching clams at a rate of less than two cages an hour. He was spending too much time at sea, using too much fuel, and making less money. He expected the new pump to change that.

But the change had not come, so after he talked with Giverson, Evans went down to the engine room. There he found that one of the deckhands had failed to open the valve on the clam pump completely. That could cause inadequate pressure to the nozzles on the dredge, so Evans opened the valve all the way—a couple of turns. It seemed then that the dredge came up with more clams. But Evans was not certain.

A few hours later, Giverson was eating his lunch and was watching the noon television news when his phone rang. Evans said he finally had his cages full and was steaming down the beach. He expected to arrive in Atlantic City at about seven o'clock.

About one o'clock in the afternoon, Evans called again. He told Giverson that he had been catching poorly, and he asked the dock manager to arrange for a diver to look underneath the *Adriatic* sometime the next morning. Perhaps a month in Point Pleasant had allowed barnacles to grow over the intake for the pump.

Giverson called Jack Keith, a local diver, who agreed to inspect the *Adriatic*.

"Everything's set," Giverson told Evans at 1:30 P.M. when the captain answered his cell phone. "Jack will be here at seven o'clock tomorrow morning, ready to dive on you and check your valve."

"Okay, no problem, Bub. I'll see you when I get in tonight, if you're going to be there."

The sky that a day before was cloudless had now grown overcast. To the southwest, a front was racing toward the Atlantic Ocean, crossing Maryland and Delaware first and then aiming for the Delaware Bay and the lower lobe of New Jersey. The front was marked by a darkened sky, screaming winds, and lightning. The bad weather that had been predicted for later Sunday night was ahead of schedule. At three o'clock in the morning, the

National Weather Service had issued a revised forecast for coastal waters from Sandy Hook, New Jersey, to Fenwick Island, Delaware, and out to sea 20 nautical miles. The headline on the forecast was: "Small craft advisory." The forecast called for "southeast winds fifteen to twenty knots, becoming south and increasing to twenty-five to thirty knots with higher gusts this afternoon, seas three to five feet, building to five to seven feet. The visibility occasionally one nautical mile or less and showers and fog, and there's a chance of a thunderstorm this afternoon." By one o'clock in the afternoon, a sea buoy off the mouth of the Delaware Bay—about 100 miles from the *Adriatic*—was recording peak winds of 28 knots with steep, five-foot waves, an air temperature of 53 degrees, and a sea temperature of 44 degrees.

The *Adriatic* was not a small craft, and the predicted conditions—up to 30-knot gusts—would not dissuade most clam boat captains from completing their trip. George Evans in recent years had been known to be a conservative seaman, however, who would be driven to shore by weather that others might endure.

Regardless, the *Adriatic* was on a collision course with the very storm Evans had planned to elude. The waves were coming from the southeast and the boat was traveling southwest, which meant it was in a beam sea, with the waves hitting it from the port side. The outriggers were still deployed, but the birds were retracted and the ride was becoming uncomfortable, even for those whose time it was to sleep.

Frank Jannicelli just wanted to get home. As the clam boat heaved one way and then the other, he borrowed a cell phone and dialed Amy Cavanaugh's number. He got her answering machine.

"We're going to be in Atlantic City probably around five, five-thirty," he said. "Please make sure somebody's there to pick me up, because I don't want to get stuck for a ride."

Then he got in his bunk and, exhausted, tried to sleep. Mike Hager did the same.

By midafternoon, the seas offshore from Atlantic City were running at six feet, with steep waves and steady 30-knot winds. There were gusts to 50 knots and blinding rain.

William Parlett, the first mate on the clam boat *Richard M*, was 90 minutes ahead of the *Adriatic*, steaming along the same course, and was nearing Atlantic City. He saw squall lines coming across the sea in close ranks—perhaps a mile apart. Lightning shot from the darkened sky and waves broke over the side of his boat. Parlett was sufficiently concerned with the conditions that he woke his crew, just in case.

James Charlesworth, the first mate on the *Timberline One*, was about 22 miles away from the *Adriatic*, dredging clams. The boat was occasionally punching into waves that sent green water over its 12-foot-high bow, and although the *Timberline One* was a large boat that could take most seas, Charlesworth was pondering whether to lock his dredge in place and quit.

The weather was sending shivers across the land as well as the sea. Richard Hager was lying on his couch, looking out the apartment window. He saw clouds racing across the sky and, with a fisherman's experience, he knew what that meant. But he suspected the *Adriatic* was already in port, given Evans's reputation for conservatism.

Joan Nowicky had stayed home from work on Monday because she was having new carpet installed in her town house. She saw the turbulent sky and she thought of calling the *Adriatic*. But she left the phone in the cradle. She often took business trips and she would expect Evans to trust in her ability to take care of herself. She owed him the same respect, and so she stifled the urge.

Fifty miles to the north, Christine Jannicelli was at work at three o'clock, but she was growing so agitated that her boss sent her home for the day. She gathered all the laundry in her home and began washing, driven by some impulse.

Amy Cavanaugh was napping in her apartment when a thunderclap outside awakened her. She sat up in bed and thought about her roommate, Frank.

It may have simply been the recent experience in the clam boat fleet that gripped these people. Three boats down, six men lost in a dozen days was a frightening string of coincidences. But in fact, somewhere in the belly of the *Adriatic* something was terribly wrong. Water was pouring in—somewhere. There were no television cameras on the *Adriatic* to alert those in the wheelhouse to a problem. There were no watertight bulkheads beneath its deck. A gallon of water spilled in the bow soon found its way to the stern. And now water was coming in not by the gallon but by the barrel. It happened so fast that there was no time to react, no time to sound an alarm.

Evans grabbed his microphone.

"Mayday! Mayday! *Adriatic*!" he called on channel 16.

Douglas Oland, because he was a fresh hand, may have stayed in the wheelhouse to learn more about clamming and the sea during the trip to the dock. The youth who romanticized the sea and its peacefulness found instead its wrath. Punched by the waves, the *Adriatic* was on the precipice of destruction.

THERE IS NO question that the *Adriatic* took on seawater at a catastrophic rate. The still unanswered question is how that occurred.

A coast guard engineer, Lt. Jerry Dewayne Ray II, examined videotapes made of the vessel on the ocean floor by divers. He found that the flexible coupling—essentially a hose that is clamped between two sections of 12-inch pipe leading from the clam pump to the deck—was at some point torn from the pipes. Moreover, in the same pipeline, where flanges at the ends of two sections were joined by several bolts, the bolts were either stripped or their nuts were loosened by someone, and several bolts were missing entirely, resulting in a gap between the flanges. In any case, the main valve that let seawater into the clam pump had been left open after the pump was turned off and the *Adriatic* was headed toward the dock.

All of the breaks in the piping system could have occurred when the boat hit the ocean floor, Ray concluded. Or a weld holding the clam pump or its piping system could have failed

while the boat sailed across the building seas, causing a thrash-
ing of the piping that ruptured the flexible coupling and parted the flanges.

If the flexible coupling failed, the boat would sink within
four to nine minutes, Ray calculated. A parting of the flanges
would have taken substantially longer.

Another explanation considered by Ray for the missing and
untightened flange bolts was that someone had gone into the
engine room and loosened the bolts while the vessel was at sea.
Leaving the bolts untightened and missing could have led to
the separation of the flanges and the eventual flooding of the
boat. At the same time, a person who would have done this
would have been aware that water was spilling into the boat
because of that open valve. No one could suggest why anyone
aboard would have been working on those bolts or would have
left them untightened.

If all of these failures occurred when the boat hit the bottom, there are two more possible explanations for why the boat
sank. One is that, in the rough seas, the dredge fell over the
side, tipping the *Adriatic* so that the seas washed over its decks,
flooding the holds. Another possibility is that the clam hose,
trailed behind the boat, was caught in the propeller and
stopped the engine dead. With no engine, there would also be
no way to steer the boat and, foundering in steep, green waves,
it could have become swamped.

CAUGHT IN VIOLENT seas and taking on water, the *Adriatic*
rolled hard. One outrigger plunged below the waves as the
boat fell onto that side. The windows of the wheelhouse
smacked against the ocean surface, and if the dredge was still
on deck, it now fell into the sea, and the six clam cages that had
been opposite the dredge on the deck now tumbled as well.

If they were still sleeping in their bunks below the wheelhouse, Hager and Jannicelli became immediately aware that

the boat was on its side. They had either been thrown from their bunks or were trapped in them as the side of the boat became its low point. If the boat was on its port side, then escape through the watertight door was impossible. They had to make their way to the forepeak, where the two wooden doors leading aft and the ladder to the hatch before the wheelhouse were their escape options. The friends clawed their way forward along the spinning hallway, Hager dressed only in dark denim trousers, jockey shorts, two pairs of gray socks, and one black rubber boot, Jannicelli barefoot in a white T-shirt, black sweatpants, and boxer shorts.

By now, the other outrigger had whipped across the sky, and its weight was helping to roll the *Adriatic* upside down. The port windows of the wheelhouse were smashed. Whether Evans was still in the wheelhouse is unknown. Oland's location at this point is also unknown. The captain and the fill-in deckhand had no time to retrieve survival suits from the crew quarters at the foot of the stairs. Perhaps they had already stepped out into the frigid sea in hopes of catching the life raft when it inflated. But the boat continued to roll and sink, and as the hydrostatic release on the life raft was activated and the lid came off its case, the raft inflated, only to get caught in the boat's rigging. Evans and Oland were in the water with no survival gear, and help would not be coming soon. The brief Mayday that Evans had sounded came in garbled, and coast guard watchstanders were only able to decipher the repeated word *Mayday*. The watchstanders called out several times, asking for the vessel that issued the distress call to respond; but when they got no reply, they stopped calling. Moreover, when the boat slipped beneath the surface, the hydrostatic release on the EPIRB failed because the white nylon pin was too tough to be sliced by the mechanism's razor. As a result, the lid stayed attached to the case and the EPIRB never floated free and never transmitted.

All but three of the clam cages fell from the *Adriatic*'s hold as it spun down to the ocean floor. And inside the crew quarters, the water rushed in, filling every void and trapping Hager and Jannicelli in the forepeak, seizing them in its frigid embrace and stealing the breath from their lips.

In seconds, the *Adriatic* had rolled down through 60 feet of water, turning more than 180 degrees and hitting the muddy ocean floor hard, crushing its port side. The earthly form of Michael Hager, who had wanted nothing more than to raise his son, Mikey, and to fish, floated lifeless in the forepeak beside the body of his friend, Frank Jannicelli, a boy just becoming a man.

EPILOGUE

AROUND three o'clock on the afternoon of Monday, January 18, 1999, I was following Louis Lagace across the huge boulders of the north jetty of Manasquan Inlet. He had driven from Rhode Island to inspect the remains of his boat, the *Ellie B.* A few planks, painted red, were floating in the surf beside the jetty, and a heap of steel—the boat's machinery—was already rusting where it had settled at the jetty's end. The sea was rougher now than it had been the day before when the boat hit the rocks, and the sky was a dismal, high overcast, with cold, sprinkling rain blowing in gusts. As we stood looking down at the wreckage, lightning appeared to the south, moving toward us with a squall. I felt exposed, and I thought Louis did as well, because he headed back over the rocks toward shore. But where the jetty met the sand, Louis turned north and walked up the beach to a spot where more of the planks rocked in the surf.

At about this time, unknown to us, George Evans was grasping the *Adriatic*'s microphone, crying out a Mayday that could barely be heard. And within minutes, Michael Hager and Frank Jannicelli were gone, while Evans and Douglas Oland were never to be seen again.

At seven o'clock the next morning, my home phone rang. Kathy Becica, who had called me from the clam dock 24 hours earlier with word about the *Ellie B*, now told me the *Adriatic* was down and all hands were missing. The news felt like a punch to the chest.

On Friday, three days earlier, I had been looking for someone who could tell me about the *Beth Dee Bob*. Bill Becica, who after five days of seeing me loitering around the dock apparently decided I wasn't going away, had suggested I speak with Mike Hager, whom I could find over on the *Adriatic*. I had walked east along the dock and found a man just climbing up from what appeared to be the hold, a welder with his mask tilted back. When I asked for Hager, he went in the wheelhouse and returned, followed by a lanky young man with a dark blue baseball cap holding down shaggy blond hair. Mike Hager said he would take a smoke break to talk with me, and because the wind was blowing a frigid mist, we went inside the shed of the clam dock, where we found an unused office. Standing there, smoking two cigarettes in perhaps ten minutes, Mike answered my questions about the *Beth Dee Bob*, upon which he had worked before. He described the locations of the boat's engines, the television system that kept watch below deck, and the work rituals aboard that clam boat. He talked about the crew accommodations, noting: "On the *Beth Dee Bob*, that was one thing that was a little strange. When you were in the [bunk], you were below the waterline." Then he startled me with the fact that he had been invited on the doomed voyage. His eyes were the hollowed caves of one who sees his own grave open before him. He spoke quietly, staring off over the opaque green current of Wills Hole Thoroughfare. "If I went on the New Year's trip, they would have taken me" on the final voyage, he said. "I'm still amazed about it."

Not a week later, with Mike Hager still missing at sea after the sinking of the *Adriatic*, I sat at the dining room table in Dick and Judy Hager's apartment, listening to the story of their youngest son's life. Dick's eyes were red and grief tugged at his voice, already weak and hoarse from his infirmities. Judy stood quietly behind her husband at times, or sat at his side, the two of them surrounded by their three surviving sons—Richard Jr., Jeffrey, and Timothy—and two daughters—Terri Ware and Penny Pownall. Sean Domingo, Mike's best friend, and Susan Cornell were there, as was little Mikey, who was too young to understand the tragedy and seemed happy just because there was such a great crowd of family gathered.

Divers had found Roman Tkaczyk's body five days earlier at the foot of the stairs in the galley of the *Beth Dee Bob*. Other divers would bring up the bodies of Mike Hager and Frank Jannicelli from the forepeak of the *Adriatic* about a week later.

On January 22, a bagpiper played at the memorial service for Edward J. McLaughlin. More than 250 clammers, fishermen, friends, and family filled a church. "No earthly father would will such a death," the priest said, "nor would God. [But] He can't take away our free will."

Then the priest had some advice for the mourners: "It is a time to learn so that this type of work can be made safer."

Funerals for Michael S. Hager and Frank Jannicelli III followed, as did those of Jay Bjornestad, his shipmate Roman Tkaczyk, and Paul Martin of the *Cape Fear*. The bodies of McLaughlin, Grady Gene Coltrain, Steven Reeves, George Evans, and Douglas Oland were never found.

Separate coast guard investigations of the *Beth Dee Bob* and *Adriatic* sinkings, required because of the loss of life, began in Philadelphia on January 28. An investigation of the *Cape Fear* sinking had begun on January 20 in North Dartmouth, Massachusetts. There had been no injuries or death in the wreck of the *Ellie B*, and no coast guard investigation was required, although John Babbitt had been issued a ticket by a state trooper a few hours after the sinking as he stood on the beach, looking at his wrecked boat. The ticket was for failure to keep a proper watch.

More than a score of lawyers were hired by surviving crewmen, the families of the lost men, boat captains, and boat owners. The hearings, each with dozens of witnesses, stretched over many sessions. Decorum prevailed in the *Adriatic* and *Cape Fear* hearings. Commander Michael D. Kearney had a brawl on his hands, however, when he attempted to investigate the sinking of the *Beth Dee Bob.* With grieving relatives looking on, lawyers attacked each other and the coast guard as if their jockeying could assist their clients in future suits. In fact, use of the record of these proceedings in civil cases was specifically prohibited by law. The whole purpose of the inquiries was to determine the facts by encouraging witnesses to speak freely, and then to learn from those facts in the hope of making the industry safer.

As testimony unfolded before Com. Mary E. Landry, who was charged with investigating the loss of the *Adriatic,* it became clear that the captain and crew were not going to be relieved of suspicion that they contributed to the boat's loss. A coast guard naval architect accepted the possibility that someone aboard had been working on the clam pump system while at sea, and had loosened the nuts and bolts holding the flanges together, and that this had allowed the flooding that sank the boat.

Dick Hager, torn by sadness over the loss of his youngest son, now boiled with anger. "No! That didn't happen," he demanded from his medical prison—the couch in his living room. George Evans never worked on the machinery but left that to his mate, Dick insisted, and Mike, the mate, and Frank were sleeping in their bunks on the way home, as they always did. How could they—and why would they—have dismantled the piping? To Dick, the coast guard was trying to place the blame on dead men who could not defend their reputations. He became embittered.

The hearings concluded in Philadelphia and Massachusetts, and then the respective hearing officers began to analyze the information they had gathered and to come to some conclusions. Commander Landry was the first to file her report, which was dated July 23, 1999. Commander Kearney filed his findings on the *Beth Dee Bob* on August 18. Capt. George R. Matthews, who was assigned to investigate the loss of the *Cape Fear,* took nearly two years to complete his 99-page report.

But reaction to the January 1999 tragedies had not waited for the outcomes of these investigations. In April 1999, the Coast Guard Fishing Vessel Casualty Task Force, with members from the industry and the government, had looked at the events and come to some sweeping conclusions. Safety of the fishermen should be a significant consideration when regulators decide how to manage a fishery, the panel said. The experts saw a need to ensure that fishing boats complied with existing safety regulations. They wanted someone to look at the effectiveness of existing coast guard stability standards. They sought better information for fishermen and the creation of standards governing the proficiency of captains and crewmembers of fishing boats.

Immediately after the *Adriatic* sank, Kathy Becica, the office manager at the Point Pleasant clam dock, reeling with grief, looked for a way to express her feelings. She and her husband, Bill, formed a nonprofit corporation to raise money. Some of the funds were dedicated to the children of the lost clammers. But part of the fund was set aside for a more visible memorial. On October 8, 2000, a crowd of several hundred gathered beside the Manasquan Inlet for the unveiling of a life-size bronze statue of a fisherman holding a lantern aloft and surrounded by a low fence with bronze plaques attached to the top of its railing. Each of the 38 Point Pleasant boats known to have been lost at sea, dating to 1931, was represented with a plaque on which the names of the men lost were inscribed.

In late 2000, the Society of Naval Architects and Marine Engineers decided to form an ad hoc committee to look into the issue of commercial fishing boat safety. The committee's members turned an unflinching eye on their own profession, looking for ways to improve fishing vessel stability and to convince fishermen to pay attention to how they load and handle boats.

By early 2001, Capt. Tom Dameron had begun to experience some new interest from clam boat owners in the little business he had formed in 1994. A licensed captain, Dameron had seen that the various safety drills captains are required to perform every month were being widely ignored. He formed a company—

Shipboard Emergency Action Corp.—and offered, for a fee, to conduct that training for boat owners. He was met with intense uninterest by owners, who saw his proposal as just another unnecessary expense. Nor did they flock to him even after coast guard inquiries showed that the most basic drill—donning survival suits—was almost never conducted on any of the lost clam boats. But slowly, a few boat owners did respond to Dameron's offer, and by the spring of 2001, he was working as captain of the *Christi Caroline* only two weeks a month so that he could conduct drills on other clam boats.

As if preparing to begin a new era in commercial fishing, the final reports of the three coast guard inquiries started to become available just as the new century was arriving. None found absolute evidence of catastrophic mechanical failure. Each attributed some blame for the tragedies to human error.

THE *BETH DEE BOB*

COMMANDER KEARNEY CONCLUDED that the practice of double-stacking clam cages in the forward hold doomed the *Beth Dee Bob*. In rough seas, the clam holds filled with water and no one turned on the pumps to empty them. As a result, the rear of the boat, where a watertight door was left open, settled low in the sea. Water flooded through the door and filled the engine room, causing the boat to slide backward down into the sea in 115 feet of water, Kearney theorized. He found no evidence of equipment failure, but he wrote that "The crew's lack of understanding of stability was a hazardous precondition that contributed to the vessel's sinking."

Among other criticisms, Kearney wrote that the practice of paying crew members a share of the catch "encourages overloading," as did the pressure to load the boat with enough cages to fill tractor-trailers at 14 cages per trailer.

Kearney recommended that all clam boats be required to have stability letters. He urged that all captains be licensed and their crew hold merchant mariner documents attesting to their proficiency as seamen. Alone among the reports, Kearney's suggested that the coast guard consider an alternative to the cumbersome survival suits that fishermen cannot wear while they are working and cannot get to or get into in a sudden emergency.

The Cape Fear

CAPTAIN MATTHEWS FOUND that "the cause of the capsizing and sinking of the [fishing vessel] *Cape Fear* was downflooding from following seas into the clam tanks through hatch covers that were not weathertight." He found that the *Cape Fear* was overloaded and that the crew failed to operate in accordance with the boat's stability letter.

The investigator said there was "complacency or inattentiveness of conditions aboard the vessel." There were no safety drills, he noted, and three of the four crewmembers tested "were found to be drug users."

Matthews noted the lack of any company policies concerning operation of the boat, hiring crew, or any of the practices required to gather clams, for that matter. He wrote that the very design of the *Cape Fear* "increased the risk" of sinking.

The captain recommended that the coast guard consider requiring licenses for captains and mates, as well as merchant mariner documents for other crewmen. He suggested regular mandatory inspections of the clam boats as opposed to the voluntary inspections now offered by the coast guard.

Matthews was the only one of the three investigating officers to suggest that the coast guard consider imposing civil penalties against crewmembers. He said Capt. Steven Novack might be cited for negligent operation of the *Cape Fear*, for failing to conduct safety drills each month, for failing to maintain his lifesaving equipment, and for using drugs. The investigator also suggested that James Haley be pursued for his drug use and that a civil penalty be sought against Warren Alexander for operating the *Cape Fear* "in a negligent manner that endangered life."

THE *ADRIATIC*

"THE ROOT CAUSE of this casualty," Commander Landry wrote, "is the lack of a high standard of care in maintenance and operation of the F/V *Adriatic*." She went on to note the boat's history of problems, including the failure of a hydraulic line whose deterioration had been masked when it was painted, and a citation against George Evans in 1996 for operating with an expired hydrostatic release mechanism on either the EPIRB or the life raft, though the record was unclear which device was involved.

The investigator concluded that someone had hooked a come-along—a set of blocks and cable—to the wheel used for closing the valve between the bottom of the boat and the clam pump, and that the valve was open when the boat sank. In an emergency, she said, the valve could not be easily closed.

Someone failed to close a watertight door to the *Adriatic*'s engine room, Landry wrote. "This door being left open had tragic consequences and severely hampered the time available for the crew to respond in this casualty."

The commander blamed Evans for failing to follow instructions when he updated the hydrostatic release on the EPIRB. Had the proper pin been in place, she said, the EPIRB would have broadcast its alarm.

The *Adriatic* was not overloaded, Landry ruled, and it had adequate stability for the load it was carrying.

Landry, like Kearney and Matthews, recommended the licensing of captains, and she suggested that all clam boats be required to have stability letters. She also called for more stringent coast guard inspections of the boats. And she called on the coast guard to work with EPIRB manufacturers and service companies to expand the inspections of the devices.

Although the coast guard hierarchy agreed with many of the investigating officers' recommendations, none of the more demanding suggestions had been implemented as of the writing of this book. Some changes required legislation. Others, such as licensing, were politically difficult to enact due to the entrenched opposition among members of the clamming industry. But in the fall of 2000, the coast guard began Operation Safe Catch, an aggressive boarding of commercial fishing boats in search of safety violations. A few vessels were immediately ordered to port and prevented from returning to sea until the violations were corrected.

AMONG THE MEN who survived the four clam boat sinkings, only two had returned to the sea two years later. Steven Novack became captain of the *John N*, another of Warren Alexander's boats. Alexander sold the boat and Novack went with it to Ocean City, Maryland, not far from his home in Virginia. In the summer of 2001, the *John N* suffered a major fire while at sea, and the boat was hauled out in Norfolk, Virginia, for extensive repairs and improvements.

Gary Sylvia, who survived the *Ellie B* sinking, was the only other clammer to go back to sea. He went lobstering near his Rhode Island home. But then, plagued with emphysema, he applied for disability benefits and returned to shore.

Jason Wilson, Sylvia's neighbor, stayed onshore and was said to be painting houses and going to bartending school.

John Babbitt, who had been fishing since he was 16, decided he no longer wanted to be on clam boats. He had diving and welding to keep him busy. "If you're supporting a family, you don't want to be out there," he said.

James Haley, Novack's first mate on the *Cape Fear*, could not get over the terror he had experienced in the black ocean or the sound lingering in his ears of Steven Reeves's last desperate cry for help. He tried finding work on land near his home in Oak Hall, Virginia, but nothing paid him the big money he had made at sea. The fisherman was left to rely on his wife, who had a business of her own.

Joseph Lemieux, the other *Cape Fear* survivor, sued Warren Alexander's company and got an undisclosed settlement. Friends said he was working at the Sea Watch dock in New Bedford as a forklift operator.

In her boutique-neat town house in Brick, Joan Nowicky kept the only photograph she had of George Evans in a place where she could always see it. Two years later, she still glowed when she talked about the one man who, in so short a time, had come to mean everything to her. Her memories had been spared of any discord by the briefness of their time together. They had not had time for a fight. At night, when she went to bed, she lay beside a teddy bear that wore one of George's shirts.

Michael S. Hager Jr. was eight years old as 2001 ended and had moved with his mother, Susan Cornell, back to New Bedford soon after his father's death. Once a month since then, his grandparents drove to Massachusetts and brought Mikey back to New Jersey for the weekend. And during the summer, Mikey visited Dick and Judy Hager for several weeks.

And each day, Dick's bitterness and grief seemed to grow. He believed that he was responsible for his son's death because he had led him into the fishing life. He was distressed that Mikey no longer lived nearby, and he was angry with Cornell for having taken the boy away. He fumed that men he had known for much of his life would not tell him what he believed to be the

truth concerning the loss of the *Adriatic*—that new welds had
failed, causing the clam pump piping to flood the boat.

Judy Hager continued to go to her second-shift job at a phar-
maceutical company, and on the night of March 1, 2000, the
day before what would have been her son Michael's thirty-third
birthday, she arrived home as usual after midnight. Dick had
fallen asleep on the sofa with his oxygen supply. They ate dinner together. Then she went into her bedroom to watch television while he fell back to sleep in the living room. Judy was
awakened by Dick's voice at 4:45 A.M.

"Judy! Judy! Wake up! There's a fire downstairs!"

Flames and smoke were leaping outside from the apartment
below the Hagers', but there was little smoke in their second-
level apartment. Dick was too weak to make it down the long
fire escape, so they headed for the stairwell, which reached the
front door in only eight steps. When they opened the door, they
found dense, black smoke. Judy thought she should go get a wet
facecloth to help ease Dick's breathing, but she said nothing as
her loving husband tugged her by the hand and, carrying his
oxygen supply, bravely led her down the steps to the front door.

A teenage girl had moved into the third-level apartment
above the Hagers' a week before, and Dick was concerned that
she had not escaped. He tried to tell the arriving firemen about
it. As he and Judy stood in the parking lot, talking to a fireman,
without a word of complaint, Dick collapsed in front of Judy.

Medics could not revive him. An autopsy determined that he
had succumbed to the effects of smoke inhalation.

Brokenhearted and embittered by the loss of his son at sea,
the old sailor finally was at rest.

ON ANY GOOD day, when the wind is moderate and no storms are
forecast, the clam boats still head to sea from Point Pleasant and
New Bedford, from Atlantic City and Cape May and Barnegat
Light and Shinnecock. They are the same boats that shared the

ocean with the *Beth Dee Bob, Cape Fear, Ellie B,* and *Adriatic.* Some of the captains have retired and some have moved to other vessels. The deckhands come and go. Some go on to become mates; some go ashore to find drug dealers.

One boat owner has reversed his course. Louis Lagace took his insurance money and invested it in a new clam boat. He bought the boat in New Bedford, but he moved it to Point Pleasant. He renamed it the *Mariette,* after his mother. And, no longer content to remain ashore, he returned to the sea as a part time clam boat captain.

The dream lives on.

And yet peril lurks offshore, awaiting a clam boat, alive with men and loaded for money, heading for the dock.

ACKNOWLEDGEMENTS

A STORY, whether fiction or fact, is never the possession of an author but that of those individuals whose lives either inspired the writing or were its subjects. The owners of this story are the intrepid men who set out on a winter sea, some of them never to return: Edward McLaughlin, Jay Bjornestad, Roman Tkaczyk, Grady Gene Coltrain, Steven Novack, James Haley, Joseph Lemieux, Steven Reeves, Paul Martin, John Babbitt, Gary Sylvia, Jason Wilson, George Evans, Michael Hager, Frank Jannicelli and Douglas Oland.

I owe a debt of thanks to the families, friends and lovers of these men, individuals whose names are found throughout the story. In many instances, they welcomed me in the midst of their grief as well as over the years that have followed the tragic winter of 1999.

Bill and Kathy Becica, who knew most of the men and who together had been at the heart of the clamming industry for decades, were extraordinarily helpful. I am indebted to them for their advice and guidance, for their warmth and their humor.

Capt. Ed Platter helped put a face on the men about whom I would write by agreeing, when no one else would, to take me to sea on his clam boat, the *Debbie & Jeanette.*

I found the United States Coast Guard officers and enlisted members uniformly helpful when I needed their assistance. Rescue Swimmer Richard Gladish, Commander Michael Kearney and Commander Mary Landry went far beyond their official duties to help me understand these events. Each showed a very human concern for the commercial fishermen they are charged with policing and protecting.

Similarly, naval architects Bruce Johnson and John Womack took me beyond the mathematics of their profession, eager to help explain the hazards of unstable fishing boats because they genuinely cared about the safety of the men who sail those craft.

A special thanks is due the editors of the *Philadelphia Inquirer,* who gave me the time and freedom to pursue a story that might have been told briefly and then forgotten, and to the dozens of *Inquirer* readers who urged me to expand the January, 2000 newspaper series into a book.

My most unflaggingly harsh critic and the best editor I had the pleasure of working with at the *Philadelphia Inquirer,* Robert Fowler, read the entire manuscript and offered unsparing advice that resulted in a solid first draft worth delivering to Carroll & Graf. And *Inquirer* photographer David M Warren, recognizing my incompetence in his art, volunteered to help me assemble the pictures that would be used in the book.

Finally, I am grateful for the insights of Executive Editor Philip Turner and his assistant, Keith Wallman. Together, they helped shape a book that I believe is a fitting tribute to the men of the *Beth Dee Bob,* the *Cape Fear,* the *Ellie B* and the *Adriatic.*

INDEX

Abescon Inlet, 91
Adriatic, 4, 243, 255, 270–272
    clam pump, 248
    crew, 5–9
    investigations, 275–276
    rust, 49–50
    sinking, 264–267
Alexander, Warren, 70, 163–164,
    216, 276
Allen, Sue, 167–168, 215, 217
Andrea Gail, 62, 239–240
architects, 194–195
Ascoli, Dominic, 7
Ashton-Alcox, Kathryn, 39–40

Babbitt, John, 230, 236–239, 240,
    257, 270, 276
Barenegat Inlet, 40
Barlow, Millie, 80–81
Barnes, Marilyn, 223
Bart, Justin, 79
Bart, Rodney, 11, 27, 79, 103, 104

Bart, Sarah, 79
Beale, Edward, 115
Becica, Bill (William), 42–43, 104,
    176
Becica, Kathy, 42, 68–69, 104, 269
Becica, Sean, 43
Becica, Tom, 215
Becica, William J., 43
Beth & Lisa, 68
Beth Dee Bob, 3, 145, 269, 270–272
    classification, 30
    crew, 18, 72–79
    investigations, 273–274
    loading, 4, 33, 273–274
    radio, 33
    routine, 18
    sinking, 131–133
    solenoid malfunction, 31–32
    stability letter, 36–37
    stern ramp, 36
Bettie T, 71
Billy Jo, 109

Birchall, Patti, 96, 121
Birchall, Tom, 96
"birds", 19
Bjornestad, Jay, 18, 31, 73–74, 95,
    137–138, 140, 270
boats. *See* clam boats
Brayton, Charles, 80
Brayton, Roger, 65
Broadway Bar & Grille, 44
Browder, Horace, 101
Bryan, James S., 115
Buzzards Bay, 70

Cabral, Stephen L., 81–82
Cape Fear, 62, 144, 145, 162,
    199–210
    crew, 164–171
    investigations, 270–272,
        274
    rescue, 211–214
Cape May, 40
Cavanaugh, Amy, 7–8, 156,
    158–160, 263
Charlesworth, James, 263
cherrystone clam, 38–40
Christi Caroline, 61, 103
Christian Alexa, 44, 102
Christina, 102
Christopher Snow, 59
clam boats, 184–187, 191–194
    clam dredge, 50, 84, 86, 88
    clam pump, 50–51
    design, 196–198
    insurance, 197–198
    loading, 185
    stability, 195–196
    See also clam fishing; commer-
        cial fishing
clam fishing, 11–12, 30–31, 38–40
    captains, 60–61

economics of, 12, 52
fatalities, 14–15, 63–71,
    107–108
logbooks, 56
regulations, 11
See also clam boats; commercial
    fishing
coast guard, 129–131, 172, 272
    investigations, 270–272
coastal upwelling, 54
Cohen, Daniel, 104
Coltrain, Grady Gene, 18, 75–79,
    104, 270
commercial fishing
    accidents, 4
    drug use, 80–82
    environmental concerns,
        54–55
    fatalities, 9–10
    inspections, 108–109
    regulations, 53–58
    safety, 272
    See also clam boats; clam fish-
        ing
Cooper, Porus, 13
Cora Jean Snow, 59
Cornell, Susan, 8–9, 46–47, 277
Cornett, Daniel, 126
Cornett, Michael, 125–129
Cornett, Paul, 126

Dameron, Tom, 61, 272
Danielle Maria, 59, 90, 102
Davidson, Hans, 168
deadweight, 194
Debbie & Jeanette, 88, 103, 111
Discovery, 46
Dolphin helicopter, 134
Domingo, Christina, 247
Domingo, Sean, 45, 152, 247,

270
drugs, 80–82

Eastern Shore, 120
Edgartown, 168
Eleanor Marcher, 68
electronic position indicating
        radio beacon (EPIRB),
        35–36, 275
Ellie B., 65, 105, 228, 231, 270–272
        crew, 237–240
        sinking, 250–254, 257
Enterprise, 104
EPIRB (electronic position indi-
        cating radio beacon),
        35–36, 275
Evans, George Whitely, 5–6,
        51–53, 58, 177–182,
        220–227, 243, 247–249,
        255–262, 268, 270
Evans-Mizrachi, Patricia, 220

fill-in, 12–13
Fisheries Conservation and
        Management Act, 54
Fishing Vessel Casualty Task Force,
        272
Flicka, 105, 156
Freeman, Richard, 222–223

Gallagher, Thomas, 255
Giverson, Everett "Bub", 260
Gladish, Richard, 113–121,
        135–138, 141
Goodwin, Richard E., 107
Goulart, John, 63–65
Gower, Teresa, 224
Great Egg Harbor, 40
Group Woods Hole, 211
Gulf Air, 70

Gull Island, 41
Gumby suit, 34

Hager, Dick, 45, 148–151, 269,
        271, 277–278
Hager, Jeff, 148–151
Hager, Judy, 45, 148–151, 244,
        269, 277–278
Hager, Michael Scott, 8–9, 13,
        16–17, 43–48, 103, 148–151,
        159, 246–249, 256, 267–270,
        243, 277
Hager, Richard, 16, 263,
        270
Hager, Terri, 45
Hager, Timothy, 44, 55, 270
Haley, James, 145, 166–167, 173,
        184, 188–190, 208, 218–219,
        276
Hammerhead, 214, 217
Heaton, Clay, 55
Higbee, Harry, 110
Hill, Thelma, 225
Hurd, Bobby Lee, 126
Hutton, Michael, 105–106
Hutton, Rita, 105, 107–109
hypothermia, 139–140

ICW (Intracoastal Waterway), 40
immersion suits, 34–35, 274
Indian River, 165
ITQ (Individual Transferable
        Quota), 53–54, 57

Jamaica, 102
Jamaica II, 95
Jannicelli, Christine, 263
Jannicelli, Frank, 6–8, 103,
        156–161, 243, 245, 256,
        267, 268, 270

Jersey Devil, 163
John N., 43, 163, 169, 203, 276
Johnson, Bruce, 191, 192, 194
Judy Marie, 59
Junger, Sebastian, 24, 62

Kane, William, 107
Kayle, John, 104
Kearney, Michael D., 271, 273
Keith, Jack, 261
Kelleher, Beth, 71
Kelleher, Robert, 71
Kelly, Douglas Miles, 145, 171
Kessler, Frank T., 63–65
Kime, J. W., 108
Kirk, Larry, 94, 100, 124, 131
Kodiak Island, Alaska, 118

Lagace, Louis, 30, 228–235, 240,
    268, 279
LaMonica, Peter, 58, 59, 61, 91
Landry, Mary E., 271, 275
Lanseardia, William, 66
LaPlante, Kim, 146, 169–171, 215
Laurelton Welding, 17
LaVecchia, Daniel, 58, 91
Layton, Richard, 107
Lemieux, Joseph F., 146, 171, 173,
    200, 219, 277
lightship weight, 194
Lima, Robin, 169
Lisa Kim, 59
Little Egg Harbor, 40
Little Gull, 165
Loy, James M., 130

Mae Doris, 105, 106, 107, 151
Manasquan Inlet, 40–41, 98
Manasquan River, 41
Marie Kim, 44, 151

Mariette, 279
Martin, Anthony, 171
Martin, Mary, 171
Martin, Paul, 146, 171, 173, 200,
    217–218
Marvin John, 165
Mathis, John, 203, 211
Matthews, Eric, 111
Matthews, George R., 271
Matthews, Pete, 111
McFarland, Scott, 113
McLaughlin, Ed (Edward J.), 3,
    17–18, 21–27, 31–32, 58, 62,
    123, 176–177, 270
McLaughlin, Kevin, 25
McLaughlin, Liam, 21
McLaughlin, Lisa, 21–23, 176–177
Mid-Atlantic Fishery Management
    Council, 53, 54
Miss Merna, 163, 203
Misty Dawn, 163, 203
Montauk, 165
Morning Dew, 126–131
Mud Hole, 20, 97

National Geographic, 234
National Marine Fisheries Service,
    55, 56
National Oceanographic and
    Atmospheric
    Administration (NOAA), 35
New Bedford Standard-Times,
    80–81
New Jersey coast, 40
NOAA (National Oceanographic
    and Atmospheric
    Administration, 35
Novack, Steven Craig, 62,
    144–145, 164–166, 173,
    188–190, 199–210, 276

Nowicky, Joan, 5–6, 177–182, 227, 256, 263, 277

Ocean Quahog Corp., 59
Oland, Douglas, 244, 257, 264, 268, 270
Oliveira, Ric, 80
Orkapski, Bronislav, 31
O'Sullivan, Robert William, 197

Parlett, William, 190, 263
Patrick, Christi, 225
Pearl Ace, 128
Philadelphia Inquirer, 13
Platter, Edward N., 88–89, 109, 110
PMD Enterprises, 18
Poggie, John J., 82
Point Francis, 214, 217
Point Highland, 156
Point Pleasant Beach, 40, 43, 104
Point Pleasant Packing, 17
Pollnac, Richard B., 82
Pownall, Penny, 270
Predator, 19–20
Puglisi, Anna, 75–78

quahogs (Arctica islandica), 4, 38–40, 52, 85

Ray, Jerry Dewayne, 264
Reedy, Colin, 100, 154
Reeves, Steven Mark, 146, 167–171, 173, 200, 270
Rencurrel, Amber Lynn, 165
Rencurrel, Andrew B., 66–68, 70, 165
Rencurrel, Karen, 165
Rencurrel, Lesley Lee, 165
Riccio, Ernest, 32

Richard M., 190, 263
Rosenthal, Robert J., 13
Rubin, Bernard, 53, 58, 225
Rutgers University, 39

Sacchi, Helen, 47
Salty Sea, 69
Sandy Hook, 41
Sartori, 117
Savage, Ricks, 191
Sea Watch International Limited, 58
Senger, John, 31, 71
Shell, Jeff, 111
Shinnecock, 165
Shipboard Emergency Action Corp., 273
shucking, 58
Smith, Fred, 24
SNAME (Society of Naval Architects and Marine Engineers, 191, 272
Staab, Michael, 66
stability letter, 36–37, 172–173, 190, 273
Stephanie D., 165
Stevenson, Joel, 90
Studds, Gerry E., 108
surf clams (Spisula solidissima), 38–40, 85
Surfside Packing, 91
survival suits, 34–35, 274
Sylvia, Gary, 239, 251, 276

Tammy D II, 71
The Perfect Storm, 24, 62, 239
Thom, Stephen, 139–140
Tirella, Nicholas, 160
Tkaczyk, Roman, 18, 72–73, 104, 132, 270

Troydon, 66–68, 70, 165

Tuisu, 44

University of Rhode Island, 82

Victoria Elizabeth, 11, 75, 79, 103, 105

Walker, Keevan, 99, 154

Wallace, David, 191

Wally Fox, 71

Ware, Terri, 270

Welding, Laurelton, 51–53

wheelhouse, 84

White, Lynn T., 36

Wills Hole Thoroughfare, 17, 41

Wilson, Jason, 239–240, 276

Womack, John, 191, 194